Depression Winters:
New York Social Workers and the New Deal

American Civilization
A series edited by Allen F. Davis

William W. Bremer

Depression Winters: New York Social Workers and the New Deal

Temple University Press   Philadelphia

Freed. 29.95 / 26.96 / 7/1/85

Temple University Press, Philadelphia 19122

© 1984 by Temple University. All rights reserved

Published 1984

Printed in the United States of America

Library of Congress Cataloging in Publication Data

Bremer, William W.
  Depression winters.

  (American civilization)
  Bibliography: p.
  Includes index.
  1. Social workers—New York (N.Y.)—History.
2. Public welfare—United States—History—20th
century. 3. Depressions—1929—United States.
I. Title. II. Series.
HV99.N59B74 1984   361.3'09747'1   84-2572
ISBN 0-87722-350-5

To my mother, Marie Walling Bremer,
and to the memory of my father, John Thompson Bremer, 1912–1975

Contents

ix   Preface

xiii   Acknowledgments

3   1. Together at reform's East River

15   2. The crusade for Neighbor Smith

25   3. Two winters' deepening chill

38   4. Starting with business, where the jobs are

54   5. Unemployed men, morale, and emergency work

63   6. An icy winter's blast for federal action

76   7. Embedding professionalism in public programs

88   8. The President out in the cold: Herbert Hoover

101   9. FDR: the social workers' choice

114   10. Interlude: waiting out the longest winter

126   11. Jobs for Americans: from springtime bliss to winter blues

142 12. Better half a social security act than none
158 13. Harmonies in depression counterpoint
171 14. The American way of welfare
181   Notes
217   Bibliographical note
223   Index

Preface

Frances Perkins maintained that a group of New York social workers influenced federal policy toward unemployment during the Great Depression. In her memoirs, the former Secretary of Labor argued that the New York social service community set the pattern for the New Deal's innovations in public welfare.[1] "There was not any close social life between the social workers in New York City," she decided, "but what with one agency helping another agency most social workers got to know each other in one way or another." Their sense of community was based on their early associations and on their professional commitment to help others.[2] She wanted to write a book about the New York social work group called Children of Light.[3]

Perkins never got around to write her book, but others have noted the way the New Deal borrowed from the city and state of New York, and that individual social workers including Harry Hopkins, Molly Dewson, and Perkins left New York to join the federal government. New York was the crucible in which "national policies were formed," Clarke Chambers has written.[4] But no scholar has examined in detail the way New York social workers interacted with each other, and how they influenced government policy in New York and Washington.

This book describes the New York social work community and its influence. Perkins implied that the group was small. My own estimate, based on reading private papers, is thirty to forty people. Eight of them—Lillian Wald, Homer Folks, William Matthews, Paul Kellogg, Mary Dewson, William Hodson, Harry Hopkins, and Frances Perkins—appear most frequently because they were principal movers and shakers. About twenty more are included as major figures. My list, however, is scarcely definitive; nor have I been fair in giving sufficient treatment to everyone. The community is more important than the individual members.

I am convinced that the New York group formed a community. Historian Thomas Bender has argued that historians must give attention to "the network of social relations in which the individual is embedded" if we are to comprehend the manner in which "the qualities of mutuality and sentiment associated with community" have taken hold in twentieth-century urban society. By working from the anthropologist's "interior view" of social contacts, he suggests, we can reconstruct the experience of community among city dwellers, including members of urban-based professional groups.[5] An "interior view" reveals that the New York community maintained qualities of mutuality and sentiment regardless of differences of opinion, personal rivalries, and dissent. As Frances Perkins sensed, the leaders trusted, respected, supported, and learned from one another because they shared an extraordinarily rich professional experience. In addition, the dynamics of their community life drew people together. As John McClymer puts it, "If communities provide emotional sustenance to their members, they also inculcate values and customs; they influence perceptions by organizing expectations about the course of daily life; and . . . they demand active participation."[6] Perhaps the key factor was the New Yorkers' ready identification of themselves as a distinct community of people with common loyalties.

Through seven winters of crisis, beginning with the winter of 1929–1930 and ending with the winter of 1935–1936, New Yorkers launched unemployment programs, tested their results, and initiated a process of trial and error that both anticipated and directed changes across the nation. The city's settlement houses and charity buildings resembled naturalists' field stations where social workers gathered information, made observations and decided what action to take. News about mounting unemployment reached the dining halls at Henry Street settlement, the meeting rooms at the Association for Improving the Condition of the Poor, and the editorial offices at *Survey* magazine before national government organizations and media learned the facts.

The New York social work community functioned most effectively from 1928 to 1934. In addition to publicizing ideas and lobbying for new laws at all levels of government, New Yorkers led the politicization of social work itself. They supported the presidential candidacy of Al Smith in 1928 and renewed a commitment to political action that had waned about a decade before at the close of the Progressive Era. They gained political power under Governor Franklin Roosevelt, and as they responded to the crisis of the Depression, they became convinced that only government action, not private philanthropy, could solve the problem of unemployment.

In 1933 President Roosevelt called Perkins and Hopkins to Washington; other New Yorkers joined them, and much of the New York program became federal law. Social workers in other cities—Boston, Chicago, Philadelphia—contributed also, but to a lesser extent, particularly in the critical years of the early New Deal. Some of the group became disenchanted during 1934. A few moved to the left and became critics of the New Deal. By 1936, the New York social work community was fractured, but its influence survived.

Acknowledgments

My former wife, Sidney H. Bremer, devoted her considerable knowledge of Americana to the development of my ideas, and in addition labored on my prose. My thanks begin with her. The book itself began over twenty years ago, when Otis A. Pease welcomed an insistent student into an honors section of a course on the 1920s and 1930s. David M. Potter never saw more than drafts of a dissertation, yet his comments, criticisms, and line-by-line dissection of my writing still guide me. His wisdom about life's paradoxes has also proved a constant aid. William R. Taylor endeavored to teach me intellectual and cultural history; Barton J. Bernstein worked to impart social history. Even though he has not known it, Clarke A. Chambers became my mentor, counseling me from the day in 1969 when I first entered the Social Welfare History Archives.

Work in archives incurs great debts to curators and research librarians. Rather than list everyone, I want to acknowledge the special attention given me by Andrea Hinding of the Social Welfare History Archives, Joseph Marshall of the Franklin D. Roosevelt Library, Nancy Hauser and William Liebmann of

Columbia University Libraries, Elizabeth Mason of the Columbia Oral History Collection, and Paul Rugen of the New York Public Library. Two Lawrence University librarians, Harriet Tippet and Kathleen Isaacson, demonstrated patience as well as helpfulness in response to every request, including information regarding street addresses of fifty years ago. A Lawrence student, Keith Hempel, also contributed to my research.

Many historians and friends read the manuscript. Barton Bernstein, Frank Freidel, Robert H. Bremner, and Richard Polenberg critiqued it in its dissertation form. Clarke Chambers, Otis Pease, Thomas Bender, Walter I. Trattner, Allen F. Davis, and former Lawrence University colleagues S. Douglas Greenberg and Morton (and Mina) Schwartz criticized the book manuscript. My fellow Lawrence historian, Anne J. Schutte, has labored on each of its versions. The interest of Holly J. Lyon kept my writing "humming along," and her comments as reader showed that she knew my voice. None of these scholars and dear people bears responsibility for my faults; any mischief is my own.

Research grants and travel fellowships from the Social Welfare History Archives in Minneapolis and the Eleanor Roosevelt Institute in Hyde Park made it possible for me to expand my work. The support of Lawrence University was also a great help. Wendell Tripp and the 1982 manuscript award of the New York State Historical Association aided my publication.

Depression Winters:
New York Social Workers and the New Deal

**Together
at
reform's
East
River**

1

Since the end of the nineteenth century, social workers had struggled with the inequities of urban progress. While others hung their names in lights on Broadway, erected skyscrapers, built factories, tunneled subways, and amassed Wall Street's billions, a band of settlement house and charity workers devoted themselves to the human debris left behind in the rush for riches. They worked in overcrowded tenements, dingy sweatshops, and oppressive slums, and their clients included disabled workers, helpless widows, dependent children, craftsmen displaced by mechanization, the indigent elderly, the ill, the illiterate, the unemployed, and the poor of every race, nationality, and description. Yet despite an abundance of misery, New York's ability to create great wealth fostered their hopes of raising the standard of living for all.

3

The twenty-five years in age that separated the oldest welfare reformers (Lillian Wald, Homer Folks, Mary Simkhovitch, and Edward Devine, all born in 1867) from the youngest (Helen Hall, Abraham Epstein, Jane Hoey, and Harry Lurie, all born in 1892) was bridged by their mutual participation in a re-

form movement that stretched from the Progressive period to
the Depression era. The reformers never formed a monolithic
community, however, even when advancing their reforms. Certainly their backgrounds were similar. Most were Protestant and
middle class, and the majority came from rural areas and smaller
cities, often in the Middle West. Their fathers had been comfortable farmers, merchants, doctors, and ministers. Their early
lives were distinguished by the still exceptional experience of
college education, often at home-state institutions. Most also
did some graduate work, coming east to study at universities in
metropolitan centers. They were Protestants who had grown up
in homogeneous communities and who joined the rural-to-
urban migration in search of new opportunities for careers.
They earned degrees in law, medicine, education, and the ministry. Very few studied social work or began careers in that occupation. Many started out as teachers, civil servants, and journalists.
Of course there were many exceptions: the outer circle of this
group included immigrants and the children of immigrants, Jews
and Catholics, eastern urbanites, people who lacked formal edu-
cations, and the sons and daughters of working-class parents.[1]

All were social workers of sorts, but they labored in the
transitional years before social work had developed into a distinct profession. Some worked in charities and others in settlement houses. They were joined by others, including journalists
who edited social service magazines, researchers who took jobs
in philanthropic foundations, and social scientists who worked
in civic action organizations, most of whom entertained the label
"social work" to designate their calling because neither it nor
they were specialized and discrete. All sought to solve society's
problems by improving the quality of urban, industrial life. Social workers in name, they were reformers by disposition. Lawyers, doctors, nurses, ministers, and other kinds of professionals
found places somewhere in this newly emerging field. Bruno
Lasker, a resident at Henry Street settlement, recalled that
Lillian Wald pioneered new services "simply by adding to her

4

house-mates people . . . who, she thought, had something important to contribute."[2]

Many found opportunities in the various social work agencies. Some stayed a few years and then took jobs in government, business, or the university. Others remained to become social work executives. Nearly all the important New York figures achieved leadership positions by the age of forty, and many moved from a first job into an executive post in less than ten years. Most had become executives by 1917, when the United States entered the war in Europe, and they constituted the managerial class of social work.

New York social workers were in many ways similar to colleagues in Chicago, Boston, and other cities because social work grew up in the same manner everywhere. But they benefitted from a uniquely favorable reception given their efforts by three governors of New York—Theodore Roosevelt, Charles Evans Hughes, and William Sulzer—along with two mayors of the city—Seth Low and John Purroy Mitchel. New York's politicians, including Al Smith, who became governor in 1919, sought social workers' advice, selected them for commissions, and appointed them to administrative positions.[3] Welfare reformers in other cities and states fared less well.

During Mayor Mitchel's administration, which lasted from 1914 to 1918, the city faced an economic slump that gave social workers a prime opportunity to act: John Kingsbury was Commissioner of Public Charities, and William Matthews, Harry Hopkins, and Jane Hoey ran the Board of Child Welfare. Several others served on a Mayor's Committee on Unemployment that produced a report setting forth a comprehensive plan to combat joblessness. Little came of it because the outbreak of war in Europe spurred economic recovery. Nonetheless, a plan that anticipated later innovations had been drafted. Reformers had also suggested a new view of the unemployed: they were victims of economic conditions, and therefore not responsible for their joblessness; for this reason they deserved the kind of help that

5

would retain their self-sufficiency and sense of personal worth.[4] As Frances Perkins noted later, the actions taken in New York after 1929 were "based upon what we had done in Mitchel's administration," when her husband, Paul Wilson, had also worked in city government.[5]

The war years were a midpoint in a forty-year evolution in social worker perceptions of poverty. Nineteenth-century charity leaders had focused their attention on the degradation of the individual and destruction of the family. They feared the poor because of their potential for violence, and they sought moral correctives to pauperism, trying to instill virtues of hard work, thrift, and sobriety. They held the individual morally responsible for being poor. Progressive reformers, who were influenced by the new settlement movement, switched attention to the environment. They saw the causes of poverty in faulty structures of the economy, society, and urban-industrial life, and believed that poverty could be eliminated by changes in institutions. They sought to create more effective community organizations, to enact better social laws, and to make social expertise important in the administration of government. Because the poor were not directly responsible for their poverty, society—as an act of social justice—was to ensure opportunity for people who could grasp it, while protecting those who could not.

But the able-bodied unemployed posed a special problem: their poverty was temporary and they had to be ready to grasp opportunity when it came their way again. If welfare systems simply relieved their distress, they might relax into a state of nonproductivity. On the other hand, if punished, they might become demoralized and useless. New employment for them depended on their psychological as well as physical ability to return to jobs. Thus, a more complicated view of poverty had begun to appear by the close of the Progressive Era: reformers still sought social justice through institutional changes, but those changes had to include devices to sustain the morale of the unemployed. Later, during the Great Depression, devices to maintain the productive skills and habits as well as the morale of unemployed

Americans became the central features of the reformers' new welfare programs. Of course, New York social workers were not the only ones to discover a psychological approach to the problem of unemployment. In every place where a work relief project was started or unemployment insurance was debated, other social workers were expressing similar concerns. Yet New Yorkers had been working on the idea since late in the nineteenth century, and they usually took the lead.[6]

The New York social workers' sense of community appears to have developed out of professional rather than recreational friendships. Their letters and notes make few references to time spent in one another's homes, at concerts, the theater, or at informal gatherings. Except for Harry Hopkins, they did not become involved in sports, either as participants or spectators, although Paul Kellogg and his brother Arthur did share hiking adventures in the mountains of New Hampshire and Vermont. Some traveled together as companions to the British Isles and Europe. Unmarried women gathered each summer at a retreat kept by Lillian Wald in Connecticut. But most of those who were married vacationed with their families. In addition, there seem to have been few affairs or romantic attachments within the group. There were some deep friendships, but most were more committed to their work than to their social activities. After 1929 that work became an obsession.

A settlement house resident was on duty twenty-four hours a day. A settlement was home, social center, and classroom as well as business office. Distinguished visitors were common. Columbia University professors Adolph Berle, Raymond Moley, and Rexford Tugwell were frequent settlement guest lecturers; they became FDR's first brains trust. Poets from Greenwich Village and novelists leading a Renaissance in Harlem entertained and enlightened settlement guests with programs of verse and prose. Politicians, philanthropists, and public servants showed up at parties, exchanging ideas with constituents, beneficiaries, and clients from the neighborhood. No clear line separated a resident's work from his play. Bruno Lasker knew Henry Street

7

as "a house in which and through which people of different backgrounds might meet informally, as well as through organized activities, to help each other to a fuller understanding of our complex community life, and to work together in common cause for its betterment."[7]

The work center for most leaders was the 100 block of East Twenty-second Street. The United Charities Building occupied the corner of Twenty-second Street and Fourth Avenue; its address was shared by the Charity Organization Society (COS), the Association for Improving the Condition of the Poor (AICP), the State Charities Aid Association (SCAA), and the New York School of Social Work. The building also housed an important research library, and as Frances Perkins recalled, "Everybody who was in social work . . . went to the Charities building to the library."[8] The School of Philanthropy began there in 1898, holding its first classes under the auspices of the COS; later, after it became the School of Social Work in 1919, it moved, but only across the street to 122 East Twenty-second Street. The magazine *Charities*, which became *Charities and the Commons* and then *Survey*, started there too, again because of initiatives taken by the COS. Its general secretary, Edward T. Devine, inspired creation of both school and publication. After the School of Social Work moved, it occupied six floors of an addition attached to the Russell Sage Foundation Building. The main building, which stood a few steps farther east, at 130 East Twenty-second Street, housed the offices of the American Association of Social Workers (AASW), the Family Welfare Association of America (FWAA), and the Russell Sage Foundation (RSF), which was a national center for study of social issues. Those were just a few of the organizations headquartered in those two buildings; a change in jobs often involved no more than a change in floors or a move across the street. Just about everyone who was doing anything was there, looking in on others doing similar things. Florence Kelley loved to tell a story about a man who stuck his head through a crack in a conference room door and asked, "Ah, what's this bunch call itself today?"[9]

8

Led by editor Kellogg, the *Survey* staff understandably sought quieter surroundings for its labors, and settled at 112 East Nineteenth Street—all of three blocks away. The offices of the American Association for Labor Legislation (AALL), the American Association for Old Age Security (AAOAS), the National Child Labor Committee (NCLC), the National Consumers' League (NCL), and the Welfare Council of New York City, the first organization that sought to coordinate the city's private social services, were located within one to five blocks of the Charities Building. The concentration of activity around East Twenty-second Street nurtured close, lasting professional relationships.

At one time or another, many of the nation's welfare leaders worked together in the Twenty-second Street neighborhood. Edward Devine, Joanna Colcord, Gertrude Springer, and W. Frank Persons, who directed the New Deal's federal employment service, started out at the COS, as did Kellogg, who began his editorial work with *Charities* in 1901. The AICP was the early social work home of John Kingsbury, William Matthews, and Harry Hopkins, who was administrator-in-charge of the New Deal's relief programs. Frances Perkins's career began as executive secretary of the NCL's New York chapter; in 1927, the chapter president was Molly Dewson, who later was a close adviser of Franklin Roosevelt. Allen Burns worked at the nearby National Information Bureau before becoming director of the Association of Community Chests and Councils. Porter R. Lee directed the School of Social Work, and I. M. Rubinow, Eduard Lindeman, and Mary Simkhovitch were on its faculty. The AALL's John Andrews, the RSF's Mary Van Kleeck, the AAOAS's Abraham Epstein, the FWAA's Linton Swift, the AASW's Walter West, and the SCAA's Homer Folks worked in or near the Charities Building; most served Roosevelt's administration in an official capacity. William Hodson joined the RSF one year before becoming executive director of the Welfare Council; during the La Guardia mayoral years, he served his city as Commissioner of Public Welfare and worked closely with New Dealers. Hodson's chief assistant at the Welfare Council, Jane Hoey, was appointed

9

director of the Bureau of Public Assistance of the Social Security Administration. At least sixteen leaders from the neighborhood of the Charities Building ended up in Washington, working for the New Deal in some official way.

Since their offices were nearly adjacent, New York's leaders neither wrote many letters nor depended on telephones when communicating with one another. Their experience at East Twenty-second Street produced closer interaction—chats in corridors, strolls into colleagues' offices, conversations on elevators, exchanges of ideas over quick lunches, chance meetings on the street, evening meals before returning to the office. Reformers who worked there became a kind of interlocking welfare directorate. When Franklin Roosevelt took Perkins and Hopkins to the nation's capitol, it was a matter of habit for them to call on the talents of old colleagues in the Charities Building crowd.

East Twenty-second Street was the stronghold for Protestant, middle-class social work in New York. The principal Jewish charities and foundations were located at 71 West Forty-seventh Street, many blocks away. The center for Catholic charities was equally distant. Jewish social workers such as Solomon Lowenstein and Frances Taussig as well as Catholics such as Mary Gibbons frequently came into the East Twenty-second Street area (for example, to work as members of the executive committee of the Welfare Council's influential Coordinating Committee on Unemployment), but ideas as well as physical distance sometimes separated them from their Protestant peers. Several Jewish leaders had immigrated to the United States, and their intellectual roots lay in Eastern Europe and Russia, where socialist doctrines had taken hold late in the nineteenth century. In addition, they worked with socialist labor unions and political parties on New York's lower East Side. Harry Lurie was one of them. He was a critic of capitalism and of social work theories that accepted its economic system. Catholics also took an independent course, assuming less separation between church and

10

state and sometimes insisting on state aid for parochial institutions, positions that made Protestants balk. Jane Hoey was the only Catholic from New York to serve the New Deal in a major welfare post; there were no Jews.

The New York-New Deal connection, then, was based on a Protestant, middle-class establishment, but this group still contained diverse elements. Several middle-class Protestants voted for and sometimes called themselves socialists. Others were surely influenced by Abraham Epstein and I. M. Rubinow, whose ideas on unemployment compensation derived from socialist theory. Moreover, mutual goals never overcame all personal differences. Lawson Purdy of the COS simply disliked Harry Hopkins, and William Matthew's contentious ways aggravated people. Leaders managed to work together, but they did not always love one another.

All social work leaders of this period—Protestants, Catholics, and Jews—shared some basic assumptions. Their welfare programs were designed to save the traditional family. They focused on the male's role of producer and provider, and usually relegated married women to dependency on their husbands; the plight of single persons was virtually ignored. Hence a paradox: in New York as in other cities, men and women in social work shared leadership duties, but devoted themselves to preservation of the male-dominated family. This paradox was hardly new; reformers had always tried to protect women in their roles of wife and child-bearer. The two organizations most responsible for protective legislation were the National Consumers' League and the Women's Trade Union League, each of which maintained national headquarters and local chapters in New York. The NCL and WTUL, which were led by women, offered supportive groups to other female leaders in social work. In this way Florence Kelley and Mary Dreier had been mentors to Perkins, Dewson, and Rose Schneiderman, all of whom joined the New Deal. (Eleanor Roosevelt was intimately associated with both groups too.) Although most of these women never mar-

11

ried, they drew no conclusions from the evidence of their own careers, and generally failed to insist on female independence or equal treatment with men under the new welfare programs.

Social work was not exclusively a woman's profession, though it was often perceived that way. Female leaders were usually associated with settlement houses and agencies engaged in research and publication. Men headed the wealthier and more powerful charity organizations and civic action groups. Even when the executive committees of groups such as the Welfare Council were mixed, males appear to have dominated. Perhaps they used their positions to put their values into effect (nearly all headed traditional families). But female leaders rarely protested a policy; they seemed content with programs that preserved the family as it was.

During the 1920s, social workers were fighting merely to keep the reform tradition alive, in part because working and living conditions improved rapidly during the decade. Some enlightened employers were reforming their business practices, building safer factories, providing free health care, instituting pension plans, and offering bonuses as incentives to productive employees.[10] Meanwhile, the familiar clients of the settlements and charities—the immigrant poor, whose numbers were shrinking anyway because of new immigration quotas—were migrating out of Manhattan to middle-class outer boroughs and suburbs. Growing prosperity seemed to assure the eventual amelioration of most social evils.

12   Only in the area of workmen's compensation, which provided employees with some protection against losses due to on-the-job accidents, had the progressives secured permanent state legislation. Other losses, whether due to old age, sickness, or joblessness, were left "at loose ends," as Paul Kellogg acknowledged.[11] The state helped the most helpless—the insane, the handicapped, orphans, widowed mothers, the indigent sick, and the indigent elderly—but public aid often meant institutional care in asylums, almshouses, and the like. For the vast majority

of Americans as well as New Yorkers, there was no assurance that prosperity would continue, and little protection if it did not.

Even local reform initiatives fell short of success. In 1925, New York joined a movement among private philanthropies in cities across the nation to create welfare councils. The Welfare Council of New York City was to provide an integrated social service program that would allow for "a concerted attack upon fundamental causes of poverty, sickness, and other forms of human suffering," according to William Hodson, its first executive director.[12] By 1928, six hundred and forty privately-run welfare agencies from the city's count of over eleven hundred had joined the Council. They were to work together, reaching decisions by mutual consent through a "conference method" of mediation and compromise. But getting hundreds of different private agencies to cooperate was no easy task. Even when a policy was recommended by the executive committee, compliance was voluntary and not always forthcoming. The Welfare Council turned in aimless circles during a period of economic growth. "I wish we could carry over into non-emergency times something of the enthusiasm for team play that can be marshalled when an emergency arises," Hodson lamented in a letter to Lillian Wald.[13]

Reformers were also confronted by theories of modern psychology that stressed the old idea of individual responsibility. New specialists—psychiatric caseworkers—began to describe the poor in terms of diseased mental conditions. They talked about maladjustment and abnormal behavior, and stressed with vigor the deficiencies of the individual. Growing economic prosperity added credence to their theories, since millions of formerly impoverished people were moving up the economic ladder. What was wrong with those left behind? An individual's success seemed to depend on his personality; even settlement houses began to use "character-building" programs to help people get into step with middle-class ways of living.[14]

Paul Kellogg believed that "a very small tail was wagging

13

a large dog," but psychiatric casework threatened the assumptions of reformers, especially their view of human psychology.[15] The reformers agreed with William Matthews, the director of the family welfare department of the AICP, that it was better to emphasize "the normal part of a man, not the unhappy, abnormal part."[16] They regarded their typical client as mentally able and healthy, willing to work and manage his own affairs, given the chance. They still had a program they hoped to enact for that kind of person; it involved public works, a system of public employment bureaus, unemployment insurance, old-age benefits, and health insurance, but the achievement of these goals seemed a long way off.[17]

Social workers in 1928 had little presentiment that a national crisis lay dead ahead. They were preoccupied with problems of their own. They had not yet achieved a discrete identity as professionals. Two different, competing theories about poverty, one environmental and the other based on the individual, tore at their thinking. The services they provided were insufficiently coordinated. Also, they had no political home. Yet some displayed a touching optimism: "I have complete confidence," the SCAA's Homer Folks declared, "that there is such a thing as a social program; that somewhat blindly and unconsciously, we are all striving for it, and that it is thoroughly wise and thoroughly practical and . . . thoroughly conservative, meaning by that, a wise conservation of human resources."[18] Nobody knew that the inauguration of a new president in 1929 would precede an economic catastrophe. Four consecutive winters, each more terrible than the last, each leading toward the depths of a Great Depression, each shattering earlier assumptions and teaching new lessons, would exert a galvanizing effect on New York's leaders, strengthening the interpersonal ties that bonded them together and giving them a welfare program to present to the nation.

14

2

Alfred E. Smith grew up on the lower East Side. His family home stood only blocks from Henry Street, where Lillian Wald founded her settlement house. Although the Smith family was not poor enough to attract social workers' attention, Al Smith caught their eye during his early days as an aspiring politician. People like Wald and Mary Simkhovitch remembered him as a young city alderman, and they called him neighbor.[1] Until the end of the 1920s, Smith maintained his family residence in his old neighborhood. Its character changed from middle class to working class during his lifetime; thus he shared with social workers a similar perspective on the problems of his city. From his years as a state assemblyman, and then as governor, he also displayed "the sure, unabashed and eager habit of seizing upon those who knew more than he did about any question with which he was confronted," as Paul Kellogg put it, and that habit of consulting experts brought social workers into his circle of advisers.[2] Smith's personality and his easy ability to get along with all kinds of people made him a favorite of the social work crowd. In 1928, when he ran for president, he was their hero.

15

Social workers did not easily form attachments with politicians or political parties. Lillian Wald was always a Democrat, Homer Folks favored the Republicans, Mary Simkhovitch switched from Republican to Democrat, and Paul Kellogg voted for socialists about as often as for either major party. Yet a gap existed between personal preferences and public endorsements, and for practical reasons. Social work's dependency upon philanthropists made nonpartisanship a good policy, since a host of contributors might be alienated by unacceptable endorsements. In addition, if social welfare programs became the exclusive property of one political party, they would invite partisan opposition. Moreover, a spirit of professionalism demanded that programs be developed objectively, adopted on the basis of merit, and administered impartially. For these reasons Lillian Wald refused to endorse Al Smith's bid for reelection as governor in 1926.[3]

Politics also smacked of the unsavory. Social workers wanted welfare programs to be run professionally, with equal justice for all regardless of party. They knew that local political machines like New York's Tammany Hall did not meet those expectations. Often, social workers competed with ward leaders, who distributed groceries to the needy and jobs to the unemployed. Such services were rendered by the machine in order to build support at the polls, and benefits went to loyal party followers. In addition, most of the county's public welfare administrators and many staff personnel were political appointees. Frequently, they lacked the training and skills of the professional social worker. "We have not discovered in this country," Porter Lee declared midway through the 1920s, "how to eliminate political considerations in the vulgar sense from public [welfare] administration," because what was true of Tammany Hall pertained to the actions of political organizations generally.[4]

The reformers among the social workers, however, argued that they had a legitimate interest in government, which implied a legitimate role within politics. In William Hodson's estimation, the future of social service depended on "the gradual

16

acceptance of the social worker by the community as one skilled in the *art* of adjusting human relations, and the recognition that there is inherent in that skill a measure of *authority and expert judgment* in public welfare questions."[5] Others argued that their experience and insight justified not only their participation in government, but the expression of their personal political convictions as well. Mary Simkhovitch of Greenwich House settlement insisted that "those who have lived the life of their time & lived it with the deepest sense of responsibility are the very persons whose convictions are worth having."[6]

In this manner reformers gradually became political partisans. Usually they committed themselves to individual candidates rather than parties. As activists whom Simkhovitch called "searchers for the unifying & vital truth-in-action," they sought out candidates who were sympathetic to their cause and ready to act on their recommendations.[7] Among New Yorkers, Al Smith compelled avid support. Indeed, Lillian Wald cast aside her nonpartisanship in 1928, leading a crusade to elect Smith to the presidency. The confrontation between the New Yorkers' favorite warrior for welfare, Al Smith, and the hero of European war relief, Herbert Hoover, aroused more enthusiasm and controversy in the nation's social work circles than any other election since 1912.

In gathering under Smith's colors, New York City's leaders did not place themselves under a distinct ideological banner. Each major-party candidate displayed strong progressive tendencies as well as explicitly conservative leanings. When social workers clustered together in support of Al Smith, they merged their forces near the ambiguous center of changing political, economic, and social strategies; that centrist disposition was to characterize their behavior throughout the Great Depression years.[8] In 1934, some leaders like Mary Van Kleeck would break sharply to the left,[9] while others like Lawson Purdy would dismiss "Mrs. [Franklin] Roosevelt [as] a socialist." [10] But these were exceptions. Social work's leaders remained notably loyal to the New Deal, clinging to a style of political action that rejected the ideologies of either left or right.[11] Their attachment to Al Smith in 1928 gave an early indication of this middle course.

Bluntly put, New Yorkers engaged in a politics of personalism—a politics of trusting political leaders as individuals. They applauded Al Smith as a friend and neighbor, in part because he won the confidence of social workers during his years as majority leader of the state assembly. Frances Perkins, for example, had taken both Smith and Robert F. Wagner on an instructive tour of New York state factories; she showed them how deplorable industrial working conditions could be, and suggested corrective measures. Later, when Smith became governor, he appointed Perkins to a series of terms as a member of the state's Industrial Commission. Moreover, Smith established himself as a welfare politician, advancing measures such as improved care for the insane, higher standards of public health service, increased benefits for dependent children, rent control legislation, public funding of low-cost housing, and maximum hours-minimum wage laws to protect women and children. He also reorganized the state's executive departments, achieving greater administrative efficiency and control over public welfare services.[12] The fact that he was a fiscal conservative and a strict constructionist of the Constitution who believed in state rather than federal powers (and a Tammany man to boot) hardly bothered social workers. They admired Smith's ability to clarify complex issues and inspire people to take action. "You understand him," Paul Kellogg observed; "even more, he understands you on the other side; and presto, American life has a lift of adventure to it again."[13] Smith neatly fit the description in Mary Simkhovitch's 1949 autobiography, where in consecutive chapters on "Welfare" and "Politics" she stressed the importance of a network of people over the similarity of ideas.[14]

Many old Progressives abandoned nonpartisanship during September 1928. Edward T. Devine led the way. In a public endorsement, he declared that social workers found Al Smith "interested in the relief and prevention of poverty, in the humane care of the sick and disabled; in the rational treatment of criminals." Rebuking people who scorned the Happy Warrior as "a wet Catholic, a Tammany Catholic, a Catholic from the tenements, the sidewalks and fish markets of New York," Devine characterized him as "a student, not perhaps of the classics but of affairs; not perhaps of ancient good but of shifting, changing, developing events."[15] At about the same time, Eleanor Roosevelt persuaded Lillian Wald to declare her convictions. The founder of the nation's first visiting nurses' service and of her own settlement house in 1893, she was a favorite among New Yorkers and a well known national figure as well. Wald agreed to chair the Welfare Division of the Democratic Party's National Women's Advisory Committee.[16] Then, along with John Elliott, who had founded Hudson Guild settlement in 1895, she endorsed Smith's candidacy. In an open letter published in the *New York Times* and distributed to social workers throughout the country, the two settlement leaders called Smith "a great social statesman" and a "vital humanitarian." They praised his "genius for comprehending what social work is" and described his policies as serving "all classes."[17]

A host of New York's welfare leaders followed Devine, Wald, and Elliott into the campaign. A Social Workers National Committee for Smith took shape, and three of its many New York members—Mary Van Kleeck, Walter West, and William Hodson—drafted a statement hailing Smith as "a statesman in social welfare who will make social justice a national issue."[18] Frederick C. Howe, a municipal reformer and author of *The City: The Hope of Democracy*, initiated a Progressive League for Alfred E. Smith, and Paul Kellogg agreed to serve on its executive committee.[19] The president of the New York branch of the National Consumers' League, Molly Dewson, joined one of the League's members, Eleanor Roosevelt, in stumping the state for Smith.[20] Mary Simkhovitch did the same, while Frances Perkins toured the country to give speeches on Smith's behalf.[21] Back in the city, Harry Hopkins set up a social workers' desk at Democratic headquarters and began sending campaign literature to social workers across the nation.[22]

Outside of New York, however, social workers scarcely welcomed Smith's candidacy. As Wald told Kellogg, "John Elliott's and my letter has brought upon our heads—particularly upon mine—a storm of objection."[23] A colleague from South Carolina wrote Wald, attacking Smith's stand against Prohibition: "Whenever your sympathies overwhelm you about the wash women to whom Gov. Smith has guaranteed water, don't forget that he plans to make their husbands so drunk that they will never be able to leave the tub."[24] Other letters were more comprehensible. A Pittsburgh colleague criticized Smith's association with Tammany Hall:

> Tammany Hall . . . has no sympathy with progressive scientific social methods. I do not deny that Governor Smith has been associated with some desirable legislation for social betterment but that he is a "social statesman" and in any sense a master of social science, I do not for one moment believe. . . . Tammany has given many people jobs and done things for the common people to get their support and votes—but not for humanitarian reasons.[25]

Still other social workers were far from immune to the religious prejudice that swept Protestant America in 1928, as Wald soon discovered. She described "much of" her incoming mail as showing "direct or veiled anti-Catholicism."[26] Like many other Americans in 1928, social workers could be bigots.

Many social workers genuinely favored Herbert Hoover. Soon after publication of the Wald-Elliott letter, Jane Addams of Chicago's Hull House endorsed Hoover, expressing her own conviction that he held the edge on Smith as a champion of social welfare.[27] Even Governor Smith's first social service supporter, Edward T. Devine, acknowledged Hoover's attractiveness. The 1928 election, he explained diplomatically, offered candidates who "really know more about social work, and are more interested in constructive measures for raising the standards of living and abolishing poverty, than any candidates for the presidency ever before presented by any political party."[28] For some social service leaders, of course, the attractiveness of both

20

candidates constituted a reason to avoid endorsing either. Joanna Colcord, for instance, wrote Wald, "It seems to me there is little to choose between the social service record of the two men, and certainly no reason for social workers *as such* to line themselves up in support of the one or against the other." [29]

Hoover entered government service during the war, after completing a brilliant career as a mining engineer and businessman. His work for the Food Administration under the War Industries Board and his administration of relief in Belgium and throughout war-torn Europe won him high praise in social work circles. In 1921, President Harding appointed him Secretary of Commerce, a position he used to become the nation's spokesman for the "new economics" of the 1920s. Hoover tried to bring greater stability to industry by curbing unfair competitive practices and by encouraging cooperation through informal trade associations; in other words, he advocated some government planning and direction of the economy. Hoover also chaired the first President's Committee on Unemployment, which asserted government's responsibility for counteracting major dips in the business cycle. In addition, he personally approved of independent labor unions, endorsed public works as a means of stimulating economic activity, and sought better public health and education programs. Finally, he led the successful Mississippi flood relief effort of 1927.[30] Indeed, Herbert Hoover bore impressive progressive credentials. "I have very genuine admiration for him," Paul Kellogg admitted to Frances Perkins, "and was prepared to vote and work for him if Smith had not been nominated."[31]

21

If New Yorkers' hearts belonged to Al Smith, their endorsements, committee statements, and private letters disclose that their effort was narrowly regional in its conception and impact. "[I]n New York and in Connecticut where I know people most intimately," Wald observed, "the majority of those whose opinion we respect and who are accustomed to use their reasons, are for Al," but she conceded that support was slight elsewhere.[32] She compared Smith's circle of New York backers to "a bonfire on a cake of ice," lamenting the failure of the nation's social workers to favor her choice.[33] The fact that New Yorkers in particular endorsed Smith also provoked charges of clannish provincialism and elitist snobbery from social workers in other cities. "This political campaign is responsible for many vagaries," a colleague from Detroit wrote Elliott. "One of them assuredly is the endeavor to capitalize the national standing which social workers on Manhatten [*sic*] may have in political communications to the supposed benighted residents who are social workers in the provinces."[34] His comment may have been appropriate, because New Yorkers did pretend to national influence. Another of Wald's correspondents remembered resenting a similar political endorsement made years earlier by "a member of the New York group."[35] A third associate, who respected each candidate but favored Hoover, expressed his own reservations about the New Yorkers' visibility: "If such a letter [endorsing Smith] were to be sent, it would come most appropriately from someone not a member of the community of greater New York—a city alien to the country as a whole in its ideals and opinions."[36] Instead of helping Smith, New York's outspoken reformers may have added a stigma to his candidacy.

Al Smith went down to defeat. The crucial factor determining the election's outcome was unprecedented prosperity, an issue on which Republican Hoover was unbeatable, though debate continues on whether Hoover was the more progressive candidate, or whether Smith's identification as a wet, Catholic, Tammany Hall New Yorker worked against him.[37] "Smith is a hero and will go down as a great figure, even though the majority repudiated him yesterday," a stunned Lillian Wald believed.[38] Others recognized, however, that the election had been a contest between two capable candidates, each of whom had prompted social workers to involve themselves in politics. "Throughout the campaign there was talk of social statesmanship and public welfare," William Hodson observed, "and the social worker realized, perhaps for the first time, that some of the things that interest him most have become subject matter of national politics."[39] In the months following the election, as the emotional heat of the campaign subsided, reformers pondered the choice that had faced them and adopted a conciliatory tone.[40]

New York's leaders, of course, never forgot Al Smith. Their commitment to him had aroused intense personal loyalties. In addition to respecting his qualifications as a welfare politician, they admired his understanding of the "give and take among the rank and file of folk in a democratic society," which made him a leader capable of bringing his promises to fruition.[41] Before the 1928 contest, Paul Kellogg averred, social workers and public officials "were considered like unto two species," but in Al Smith "they had actually been crossed."[42] Smith's candidacy had also aroused the reformers' moral passions. Wald and Perkins both felt that duty compelled them to defend Smith against the prejudices that swept the American electorate in 1928, and Perkins endured countless hecklers, Ku Klux Klan cross burnings, and tomato cannonades in her effort to calm people's fears.

Most importantly, the reformers knew Smith personally and were intimate with many of his advisers and governmental associates. Unfortunately for the Republican victor, the same could not be said for Herbert Hoover. Even though they expected positive results from his presidency, they suspected his qualifications as a national leader because he had never before served in an elective post. In Kellogg's estimation, this cost Hoover vital exposure to democratic ways and made his politics an artificial, "acquired characteristic."[43] Moreover, Hoover was not known personally by New York's reformers, nor were his closest aides. In his many relief activities, the new president had always acted independently, selecting his own staff and creating organizations without drawing upon the resources of the nation's established social work profession.[44] Indeed, he maintained no direct lines of communication with the national leadership concentrated in New York. Thus, Hoover had remained a

23

remote figure, known by his impressive record, but not through personal associations.

The election of 1928 challenged and defeated the doctrine that professional social work required political nonpartisanship. In their rush into one camp or the other, the nation's social workers had raised to new heights the public's consciousness of welfare programs and the cause of social justice. New York's avid pro-Smith reformers suffered a defeat, but after 1928, they came to expect political leaders to respond to their ideas. A decade of political passivity had ended. In addition, the election of 1928 afforded New Yorkers an experience that forged a stronger sense of community among them. Their isolation amid the nation's body of social workers, the intensity of their devotion to Al Smith, and the effect of defending a "city boy" against the irrational forces of prejudice and bigotry made them aware of their own distinctiveness.

3

On January 1, 1929, Franklin D. Roosevelt took the oath of office that made him Al Smith's successor as governor of New York. Less than ten months later the stock market crash plunged the country into despair. The Great Depression so often associated with the crash, however, did not come immediately. For two years following the securities debacle, Americans experienced a deepening recession. During this time the economy's decline and the reactions of people to it resembled the movement of giant glaciers; as Lillian Wald put it, the coming of the Great Depression was "no sudden avalanche, but a creeping daily change." [1]

The nation's system of private philanthropies—its charities, settlement houses, free hospitals and health clinics, and other privately funded welfare organizations—stood as the front line of defense against rising unemployment. Public agencies—municipalities, counties, and state governments—stood close at hand, but their powers in aiding the able-bodied unemployed were severely restricted by charters and constitutions. Could charities and settlements bear the weight of the unemployed? Social workers grew testy when challenged by that question. A perceptive paper written by I. M. Rubinow—which was submitted for publication to *Survey* early in the summer of 1928 and finally rejected by the editors in February 1929, after months of agonized discussion—revealed that the alternative to private philanthropy, public relief, was a bugaboo for many social workers. Rubinow argued that charity could not provide adequate relief during periods of economic crisis and massive unemployment. Only government had the "power of raising the necessary funds" and the authority to impose satisfactory programs on entire communities. Providing relief, therefore, had to become a public duty.[2] Rubinow's thesis was straightforward, and in retrospect, patently realistic, but few of his colleagues could see that in 1928–1929. *Survey*'s editors sent the manuscript to several readers, who divided sharply in their responses. Those closely identified with the settlements and their reform tradition supported his position, but agents of the community chest movement and several charity leaders adamantly opposed it. *Survey* returned the piece as too controversial for publication.[3]

The fate of Rubinow's manuscript demonstrates how strongly social workers felt about the issue of public relief. Private philanthropy and voluntary community action were traditions deeply ingrained in the social service movement. During 1929, for example, New York City expended approximately one hundred million dollars for all its health and welfare services. Seventy percent of those funds derived from private sources, including annual contributions from individuals, foundation grants, earnings on investments, and endowments.[4] Although charitable giving was not in fact widespread, most social workers defended it as adequate for New York's needs. Moreover, few social workers believed that government would provide service at philanthropy's level of competence, and many feared that the cherished spontaneity and flexibility of their work would be ruined by government bureaucracy. Government was expected to provide assistance for permanently dependent groups like the insane, but general relief was considered the preserve of private philanthropy. These established doctrines were occasionally challenged by luminaries such as Rubinow and Homer Folks, who in 1928 also called for the "authority of legislation and public action, and the resources of the public Treasury" in combatting economic distress, but they were generally ignored.[5]

A rise in unemployment, however, was attracting attention as early as 1928. "We keep getting reports of an unemployment situation throughout the country of increasing seriousness," one of *Survey*'s editors reported in January.[6] In New York, joblessness continued to increase throughout the winter months. The Welfare Council reported that the volume of family relief work rose between 11 and 17 percent above the previous winter's average; the Municipal Lodging House experienced a 15 percent increase in homeless men seeking shelter and food; and the state's employment service found it increasingly difficult to place men in new jobs.[7] Here was a substantive issue for Paul U. Kellogg. Because he was consistently quick to articulate changes in social needs, Frances Perkins later referred to him as "a live flame" among social work's reformers.[8] Kellogg asked settlement workers to "make full use of their closeness to the human matrix of unemployment to help people to see and feel, and to touch springs of action,"[9] and his *Survey Graphic* published articles in March that "grew out of a little gathering at Miss Wald's, at which settlement workers and those next of kin to them swapped testimony as to the spread of unemployment in January."[10]

Yet it was terribly difficult to get a clear focus on the problem. About a year later, in April 1929 (one month after Herbert Hoover was inaugurated), *Survey Graphic* devoted a special issue to unemployment that gave readers a glimpse of the situation that would soon beset them. "We are so accustomed to associate unemployment with prostrate industry, closed factories, and universal profound depression," analyst William Leiserson wrote, "that it is hard to revise our ideas and grasp the fact that we must also grapple with an unemployment problem that is the direct outcome of prosperity."[11] But he was preoccupied with the

27

features of technological unemployment—the joblessness that results from accelerated mechanization and more efficient production techniques. The veil of 1920s prosperity still obscured the prophetic aspect of his statement: that abundance itself would trigger a depression. Nor did analysts know how many unemployed men and women there were. The federal Bureau of Labor Statistics supplied monthly employment figures for major industries and the wholesale and retail trades, but neither federal nor state governments collected figures on unemployment. Private organizations like the American Association of Community Chests and Councils tried to gather data independently, but all such efforts relied on superficial assessments of business conditions, incomplete reports from labor unions, and impressions gained by doctors, teachers, and social workers.[12] A lack of both insight and information hampered the analysis of unemployment in 1929. Meanwhile, as industrial production outstripped increases in real earnings and the ability of average Americans to consume industry's products, the "poverty of abundance" propelled the nation into deepening recession.[13] In 1929, however, social workers knew only that lagging employment had swelled their relief rolls.

Yet unemployment hardly seemed a grave problem, even to its most sensitive observers. Social workers had experienced several recessions and minor depressions since the last major economic dislocation in 1893, and they were wary of sounding an alarm at this point. Nonetheless, the Welfare Council dusted off a plan to combat unemployment advanced by reformers in 1914. It assigned the job of dispensing relief to private welfare agencies, while recommending that the city increase public works, award new public contracts to major private employers, expand free employment bureaus, and increase aid for homeless men seeking food and shelter.[14] *Survey Graphic* followed suit, adding that state government should also engage in more public works. In addition, its editors urged the state to promote employment "regularity" campaigns among private

employers and to study unemployment insuran
None of these proposals, however, marked a rad'
from the responsibilities of government as defined anu ⌐.
dorsed by President Harding's Conference on Unemployment
in 1921. Government might stimulate economic activity through
public works programs and help people find new jobs in private
industry, but the direct relief of economic distress remained a
task for privately supported agencies. Even though Paul Kellogg
labelled joblessness "the great neglected social hazard of our
time," the profession was moving ahead cautiously.[16]

Survey barely noticed the stock market crash late in
1929, observing only that it was a portent of harder times to
come.[17] Residents at Henry Street settlement noted that some local employers were cutting payrolls, while the visiting nurses discovered more cases of undernourishment among the families
they served.[18] A handful of breadlines appeared. During the
winter of 1929–1930, however, private agencies went about
their usual business, expanding service here and there to meet
new demands. The AICP launched a small work relief program
as an experiment, employing a few hundred jobless men to work
in city parks for three dollars a day.[19] Other welfare agencies expanded their programs, until by winter's end they were spending about fifty thousand dollars a week over their allocated
budgets for relief. This seemed a substantial increase but its inadequacy became apparent when an AICP study disclosed that
city wages had fallen by at least four and one-half million dollars
a week.[20]

29

Introducing its second special issue on joblessness within
twelve months, Survey Graphic now alluded to a "depression"
that was gripping "the richest country in all history."[21] Yet writ-
ers talked alternatively about a "recession" and a "depression"
without being consistent in their definition of either word.
When social workers gathered in Boston in springtime for their
annual National Conference, John A. Fitch of the New York
School of Social Work used the growing sense of uneasiness to

question the ability of psychiatric casework to deal with the peculiar problem of widespread unemployment. Because he saw "the degree of mastery or lack of it possessed by the individual . . . over those aspects of life that are economic in character" as "the most important element in the social environment," Fitch challenged his colleagues to turn their attention once again to the problem of economic injustice.[22] The edge to his challenge had been dulled, however, by recent reports that jobs were increasing in the early summer months of 1930.

Social workers did not yet know that they had passed through the first annual cycle in a series of winter-by-winter crises that led, ultimately, to the Great Depression. Winter was the hardest season for the unemployed. Warm weather posed fewer physical hardships and also brought temporary jobs in seasonal industries such as agriculture and construction. It was the winter months, therefore, that tested the mettle both of social workers and their doctrines. Major changes in social welfare policies usually occurred just before, during, or at the conclusion of, each of four increasingly severe winter seasons.

During the winter of 1929–1930, New York's private welfare agencies had provided *ad hoc* emergency relief services without direction from a central authority and without much assistance from government at any level. The winter of 1930–1931 began with a central organization and a plan, both of which derived from private philanthropy's efforts to meet the crisis, and ended with the intervention of city government. Municipal and state governments became fully involved during the winter of 1931–1932, and winter closed with a plea for federal intervention. The resources of the national treasury flowed into relief programs for the first time during the winter of 1932–1933, the most severe of the Depression Era. With the coming of the New Deal, the federal government made ready for the winter of 1933–1934 by legislating its own national program. In the summer of 1930, however, no social worker could have predicted that a depression would turn her world upside down within four years.

30

President Hoover believed in traditions of private, voluntary action. His progressive creed dictated that he do as much as needed to activate philanthropic responses to the emerging national problem of unemployment. He embraced in principle the need to involve local and state governments as well. Accordingly, he created a President's Emergency Committee for Employment during the fall of 1930. The PECE was to advise government leaders in establishing local employment committees, spread information among private employers about stabilizing employment, encourage investments in construction and repairs by state and local governments and private individuals (businessmen and homeowners), and administer an emergency appropriation of over one hundred million dollars for federal public works.[23] Yet the president's program provided no direct means of aiding people for whom jobs were unavailable, and left to local communities the entire burden of raising funds and organizing relief services. "[W]hen it comes down to the bare facts of food and shelter," associate editor Gertrude Springer reported in *Survey*, "it is the community organization that holds the bag, the community that must measure its problem and muster its resources to deal with it."[24]

Most American cities were poorly prepared to assume that obligation. During 1929, for example, the total expenditures for relief in twenty-two cities amounted to only one dollar per resident. Twenty-three cities spent a total of only nine and one-half million dollars for relief, an amount surpassed by New York alone.[25] Moreover, most municipalities, including New York, were prohibited by law from spending public monies for anything other than institutional care of the needy. Such restrictions were inherited from the Progressive Era, when reformers had tried to curb politicians' use of tax-collected revenues for partisan political purposes. The laws also embodied a late nineteenth-century theory of "scientific" philanthropy, that social dependents should be placed in institutional environments and closely supervised.[26] As a result, the able-bodied unemployed of the early 1930s did not qualify for public modes of care. Having no legal option, municipal government left the responsibility of mobilizing local relief efforts to philanthropic agencies.

New York's social servants confidently took their cue from the President's Committee. In October, the city's two largest charities, the AICP and the COS, joined hands and named Seward Prosser to head an Emergency Employment Committee. Eleven family welfare agencies shared in the Committee's fund, including the Salvation Army, the Catholic Charities, and the Jewish Social Service Association. Each was authorized to give relief, usually food and clothing, after determining individual need. A family applying for relief was investigated by a caseworker and checked through the Welfare Council's Social Service Exchange. Once relief began, follow-up investigations could be made and special treatment—such as psychiatric care—could be provided. The Prosser Committee and four family welfare agencies also sponsored an Emergency Work Bureau, which offered jobs at five dollars a day for three days each week. William Matthews, who had run the AICP's experiment in work relief the winter before, directed the EWB, which was allotted eight and one-quarter million dollars for the winter. The Welfare Council served as an independent advisory and publicity organization. Its Social Service Exchange, subscribed to by more than two hundred agencies, maintained records on relief recipients and gathered data on unemployment. Late in the fall, its Information Service published a series of guides to help physicians, clergymen, and policemen direct the unemployed to agencies that could help them. The Council also created a Committee of One Hundred, under the leadership of former governor Al Smith, to coordinate private relief efforts in the city.[27]

Private philanthropy was well prepared for the winter of 1930–1931, but some kinds of charity did not meet with social workers' approval. Eighty-two breadlines appeared in the city. "Anyone could start a breadline and anyone did," Gertrude Springer reported.[28] Some distributors of free food were "pseudo-philanthropists," including petty political opportunists and swindlers. The Lower East Side Community Council found that a food station at the corner of Grand and Chrystie Streets was sponsored by a Tammany Hall political club and named "in the memory of a [politician's] dead relative." Another, the "Kosher Kitchen," was operated by an elected municipal judge. A third, "St. Mark's Place," was soon shut down by the police, because the public's charity was ending up in the pockets of an excommunicated priest.[29] Social workers deplored the proliferating breadlines and similar spontaneous efforts in do-good relief as often inefficient, even when not corrupt; more importantly, they thought that such uncontrolled, indiscriminate charity fostered demoralization and degeneracy.[30] Some food stations had to be and were approved by social workers—especially those operated by the Salvation Army, the YMCA, and the city's Public Welfare Department—because they maintained professional standards and directed the needy to agencies where they could receive professional help. Such "official" food stations served an estimated eighty-two thousand meals a day near the end of 1930.[31] The so-called "glorification" breadlines, however, were deplored. "It was becoming increasingly clear," Frances Perkins commented, "that the role of the charitable who established soup kitchens . . . was the role of the well-meaning spectator."[32] Social work's goal was to save people from pauperism, and social workers demanded that assistance be uniform and professional, even in breadlines.

The social settlements used their own distinctive methods to contribute to the relief of misery. The program at Henry Street was probably typical. With funds and supplies granted by the Prosser Committee, neighborhood workers distributed food, clothing, and fuel to jobless families. They also began a free milk program for children and created a small work project, hiring men to build and plant flower boxes for the neighborhood. Women received jobs as nurses' aides with the Visiting Nurses' Service, as school lunch attendants in the settlement's hot lunch program, and as housekeepers for invalids served by the nurses. Other women earned a dollar or two a day by enrolling in a sewing class and learning a skill. A training school was begun for

33

unemployed young people, which enrolled one hundred applicants during its first week of operation. All the while, settlement
workers searched for jobs for the unemployed, either with the
EWB or private employers.[33] Henry Street added these activities
to its normal services during the winter of 1930–1931. "All the
Henry Street people are working incessantly," Lillian Wald wrote
her friend J. Ramsay MacDonald, at the end of January 1931. "I
am sorry to say that the unemployment situation in America
is . . . inexcusably bad."[34]

Wald's words expressed a changing mood in social workers during that winter of 1930–1931. In October, social service
leaders had been optimistic about their plans and had rejected a
need for government action. They worried that a public assistance program might attract masses of transients seeking greener
relief pastures. They believed that much could still be achieved
in coordinating local, voluntary relief efforts. Most of all, they
feared panic if government suddenly stepped into philanthropy's relief program. As late as December 1930, in a letter to
Lieutenant-Governor Herbert Lehman, the Welfare Council's
William Hodson termed the prospect of public aid "hasty," "ill-
considered," and "fraught with great danger." An attached
memorandum from the Council urged that "there is no evidence as yet that any locality has failed to measure up to its full
duty," and requested the state to refrain from action unless local
funds were exhausted.[35] Lawson Purdy, the executive director of
the COS, wrote in a similar vein to Porter R. Lee, who was serving on Hoover's PECE. Purdy believed that a federal relief program "would interfere with local effort, exaggerate the suffering, and do a great deal of harm."[36]

At the same time, however, the Social Service Exchange
was clearing five thousand new relief applications a day from
New Yorkers who could not find new jobs. In an effort to locate
employment opportunities, the Welfare Council conducted a
"job stimulation" canvass, contacting four thousand five hundred employers who might have work. They found only eighty-
seven jobs. Even before the end of 1930, the Council's Commit-

tee on Unemployment admitted that "it seemed unlikely that all of the [city's] resources combined would be able completely to prevent distress and destitution."[37] Then, late in February 1931, the unthinkable happened: private home relief rolls were closed to new applicants and the EWB stopped accepting men from its job line. "It is almost unbelievable, the misery of the jobless masses," Lillian Wald declared, as the number of unaided people continued to mount.[38] With the funds earmarked for private relief programs virtually exhausted, the social workers' only recourse was to turn to city government for public assistance.

It had taken the leaders of social work about ten weeks to abandon a cherished doctrine: that private philanthropy should care for the poor. They had expended great effort and ingenuity in adding new programs for the unemployed to their regular services, but as Rubinow had predicted, massive unemployment demolished the theory that private, voluntary actions would suffice in a crisis. In addition, leaders had uncovered the potential of an organization that would carry new ideas to City Hall and Albany: the Welfare Council. Directors of the city's major charities and leading settlement houses, such as Solomon Lowenstein, Bailey Burritt (of the AICP), Mary Simkhovitch, and Lillian Wald worked on its executive committee, which was chaired by Homer Folks. Together with the Council's executive director, William Hodson, they had been translating the perceptions of social workers throughout the city into fresh policies. Late in February 1931, the Welfare Council turned one hundred and eighty degrees and implored government officials to act immediately. Social welfare had entered the political arena.

35

Social workers gathered in a mass meeting on February 27, 1931, and resolved that "charitable relief can never be expected to fill the tremendous void in the purchasing power that is created when payrolls stop." The assembly resolved further that the city appropriate ten million dollars for a new work relief program and expand public works.[39] Those resolutions, the first to acknowledge the inadequacy of philanthropy in dealing with unemployment, and the first to demand public intervention, went to Governor Franklin D. Roosevelt on March 2.[40] On March 13, the leaders of the Welfare Council's Committee on Unemployment presented the resolutions to the city's Board of Estimate along with more than a thousand letters from social workers throughout Gotham.[41] City officials responded by approving a plan, worked out by a joint committee of social service leaders and executives in the Department of Public Welfare, to establish a municipal work relief program similar to that of the EWB and financed by public revenues.[42] On March 30, Governor Roosevelt put his authority behind the plan, delivering an emergency message to the state legislature. That same afternoon, the legislature passed a bill enabling the city to spend public monies for relief, and FDR signed it into law the following day.

At last, social reform and political activism had come together to produce a permanent change in New York's relief policies, reducing the role played by private philanthropy and promoting governmental action. The mass meeting in February, which was followed by a demonstration before the Board of Estimate in March and by fruitful negotiations with city and state officials, seemed to prove the worth of a "spirit and practice of concerted action." William Hodson, who had hammered out the city's plan with the help of Homer Folks and other reformers, celebrated the lesson he believed social workers had learned: "Governmental participation in social work is not to be had simply for the asking," but must be won through forceful, unrelenting pressure on public officers.[43] "We are in one kind of war," Folks declared, giving voice to new energies released by the reformers' victory, "a war against economic and social disorganization and possible disaster." Private philanthropy was still important, he told social workers, "but don't make the serious mistake of thinking for a moment that private charity can take over the duty of the public authorities . . . to care for those who are in need, and are not otherwise helped."[44] In addition, Porter R. Lee now saw the social worker in a new position of responsibility and authority "as collaborator with industrial economists, industrial managers, political scientists and [public] administrators in . . . the drafting of legislative programs."[45] Indeed, a new kind of expert—an authority on unemployment and its insecurities and anxieties—was beginning to assume a role in legislative enterprises, and with his ascent, reform's prospects looked increasingly bright.

Much had transpired between late 1928, when Rubinow and Folks made controversial calls for public action, and the events of early 1931. Private philanthropy had failed in an unemployment emergency. Deeply held beliefs had been sharply reversed in a universal call for "complete mobilization," including the enlistment of government's collective forces.[46] Only one small step, of course, had been taken—that of involving city government in the battle against unemployment's hardships. But before the leaves fell from the city's trees in 1931, the state government of New York would enter the fray, and before snows had covered the city's avenues again, reformers would carry their cause into the halls of Congress. A militant note was appropriate. The reformers did not know what lay ahead, but perhaps they sensed their mission already, because the annual May meeting of the New York Conference of Social Work took its theme from a World War I military dispatch:

> My right has been rolled up.
> My left has been driven back.
> My center has been smashed.
> I have ordered an advance from all directions.[47]

**Starting
with
business,
where
the
jobs
are**

4

New York's dramatic shift from charity to public relief raised new questions. What kind of public relief—home relief, which was distributed to people because of their need, or work relief, which people earned because they were able and willing to labor for it—would better serve the unemployed? How much money was needed and from what public source? How could private philanthropy's social workers implant their profession in an alien field, public welfare, occupied primarily by political appointees? In its turn and in rough chronological order, each of those questions would receive its answer before the coming of the New Deal in 1933. But one question came before the others, and it derived from an incontrovertible proposition: the best way to handle unemployment was to eliminate it at its source in American business.

38

"Now that Unemployment has been forced upon public attention," Supreme Court Justice Louis D. Brandeis wrote Paul Kellogg, "would it not be possible for the Survey to take up vigorously and persistently the musts of Regularity in Employment? That is the fundamental remedy. All others are merely palliatives."[1] Indeed, stabilizing employment within private industry offered a first defense against a spreading recession. "A man out of work is a drag—on his family, on his community, and on industry at large which might have won him as a consumer, if he had been working," a *Survey* memorandum observed.[2] In addition, systems of unemployment insurance and old-age pensions that business adopted for its employees could keep people off relief, since benefits would be provided as a direct consequence of their labor within private enterprise. Those benefits would also help fight recessions by maintaining the public's power to consume industry's products. Moreover, unemployment insurance systems could be designed to provide employers with incentives to keep employees on the job by penalizing those who did not. All of these ideas fell within the purview of the question, what can business do about unemployment? If social workers were to see their ideas implemented, then the cooperation of businessmen was a necessity.

A mutual interest in employment stabilization, unemployment compensation, and old-age pensions united two old, close friends, Frances Perkins and Paul Kellogg. Through her work with the Factory Investigating Commission before the war and her many years as member of the state Industrial Commission, Perkins had learned to appreciate the efforts of employers to improve the terms of labor within their own companies. Indeed, she made herself an expert on progressive industrial policies. Her office location in the New York Department of Labor building at 124 East Twenty-eighth Street also kept her in touch with the nearby Charities Building crowd and their close neighbors in reform organizations such as the American Association for Labor Legislation. As Roosevelt's new Industrial Commissioner, she appointed a state Committee on Stabilization of Industry during 1930, serving as an *ex officio* member and naming another old friend from social service, Henry Bruere, its chairman. She also drafted major portions of the speech delivered by

39

Franklin Roosevelt in Salt Lake City during June 1930, in which the governor issued a headline-making call for unemployment and old-age insurance.[3]

Paul Kellogg wasted no time in circulating Perkins's message among social workers across the nation. *Survey* published her articles as features, broke the news about the recommendations of the Bruere Committee, and allowed her to report her 1931 trip to Europe, where she had studied European modes of unemployment compensation and old-age pensions. Those favors were the fruits of respect as well as friendship. Kellogg was an expert on such matters in his own right, having made himself an adept student of industrial relations. His office at 112 East Nineteenth Street also gave him easy access to the ideas of leading theorists on unemployment compensation and old-age security, such as John Andrews of the AALL and Abraham Epstein of the AAOAS. In addition, he brought to print the thinking of others with intellectual roots and personal connections in New York, including William Leiserson and Paul Douglas. In fact, *Survey* became a forum for the ideas of all; through its pages they deliberated European solutions and American alternatives. Perkins and Kellogg also viewed with optimism the good intentions of employers who wanted to improve labor conditions, probably because they drew upon the ideas of this group of progressive businessmen and their associates. Lucius Eastman and Ernest Draper of Hills Brothers Company, Gerard Swope of General Electric Company, and Winthrop Aldrich of Chase National Bank were particularly influential. Neither Perkins nor Kellogg, of course, spoke for all social service leaders, but they provided a conduit through which flowed an American reform tradition of improving capitalism from within.

When reformers turned their attention to business's role in relieving unemployment, they did not assault industrial capitalism and the profit motive. Instead they tendered an alliance with business, expecting (idealistically) that businessmen would extend voluntary welfare practices already initiated by progressive industrial managers. "The situation is not one of starting

40

from scratch," a *Survey* editor (probably Paul Kellogg) noted.[4] During the 1920s, industrial groups like the American Management Association, the Taylor Society, and the Industrial Relations Councillors had promoted measures to ensure high wages, steady work, and continuous earnings. Businessmen "have realized," *Survey Graphic* asserted in 1930, "that high wages mean more purchasers for autos, radios, refrigerators, pianos, sewing machines, houses and the like," and some employers knew that continued prosperity required stable employment and adequate workers' incomes.[5] Frances Perkins called this voluntary business approach to welfare an "American idea." When she became New York State's Industrial Commissioner in 1929, she declared, "I come into office at a time when the industrialists of the state are ready to cooperate in any plans which . . . are going to make for the economic and social welfare of the whole community."[6] Unlike European socialists, who sought to ensure welfare by using the powers of the state to control capitalism, American social workers believed that capitalists would put their own house in better order.

The social workers turned to business leaders because close ties existed between the social service and business communities. Philanthropy provided some of those bonds: often, the most charitable New Yorkers were also the practitioners of and spokesmen for progressive business policies.[7] Exposure to business-directed reforms also inspired confidence. In addition, academic economists such as Columbia University's Adolph A. Berle and Raymond Moley were articulating theories of cooperation between social workers and business leaders during the 1920s.[8] Above all, the social workers' hope for a benign capitalist economy reflected the moral idealism of the earlier Progressive Era and radiated the view of the 1920s that business was the primary agent of collective prosperity. In addition to being the capstone of abundant material wealth, a good business society could be a just society. As Frances Perkins expressed her hope to a gathering of social work colleagues in New York, "America's contribution to modern civilization is going to be the establishment

41

of an industrial order which is also a social order—an industrial order in which there is happiness and peace and security for everyone."[9]

In their special unemployment issue of April 1929, *Survey*'s editors stressed remedial business actions, featuring a number of stories on the endeavors of "employers who had demonstrated the practicability of [job] stabilization." Five thousand copies of that issue were distributed free to members of the American Management Association.[10] Later, after signs of a recession deepened, editor Paul Kellogg used his speaking engagements to spread the message. In January 1931, for example, he addressed the Industrial Relations Association of Chicago, endorsing the practices of companies like Proctor and Gamble, Eastman Kodak, General Electric, and Hills Brothers, which had achieved "advances in scientific management and employment planning, factory by factory." Their reforms often elicited coordinated, business-led community activities, and Kellogg elaborated the details of programs being developed in Dayton, Cincinnati, Indianapolis, and Rochester. "[W]e are witnessing the beginnings of a new consciousness on the part of certain of our cities," he exclaimed, "that they are each an aggregation of human beings earning their living [and] spending their money; that they are therefore an economic set-up as well as a geographical location or politial entity."[11] By collecting unemployment data, coordinating the work of employment bureaus, creating public works projects, and beginning vocational training programs, some cities were setting precedents by working with local businesses to counteract the recession's effects.

In the meantime, New York State moved in the direction indicated by Kellogg's urgings. During March of 1930, Governor Roosevelt set up a Committee on Stabilization of Industry to draft a plan for voluntary, cooperative action between the state and its private businesses. Frances Perkins undoubtedly inspired the committee's creation: "I picked all the members. I persuaded them to serve. . . . I kept it alive." She saw it as "part of my project to educate the Governor[,] who didn't know much,"

42

in her estimation, about economics and methods of employment stabilization.[12] Henry Bruere, the committee's chairman, was an expert in progressive business methods. Born in St. Charles, Missouri, and educated at five different universities, Bruere had been a lawyer and former settlement house resident, president of New York City's Board of Child Welfare, and management executive with several different business corporations, including the Metropolitan Life Insurance Company and the Bowery Savings Bank. During the Mitchel mayoral years, he had served his adopted city as treasurer, chairman of the Mayor's Pension Committee, and member of Mitchel's Committee on Unemployment. Most importantly, his career pointedly fused the roles of social servant and corporate executive. A *Survey* review noted that Bruere's most recent book, *Profitable Personnel Practice* (1930), emphasized business methods that had been "found profitable in terms of money and good-will."[13]

As instigator of the Bruere Committee, Perkins thought that enlightened business managers would augment their own self-interest by advancing the welfare of their employees. She remembered that Mitchel's Committee on Unemployment set forth that view in 1914,[14] and she believed that there existed a "disposition on the part of employers . . . to prevent unemployment" through voluntary action.[15] Echoing Paul Kellogg's appeals, she outlined three ideas for the committee to pursue: (1) employers could stabilize employment by adopting methods already tested by industrial leaders; (2) stabilization would make business operations more efficient and profitable; and (3) maintaining payrolls would support earnings and thereby help business by enhancing the power of employees to consume.[16] Stabilization amounted to more than good social welfare policy: it was a means by which businessmen could protect their companies' well-being.

Issuing its final report during November 1930, the Bruere Committee based its recommendations on the premise of voluntary compliance. "Those who seek to reduce unemployment," the keynote read, "should seek the cordial interest and cooperation of employers." Giving dozens of examples of companies that had stabilized employment through improved marketing operations, long-range production planning, product diversification, and adjusted working schedules, the report urged chambers of commerce and industrial trade associations to encourage similar practices among members of their organizations. Improved management techniques could make "industry secure for the people who work in it," and establish a bulwark against a depression.[17] "Why shouldn't American industry, as a matter of self-respect and self-dependence, [and] of long-range common sense, set its house in order?" Paul Kellogg asked rhetorically.[18]

The Bruere Committee did assign government the responsibility of mustering community actions throughout the state. Public officials were to canvass the cities, calling industrial and community groups together, distributing information, and generating support for cooperative plans. In addition, the committee recommended state and local public works programs to stimulate the economy and to create new jobs, and it asked for closer coordination of private and public employment bureaus to facilitate the process of reemployment. The state's duty was to set in motion the machinery of voluntary decision-making; after that, each community had to formulate its own plan.[19] Following the committee's final report, Paul Kellogg composed a letter to Arthur Woods of the President's Emergency Committee on Employment, in which he outlined the work of the Bruere group. "I was suggesting that [the PECE] come abreast of the New York leadership," he told Frances Perkins. "New York has pioneered, thanks to you and Bruere, and we all want to keep it in the forefront."[20]

44

The Empire State, however, failed to move swiftly on the Bruere recommendations during 1931–1932. A parsimonious legislature refused to grant proposed appropriations for continuing the committee's work. It also avoided the creation of a special agency to help organize community programs. Meanwhile, Governor Roosevelt demonstrated his own fiscal conservatism by not implementing the emergency public works suggested by his own committee. Instead, he responded to the recession by promoting cuts in government spending and maintaining a balanced budget. He still embraced a doctrine of minimal state responsibilities and hoped that business would find its own way out of the quagmire.[21] As a result, the burden of stimulating voluntary cooperation fell upon the Industrial Commissioner, Perkins, who used her office to encourage stabilization policies within various trade associations. In addition, she fulfilled one of the Bruere Committee's recommendations, achieving coordination among the state's public and private employment bureaus.[22] In the meantime, other state officials spent many months marking time and waiting for economic recovery to happen through private business initiatives.

Self-imposed business reform was doomed to failure. The Bruere Committee had based its suggestions on the latest examples of efficient management techniques, but those techniques were geared to a process of economic expansion. Many of the policies of welfare capitalism adopted during the 1920s were costly to employers as well as beneficial to workers. During prosperous times, progressive employers often gained, because programs such as pensions and free health care increased workers' productivity. When demand for products fell, employers reduced production and eliminated welfare programs in order to cut their costs of operation. Moreover, the management techniques described by Bruere and his associates pertained primarily to large companies that enjoyed consistent, predictable demand for their products and little competition. For instance, a few well-established companies dominated the soap industry, and the consumption of soap varied little from year to year regardless of economic conditions. Those circumstances made it possible for a firm like Proctor & Gamble to rationalize production, achieve maximum efficiency, maintain steady employment, and protect employee benefits. Consumption of new clothing, however, could fluctuate greatly, creating great uncertainty among competitive garment manufacturers, who found it im-

45

possible to forecast market conditions from one season to the next. Thus, industries confronted by an unstable market proved unwilling to incur the expenses of new employee benefit programs.[23] Finally, the progressive employer faced a disabling limitation in the fact that "one establishment and one owner cannot do it alone," as Mary Van Kleeck of the Russell Sage Foundation observed. The businessman "can use his science," she reported, "only if there be sufficient unity of action to bring about the balance of all related industries one to another."[24] Since there was no way to ensure the voluntary implementation of scientific business practices, no way existed to guarantee stabilization and recovery. A lone competitor's refusal to comply with new reforms could gain him an advantage, so every employer's interest in greater efficiency and consumption was thwarted by his desire to protect his competitive position. The Bruere Committee's suggestions were costly as well as enlightened. Hard times made them too risky for implementation by most employers.

As each passing month added more evidence of deterioration in the employment situation, reformers began to cast about for fresh ideas. In May 1931, *Survey*'s editors sponsored a conference of businessmen, industrial experts, and social workers to discuss proposals for broadly-conceived economic planning. The conferees debated several different strategies for economic planning and identified numerous organizations that might take action—such as industrial trade associations, labor unions, and the Federal Trade Commission. The thrust of their various arguments, however, pointed in one direction: direct government intervention in economic affairs. "Looked at simply," economist Lewis Lorwin declared, "economic planning is merely the next step in scientific management"; and business executive Lucius Eastman, at whose home the conference was held, called for "cool and authoritative discussion of the function of government in the field of economics" and study of "the place of the state in [a] planned economy." Although they did not arrive at consensus on a detailed plan, the participants turned away from piecemeal, voluntary methods of business reform and headed toward a national plan of action. As Lorwin put it, "Any real view of a plan for this country would include the economic system as a unit and show how the various industries fit in and how they can and should adjust to one another." [25] Even the implication of coercion seemed appropriate now that voluntarism had proved unable to keep business healthy.

On June 30, 1930, at the Governors' Conference in Salt Lake City, Franklin D. Roosevelt had set forth the framework of his ideas about a mandatory public system of unemployment compensation. That was one step in thinking about a plan. Invoking the term "insurance," he called for an "actuarial" arrangement of contributions and benefit payments that would balance revenues and expenditures in a "self-supporting" system. One great "social and governmental danger" in any public compensation program, he warned, was "a natural tendency to pay the cost . . . out of current revenues of government." Rejecting the use of monies from general taxes as "socialistic," "radical," and tainted by the dole, Roosevelt insisted on contributions from both employers and employees, establishing thereby an independent insurance account from which benefits could be drawn after a worker became jobless. Using that approach to attack "the basic problem [both] of unemployment and of old age," he argued, "seems to me a business proposal which is sound." The governor also suggested that such a system had to be protected against slack workers and would-be panhandlers, drawing a line against potential beneficiaries who refused "to accept an offered position" and hinting at other restrictions that would help keep the system financially solvent.[26]

With a few aptly chosen words and phrases, FDR had sketched the outlines of a program that became the core of the Social Security Act five years later. He too had taken a cue from examples provided by private business as well as from studies made by experts such as his own Bruere Committee. A few companies had installed compensation plans of their own in order to help laid-off workers, and some industrial leaders were proposing industry-wide efforts to stabilize existing employment by

47

using special funding devices such as "merit ratings" to penalize employers who failed to maintain their payrolls. "This shows to my mind," Roosevelt acknowledged in a private letter, "that we can approach the problem from a business-like point of view and work into it gradually [through the efforts of the different states] instead of starting any wholesale plan like that in England."[27] Indeed, his 1930 emphasis on state plans and on the dual goals of compensating workless Americans while simultaneously steadying employment stood at the center of FDR's conception of unemployment insurance and distinguished his approach from that used in Europe. In drawing upon the self-interest of capitalists—their desire to maximize profits and minimize costs—he also hoped to stimulate American business to defend its own enterprise, and thereby avoid Europe's "socialistic" public dole.

Roosevelt's ideas bent strongly in the direction of the most advanced position on social insurance taken by reformers, yet they also suited the economic orthodoxy that prevailed in American fiscal thinking early in the 1930s. Since well before World War I, reformers had considered it business's duty to provide protection against many of the hazards associated with modern industrial life.[28] Specifically, businessmen could build up "reserve" funds to compensate workers for industrial injuries and lost jobs. By the 1920s, most states had adopted workmen's compensation programs, and progressive business leaders accepted proposals of that kind because they conformed with the theory of allowing the incapacitated, the elderly, and the temporarily unemployed to continue as consumers. Compensation programs also dovetailed with the orthodox economic creed of maintaining balanced governmental budgets, minimizing direct taxes on wealth, and avoiding deficit spending by public agencies, even during periods of recession and depression. If business insured the welfare of its own former employees, then taxpayers could avoid the sudden imposition of higher taxes when emergencies struck, taxes that would threaten their assets and decrease their own buying power as consumers. Public deficit spending was still rejected as the quickest way into a national poorhouse, so the genius of business-backed compensation programs rested in their method of providing *extra* funds from accumulated reserves that would both aid the unemployed and stimulate economic recovery.[29] Moreover, compensation programs dramatized the right of unemployed workers to receive benefits that derived from their own former participation in the nation's industrial life.[30]

European experiments with compensation programs also contributed to this galaxy of theories.[31] Insurance experts who harkened to Roosevelt's 1930 initiative, such as John B. Andrews, the director of the American Association for Labor Legislation, Abraham Epstein, the executive secretary of the American Association for Old Age Security, Isaac M. Rubinow, the president of the National Conference of Jewish Social Service, William Leiserson, a professor at Antioch College, and Paul Douglas, a professor at the University of Chicago, used European examples as models when devising proposals for social insurance. England's law was particularly instructive. Adopted in 1911 as Europe's first national compensation program, it required contributions as a device to promote steady work. Similar motives underlay the theory behind new American compensation laws for industrial accidents. Under these laws, employers contributed to independent mutual funds (often maintained by private insurance carriers), while the states established commissions that set premium rates and regulated the cost of settlements paid for injuries. Employers had welcomed the laws, which freed them from a haphazard liability system based on expensive law suits and unpredictable jury decisions. Reformers welcomed them too, because merit ratings were usually applied to employers' contributions, providing a financial incentive to improve working conditions. Subsequent reductions in the number of industrial accidents convinced reformers that the laws had exerted their desired impact. By applying the same approach to unemployment, they might reduce the evil of joblessness as well, and with business's cooperation.[32]

49

Most European unemployment compensation pro-
grams, however, relied on public funding, not employers' contributions, thereby negating any impetus for employers to regu-
larize work. Moreover, those European plans that did include
business's participation, such as England's tripartite plan of
splitting costs among employers, employees, and the public, de-
generated rapidly into tax-supported programs during the
1920s, when high unemployment levels destroyed their actuarial
base.[33] For American reformers, that change posed a serious
problem: not only did it eliminate the employers' incentive to
stabilize jobs, it also undermined the value of insurance by mix-
ing accrued benefits with current public expenditures for relief.
Because the Americans were becoming increasingly attentive to
the morale-sustaining aspect of welfare programs, they insisted
that the source of the dole, public funds, be kept distinct from
unemployment insurance benefits. As Frances Perkins stated,
"Insurance money and relief money ought to be kept in separate
pockets," and her sentiments echoed those of her chief, FDR.[34]
In 1930, the United States stood as a latecomer in the west-
ern world's movement toward unemployment compensation,
and her reformers still hoped to install a business-based, self-
supporting, morale-sustaining insurance system that would
stand as a distinctive American way of handling the unemployment problem.

The status of elderly Americans who could no longer
work was clearly different from that of the able-bodied, temporarily unemployed, but it posed similar issues. At the close of the
1920s, only four hundred American companies offered any pension protection for retired employees. Tax-supported county
homes were the only resort for elderly people who had no jobs,
savings, or families to support them. Institutional care, which
placed old people under constant supervision and confinement,
struck social work reformers as degrading to the elderly, many
of whom remained active and capable of exercising responsibility for themselves. In addition, institutional care was "decidedly
inadequate," according to a study of county homes by the Wel-

fare Council of New York City.[35] During the 1920s, therefore, several private welfare agencies supplemented the small re-sources of elderly New Yorkers, simply to help them stay out of public institutions. In addition, organizations such as the AICP and the State Charities Aid Association began pressing for "the establishment of suitable public agencies authorized to grant al-lowances to aged persons from public funds."[36]

An old-age pension system moved to the top of Franklin Roosevelt's legislative docket soon after he became governor. In 1929, he created a state commission to study the problem and draft a bill. When testifying before this commission, social work-ers gave emphatic support to a state program, arguing that "pri-vate charity and individual thrift and likewise group insurance and industrial pensions are inadequate to meet the problems of supporting people in their old age."[37] Extending public assis-tance to the aged in their own homes, they insisted, would both reduce expensive institutional care and allow healthy older New Yorkers to lead independent lives.[38] Soon thereafter, the 1929–1930 winter of economic hardship "brought to concrete focus many of the facts that proponents of plans for old-age security have been stressing for many years," *Survey* observed, and the Assembly unanimously passed the state's first old-age assistance program in March 1930.[39]

New York's new law was not an insurance measure, how-ever. Neither employees nor their employers were required to contribute to a pension fund that would provide retirement benefits. FDR had wanted such a contributory feature, which he saw as the only way to preserve a beneficiary's sense of self-help, thereby differentiating old-age insurance from the public dole.[40] Instead of that, the new law offered a tax-supported program of home relief. It was also a "case-working law," authorizing coun-ties and cities to distribute money to the elderly according to their need, as determined by means tests and caseworkers' inves-tigations. Since it was clearly a stop-gap measure initiated in the face of a growing economic crisis, reformers viewed the pro-gram as a mixed blessing. Old-age assistance "will be a valuable

adjunct to the whole system of public social work," *Survey* edi-
torialized, making it "possible for many old people to remain for
a time in their own homes, living with greater contentment, happiness and economy than would be possible under almshouse
care."[41] On the other hand, Eleanor Roosevelt disclosed their
underlying disappointment: "Many of us do not feel that it is a
very satisfactory bill." It was not an insurance plan, and the reformers' only consolation was to believe, as she did, that "these
things come slowly and a little at a time."[42] Three months after
signing the old-age assistance bill into law, FDR implied his own
disappointment when he joined old-age pensions and unemployment compensation as parts of a unified plan of social insurance in his Salt Lake address.

By the time Roosevelt commenced his second term as
governor in January 1931, New Yorkers had prepared the
rough draft of a program—employment stabilization, unemployment insurance, and old-age pensions—that promised to
coordinate the efforts of business and government in fighting
economic collapse. Even though signs of the weaknesses in voluntary action had appeared already, the Bruere Committee report indicated a fixed commitment to the idea that business
could do its part in stabilizing employment. Reformers continued to view with favor plans such as that proposed by General
Electric Company's Gerard Swope, which anticipated many features of the 1933 National Industrial Recovery Act.[43] Moreover,
when they turned to new public measures such as unemployment insurance, they still perceived their programs as comple-
ments to capitalism's economic rationale.

In his Chicago speech, Paul Kellogg articulated the pro-
business bias of reform when he recommended "an American
system" of unemployment insurance that would impose charges
upon "industries and plants within industries" according to their
performance in stabilizing employment. A rating scheme, he
argued, would "put the economic pressure of the [capitalist] system behind stabilization—make it to the advantage of manage-
ments to steady work."[44] And as the conference at Lucius

Eastman's home indicated, the reformers' turn toward government action coincided with the changing dispositions of some businessmen. "[T]he public is beginning to work around to the position," Kellogg wrote a sympathetic Eastman later, "that unemployment is an industrial hazard and that it is up to American business to control it and carry some of the cost through reserves or insurance."[45] In 1934–1935, businessmen of Eastman's progressive kind—many of them New Yorkers—would appear in Washington as the Business Advisory Council to give their support to passage of the Social Security Act.[46]

Indeed, social work reformers continued to labor for the improvement and preservation of American capitalism, moving in tandem with their enlightened friends within the business community. They believed that uniformity in public welfare measures, such as unemployment compensation, would benefit business by helping the nation's consumers to buy industry's products. The greatest benefit of all would be a healthy industry that was able to keep as many Americans as possible in regular jobs. Yet, as Paul Kellogg noted, promoting regularity in employment was "only half of the shield" in providing protection for the American worker. "There is the other question," he continued, "of what you are going to do to give some measure of security to the residual body of unemployed men after these reductions are made."[47] Someday, unemployment and old-age insurance would offer a partial answer. For social workers during the decade of the Great Depression, however, Kellogg raised a more fundamental issue: what kind of public aid best serves the needs of unemployed Americans for whom there are no regular jobs or insurance benefits?

53

Unemployed men, morale, and emergency work

5

As every economic indicator from new home construction to retail sales slipped steadily downward, regular jobs in private industry became increasingly scarce. Eventually, about one-quarter of the nation's labor force would find itself unemployed, and the fraction was higher in urban areas. In New York as elsewhere, unemployment affected the lives of hundreds of thousands of working and middle-class Americans who had never known joblessness before. These newly unemployed were different from the traditionally disadvantaged. They were unlikely subjects for the caseworkers' theories of psychiatric abnormality. Therefore, social work reformers reasoned, they deserved an approach to relief that departed from methods developed to help paupers, the indigent, and the psychologically maladjusted. The new approach, Homer Folks counseled, involved being "more considerate of the spirit, the condition, the feelings of the people who come for relief," and should attempt to preserve their self-respect through work.[1]

The emphasis on self-respect and the psychological well-being of the unemployed became the distinguishing feature of welfare policies during the 1930s. The idea was not wholly new. As much as a hundred years earlier, observers had noted a class of "worthy poor" whose temporary dependency derived from a shortage of jobs. During the depression in 1893, when this kind of unemployment mushroomed dramatically, social workers consolidated this "new view." These new clients did not require reformation because they already practiced the virtues associated with helping themselves. Instead, they needed to be maintained in a capitalist system that was experiencing a temporary crisis. Progressives later used methods of self-help to encourage individuals to retain their sense of self-reliance.[2] Not until the Great Depression, however, did reformers take the third step, the use of public institutions to nurture a feeling of dignity.

At the beginning of the Depression Era, recipients of either private charity or public relief paid a stiff price for the aid they received. Direct relief—grocery orders, food tickets, surplus food, used clothing, bags of coal, rent vouchers (but never cash)—circumscribed a recipient's freedom to choose what he consumed. "Voluntary shoppers" often accompanied recipients to grocery stores and supervised their purchases. Luxury items—"Cigars, cigarettes, tobacco in any form, beer, near beer, soda water, candy, pies, and cakes"—could not be bought with grocery orders, and grocers were "under no circumstances to give change in cash."[3] To determine need, caseworkers investigated recipients' homes and lives. In the estimation of Harry Hopkins, who would head the Temporary Emergency Relief Administration in New York before moving to the New Deal, these investigations fostered the "wholesale degradation of [the] finest sensibilities."[4] In addition, caseworkers often told the unemployed "where and how they should live . . . [and] how they should order their relationships within the family group, with their relatives, neighbors and friends."[5] Relief was frequently inadequate—grants were small and seldom weighted according to family needs. As a result, recipients often developed a "beggar's attitude" as they trooped from one relief agency to another, trying to squeeze out "a little here, a little there in the hope that

55

in some way they will get just enough."[6] "The whole damn theory of the thing," William Matthews protested, "is to make relief giving so unpleasant, so disagreeable, in fact so insulting to decent people that they stay away from the places where it is given."[7]

Matthews, who directed private philanthropy's Emergency Work Bureau in New York City, condemned "the old methods of poor relief" because they assumed a person's inability to care for himself and deprived him of the right to manage his own affairs.[8] They reflected a nineteenth-century view of poverty as a sign of a moral flaw. Progressives and psychiatric caseworkers had altered that view somewhat, positing environmental and psychological causes of personal dependency, but much of the American public adhered to the old notion of personal failure. "Our own idea of pride for the other fellow," Molly Dewson once caustically observed of conventional attitudes, "is that he should be ashamed of being on relief. We want him to creep up back alleys . . . to the relief office."[9] Reformers were hardly surprised that the newly unemployed of the 1930s applied for relief reluctantly, grew aggravated when investigators entered their homes and asked untoward questions, and resented the degrading restrictions imposed by relief in kind.[10] Matthews was convinced that "the big proportion . . . do not need to be salvaged any more than the people who would salvage them."[11] Harry Hopkins, one of Matthews's assistants in the old 1914 park-work experiments, also believed "that the giving of relief to unemployed people has nothing whatever to do either with the technique or the methods of giving relief to other indigent people."[12]

A new means of providing assistance was needed. "I think of [the unemployed], on the whole," William Matthews declared, "as victims of conditions over which they had little or no control—victims . . . of a material progress which has failed to bring a sustained adequacy of life to all those able and willing to work."[13] The Great Depression made such a conclusion unavoidable. Upon the urging of social workers within his administra-

56

tion, Governor Roosevelt expressed this idea in a proclamation issued during January 1932:

> No one who is out of work today can rightfully feel that he or she is personally responsible for having lost his or her job. The circumstances which have brought about this most serious depression in economic history have been of a complex and impersonal nature . . . if responsibility is to be lodged at any door it cannot be and will not be lodged at the door of those who need help today.[14]

Yet it was still necessary to convince the public, including jobless Americans, that institutions rather than individuals had failed.

Throughout the 1930s, social workers expended great effort to persuade the public to accept new methods of relief. Using personal experiences, case histories, and statistical studies, they presented the unemployed as normally self-sufficient and thoroughly middle-class in their values.[15] Most important, they were "thoroughly imbued with the common-sense understanding that without work and effort the necessities of life cannot be created and [they accepted] the obligation of every individual to labor," Harry Lurie claimed. "The previous experience of wage-earners," he continued, "had demonstrated to them that only by participating in the work of the world can they achieve real economic security or feel the sense of importance which comes from belonging in the ranks of persons who really matter because they are productive."[16] Loss of work propelled people into a progression of personal disasters which social workers chronicled in intimate detail. Economic trials accounted for part of the personal tragedy, but the psychological trauma was regarded as more critical. "As one sums up the effects of unemployment on the individual," Lillian Wald testified, "the loss of the dignity of man is the first and most tragic. With this are bound up the loss of home, of ties, of position, the humiliation of the long bread lines, the appeal to relief agencies, the overwhelming sense of failure."[17]

In their search for an alternative to home relief, reformers turned to work relief, thereby creating one of the most con-

57

fusing institutional reforms implemented during the 1930s. *Survey*'s Paul Kellogg essayed an impressionistic definition: "As a hybrid [of relief and of work] it is as important an innovation as the grapefruit. 'Work relief,' the term . . . which is often used, is . . . descriptive of its blend, but does not begin to get the full psychological value . . . out of the tremendous distinction between the 'breadlines' round about and the 'job-line' at the Charities building."[18] From its inception, work relief represented the reformers' effort to eradicate the stigma associated with a charitable dole. William Hodson and the Welfare Council felt it "better to put people to work than to support them in idleness," because work helped sustain the "morale, work habits and skills" of the jobless.[19] Harry Hopkins agreed: "Give a man a dole and you save his body and destroy his spirit, give him a job and pay him an assured wage, and you save both the body and the spirit."[20]

Though others contributed, William Matthews was chiefly responsible for the development of work relief programs in New York City. A conspicuous, outspoken, even combative man who believed fervently in the respectability of unemployed Americans, Matthews founded and ruled the Emergency Work Bureau (EWB), which queued up its job line along East Twenty-second Street. The organization expressed every facet of his personality—his vigorous devotion to work, his sympathy for the unemployed, his generosity, his intolerance of psychiatric casework, and his desire to make relief humane. His dedication to work relief derived in part from his own working-class background. Unlike the majority of his colleagues, who were middle class in origin, Matthews spoke with a poignant self-consciousness about the aspirations of poorer Americans, with whom he identified.

William Matthews migrated to America with his English family when he was nine years old; at twelve, he went to work as a harness boy in a New England woolen mill.[21] By the time he was seventeen, he had learned the skills of a spinner and weaver. His earnings as a laborer, supplemented by scholarships, financed his way through a preparatory school and Williams Col-

58

lege, from which he graduated in 1899. Even as a Williams student, he found time to return to the woolen mills, where he taught English to immigrant workers. Later he prepared for the ministry at New York's Union Theological Seminary, while leading boys' clubs at Union Settlement and then at Bethany Mission. In 1901, he entered social service on a full-time basis, becoming assistant director of Union Settlement. He soon moved to Pittsburgh, where he directed Kingsley House settlement. In 1907, Kingsley House became headquarters for the Pittsburgh Survey, the first community-wide study of working and living conditions in an American industrial city. Paul Kellogg directed that study, and Matthews lent a supporting hand. In 1913, New York's Association for Improving the Condition of the Poor called him back to the city, appointing him director of its family welfare department.

An anomaly among New York's native-born, middle-class reformers, William Matthews' life offered a social worker's version of the rags-to-riches American story: an immigrant, a child laborer, and a skilled worker, Matthews pursued the dream of unlimited opportunity and returned to the tenements and factories in order to help others along the way. Certainly his own success shaped his conviction that work was the way to personal fulfillment. When the nation experienced a slump in 1914, he launched his first work relief program for the AICP. (Neither he nor his colleagues were much aware that work relief had a history stretching back to the French Revolution, and that nineteenth-century experience with work relief had already exposed many of its shortcomings.[22]) He put six hundred jobless men to work in city parks in 1914, and paid them cash for their labor. Years later he would expand on this project. In November 1930, he was named director of the Emergency Work Bureau (EWB), private philanthropy's city-wide attempt to give jobless men employment and wages. Matthews' authority extended into the public sector by default; when the city failed to appropriate public funds for the newly authorized municipal Work Relief Bureau in the spring of 1931, the EWB stepped in with both money and guidance. For the next two years, Matthews served both as a director of the municipal work program and as the co-ordinator of private and public work relief.[23]

During the nineteenth and early twentieth centuries, American charities and public agencies had often used work as a "test"—sometimes closer to a punishment—of the poor. Work would instill virtuous habits, it was believed, while forcing poor people to prove their "worth" by earning their keep at a county farm or workhouse. William Matthews and other reformers of the 1930s, however, did not view work relief as a form of charity or a test of worth. They felt that it simply made decent jobs available to people already eager to work, and paid them for their labor.[24] In addition, the EWB adopted three psychological strat- ,
agems to help sustain morale: separating the temporarily unemployed from the permanently dependent; providing cash wages so that recipients could maintain their personal independence; and offering useful work that would preserve a man's self-respect.[25]

The EWB exemplified work relief in action.[26] To be eligible for the program, an applicant had to prove need. Any man who had been employed after January 1929, qualified for work relief, with preference given to married men with children. During the winter of 1931–1932, the EWB extended work opportunities to unmarried women, and single men were added to its rolls the following winter. In order to prepare new projects and assign men work they were suited for, the EWB classified applicants according to previous occupations and skills. The less skilled—from the factories, the trades, and the construction industry—usually worked on the city's program after it began during the fall of 1931, laboring on conservation projects in parks and forest areas or helping refurbish museums, churches, and public buildings. Those with professional training or technical skills worked for the EWB in schools and colleges as research assistants, laboratory aides, and translators, or in parks and playgrounds as recreational leaders. Others became teachers, helping immigrants learn English, for instance. Jobless musicians were

60

organized into orchestras, and one group, called the EWB Band, gave concerts throughout the city. People on work relief earned five dollars a day and worked a maximum of eight days each month. Matthews called this a "stagger on" income,[27] because it was small, but it roughly doubled the amount allotted to New Yorkers on home relief and it came in the form of cash. When the EWB closed its job-line in the fall of 1933, after the New Deal's Civil Works Administration launched a national work relief program, it had employed over ninety-five thousand New Yorkers and expended nearly thirty million dollars, 95 percent of which was distributed as wages.

A brief summary, of course, fails to convey the day-to-day impact of the EWB, either on those who gave or those who earned its relief. Although only one of many urban work relief experiments begun between 1930 and 1933, it significantly influenced the thinking of New York's New Dealers who later wrote the legislation creating the vast network of federal work relief programs—the CWA, the WPA, the CCC, and the NYA. None of the New Yorkers who administered work relief programs thought them a panacea for the unemployed. "I am inclined to think that all relief is likely to be more or less demoralizing," William Matthews himself admitted, but he believed that work relief was much less likely to degrade recipients than the handouts offered by home relief.[28] It was a temporary expedient "until a revived business calls them back to regular work."[29]

The reformers' conception of work relief had always been circumscribed by their acceptance of its subordinate place within a capitalist economy. As early as 1914, and again in 1921, reformers had accepted the pro-business view that work relief should "supply aid by means of employment, at standard rates, but on part time, to encourage [the] early return [of a recipient] to [his] regular occupation."[30] Under no circumstances should a relief income match earnings for similar work in competitive industry, because comparable income could destroy incentive to regain private employment. Similarly, work relief projects should not take work that a private employer might handle, be-

61

cause that would usurp capitalism's domain, subverting profit interests and threatening regular jobs. Work relief officials, therefore, restricted projects to work that "would not otherwise be done."[31]

The reformers' commitment to handle work relief in a way that would support the nation's private businesses raised a perplexing question: how could they eliminate the stigma of relief and make work programs psychologically satisfying without undermining capitalism? An adequate program had to offer aid at a level that lay somewhere between barren subsistence and the minimum standard of living obtainable through private employment.[32] Put in a different way, work relief had to ease anxiety and fulfill a desire for work without becoming a tempting alternative to private industry. For this reason, it could never wholly lose its stigma as charity. And that was what William Matthews and the New York reformers really wanted. They shared their culture's individualistic ethic; they too measured success by private accomplishments rather than collective gains. Their goal was to return the able-bodied unemployed to private jobs, and work relief was a means to that end. The New Deal would inherit an ambiguous legacy.

**An
icy
winter's
blast
for
federal
action**

6

When the nation's social workers met in Minneapolis during the late spring of 1931 for their annual national conference, indecision marked their deliberations about new methods of financing relief, especially with regard to public funding. "A year of dealing with the results of unemployment has shown us the futility of our efforts," Jacob Billikopf of Philadelphia declared in arguing for federal aid, but his voice failed to strike a responsive nerve among the majority. On the other hand, the remarks of one of Herbert Hoover's representatives, who reviewed the noninterventionist policies of the President's Emergency Committee for Employment, "fell on coolly critical ears." In the end, the conferees followed a cautious course, approving a Hoover proposal to stimulate local philanthropic activity by mobilizing voluntary giving on a national scale. Gertrude Springer, who authored *Survey*'s report on the conference, used the word "fear" repeatedly when characterizing the mood of the delegates, but it was not yet the kind of fear that would spark action.[1]

New York's social work reformers were the first to seek public relief; they steered initially in the direction of municipal aid, then veered toward state appropriations, and finally set a steady course toward federal funding. New Yorkers negotiated those changes in ten months, from the end of February to the close of December 1931. During the spring of 1931, New York's municipal governments gained authority from the state to dispense public relief for unemployment. Late in the summer, the creation of the Temporary Emergency Relief Administration added state support to local public relief efforts. Social work reformers pioneered each of those innovations. Then, just as 1931 gave way to 1932, their leaders testified before congressional committees in Washington, and demanded federal funding. Finally, in July 1932, federal appropriations were granted for unemployment relief. The New Yorkers' struggle to involve government—local, state, and federal—in relieving the suffering of the unemployed had come to a successful end.

By July 1931, when Springer's report on the National Conference of Social Work was published, New York reformers were moving beyond municipal relief and talking about state action. Under the auspices of Franklin Roosevelt's Committee on the Stabilization of Industry (the Bruere Committee), Homer Folks of the State Charities Aid Association was preparing a study of unemployment needs in forty-five New York cities, and his report was due in August. Anticipating the report, Henry Bruere wrote the governor late in July and reviewed a number of proposals for funding public relief programs; these included borrowing by counties, local or state bond issues, and a special state tax levy. He also hinted that the state legislature might be called into extraordinary session to consider appropriate action.[2] Eleven days later, Bruere wrote FDR again, noting that President Hoover had not yet announced his program for the coming winter and counseling him "to let the national government clarify its ideas before you make public your plans."[3] On August 11 Folks issued his report, which emphasized the strategic importance of public relief funds and predicted that "State aid will probably be necessary" during the winter.[4] Three days later, Folks telegraphed FDR, calling for a special legislative session to

64

act on the relief issue.[5] His assistant at the SCAA, Elsie Bond, also contacted Roosevelt, telling him that "the present scale of public relief in many cities is so low that radical increases in the amount . . . given each family must be made next winter if acute suffering is to be prevented."[6] Other social workers' letters and telegrams, many dated August 14, poured into the governor's office; all made the same plea: new measures for funding emergency relief were obligatory and the moment for state assistance had arrived. August 14 was a significant date, because on that day President Hoover announced the formation of the President's Committee on Unemployment Relief, which was to urge the American public to donate generously to private philanthropy while leaving additional relief measures to the discretion of local and state officials. Clearly, New Yorkers were ready to have their state government implement public programs far in advance of what Hoover would advocate.

Roosevelt called the New York State legislature into extraordinary session on August 28, fourteen days after Hoover revealed his plan. Taking note of advice he had received "from many private organizations for relief and charity," he urged legislators to act—"not as a matter of charity, but as a matter of social duty"—and proposed the creation of a state Temporary Emergency Relief Administration.[7] Backed by twenty million dollars in revenues raised through personal income taxes, the TERA was approved in September. Using a system of matching grants, it offered four state dollars for every six dollars spent by local public authorities on relief. That provision incorporated into the TERA's powers a fiscal device designed to increase local public funding and thereby enhance local involvement in relief efforts. Just as important, matching grants enabled the TERA to supervise the way in which monies were spent by whom, and also to set professional standards for administrators. In addition, TERA funds were to be expended for both home and work relief, which gave impetus to work relief programs throughout the state.[8] A revolution in public welfare administration was beginning in New York: public monies for relief expenditures grew by

65

multiples; most public relief officials became professionals with social work qualifications; and work relief became a standard response to the needs of the unemployed. In 1933, when the New Deal put the Federal Emergency Relief Administration into action, the nation experienced a similar revolution, but in 1931, New Yorkers were thinking only about the winter that lay ahead.

They prepared well for the winter of 1931–1932, but not well enough. Soon New Yorkers found themselves trapped in a recurring cycle of crisis-and-response that destroyed the foundation of relief funding, even though private philanthropy, the city, and the state were all involved. During the fall, a new philanthropic committee under the direction of Harvey D. Gibson raised eighteen million dollars for relief programs offered by private social service agencies. The Welfare Council established a Bureau for the Homeless, which was to register transients, direct them to relief agencies, and curb the proliferation of breadlines by getting them off the streets. The city appropriated twenty million dollars for its new Home Relief and Work Relief Bureaus, both of which shared an additional three and one-quarter million dollars from the TERA. The Board of Estimate also allotted extra funds for operation of the city's hospitals, homes for the aged, and orphanages, and for pensions to help the elderly, veterans, and widows. A Mayor's Fund, which was supported by donations from city employees and administered by the police, and a similar School Fund promised two million dollars in aid. The sum available for emergency services totalled about forty-three million dollars.[9]

Social workers quickly discovered the harsh realities of their situation. A neighborhood survey made by Henry Street settlement's visiting nurses found 25 percent of all homes with no employed individual and another 30 percent dependent upon two or three days of work each week. The Welfare Council's Social Service Exchange announced that of all relief applications it had processed since January 1930, 82 percent came from completely new applicants. In other words, they came from the "new poor" of the 1930s. Moreover, the total clearings of the

Exchange for 1931 (over six hundred sixty-three thousand) doubled those of 1930. Such figures told the extent to which the Depression was cutting into classes who had thought themselves immune from joblessness and dependency.[10] "At present the so-called white collar people suffer," Lillian Wald wrote, "and the employment agencies have long lines of secretaries, stenographers, typists, bookkeepers—a sickening sight."[11] Confronted by overwhelming numbers—nobody knew the exact count—heads of private social service agencies such as Henry Street's Wald faced a singular problem. They had tried to maintain their regular services, adding special programs to meet unemployment, while existing on budgets raised through voluntary contributions made to each agency separately. New York, which lacked a Community Chest organization, could not ensure an equitable distribution of donations. Nor was the Gibson Committee's unemployment fund intended to cover the regular services of private agencies: it was restricted to the provision of relief and did not apply to the care of the sick, the aged, the homeless, and dependent children. Moreover, the public's preoccupation with the plight of the jobless diverted attention from other social services and reduced financial support for them.[12] As Lillian Wald wrote Harvey D. Gibson, "Unemployment and absorption of interest in the excellent organization under your leadership makes it impossible to raise our essential budget for 1932."[13] That lament became a loud refrain as fall moved into winter.

The financial pinch threatened to eliminate activities that had become accepted facets of social work. At Henry Street, for example, the Visiting Nurses' Service staggered under the burden of poorer family health and cases of prolonged sickness. During October 1931, the nurses averaged thirteen hundred visits a day, and health organizations throughout the city were referring more and more cases to them; but the Gibson Committee refused to grant a request for emergency assistance, even though the increased caseload clearly derived from the unemployment crisis. In despair and subdued rage, Wald flatly declared that "responsibility for the care of the unemployed sick

67

has gone beyond our powers."[14] Programs in the arts, recreation, and education also suffered. Created in response to prosperity, when working people enjoyed increased leisure, these activities ironically became more important once unemployment forced people to endure prolonged idleness. Yet settlements had a hard time keeping those programs going, and their situation became acute when the city announced, in an economy move, that it was cutting back its own recreation budget and eliminating evening classes in the schools.[15] As a settlement worker observed in a Welfare Council publication, "Under the strain of widespread and immediate want, there seems to be a danger that the recognized needs of man are to be limited to the bare margin of survival, that once his body has been taken care of, his spirit will need no further support."[16] Psychiatric casework also reeled before the public's preoccupation with unemployment relief. Because most of the unemployed were not maladjusted or incapable of caring for themselves, the caseworkers' services seemed less relevant and therefore less necessary, even though the Depression created psychological disorders in addition to material want. *Survey*'s Gertrude Springer observed that the "niceties of modern social work, the careful processes of building and rehabilitation [are] going overboard. The struggle is reduced to the simple elements of food and shelter for the hungry and the homeless."[17] For reformers, who had always demanded economic programs to correct social injustices, the crisis proved painfully paradoxical; the tidal shift toward public action and unemployment relief, which they had long been waiting for, carried the good out to sea along with the bad—a development that nobody found desirable.

The problems of the private agencies, however, merely foreshadowed the deeper inadequacy of all New York's welfare services once winter produced the full impact of the Great Depression. Philanthropy's home relief program, which began accepting applications on November 15, closed its rolls on December 15. Within days after they began operating, the EWB and the city's work relief program had more applicants than they could put to work during the entire winter. The Mayor's Fund and the School Fund disappeared quickly. Finally, on January 8, 1932, the city's Home Relief Bureau, "the last available bulwark against starvation, the last open avenue for relief," stopped accepting new relief applicants.[18] Revitalized by a million dollar grant from the Gibson Committee, the Bureau reopened its rolls to new applicants on January 17, only to close them ten days later. Help from the TERA got the Bureau going a third time on February 10. In short spurts between the first of October and the thirty-first of March, private philanthropy and public agencies had more than doubled the expenditure of the previous winter on unemployment relief.[19] And even this amount had proved insufficient.

By the spring of 1932, social services in New York City had been disrupted almost beyond recognition. Nearly four hundred private agencies had disappeared since 1929 (about one-third of the 1929 total). The failure of the community to support private hospitals, playground programs, settlement houses, and psychiatric casework clinics menaced many other agencies and services.[20] We "have to beg for money now," an associate of Henry Street's Visiting Nurses' Service wrote Lieutenant-Governor Herbert Lehman. "In the first quarter of this year we had 24,765 new cases, a number that we have never recorded within memory of anyone here."[21] Obviously, private philanthropy had failed. William Matthews wrote Senator Robert F. Wagner in unconcealed frustration, "Trying to turn back this tide of distress through private philanthropic contributions, is about as useless as trying to put out a forest fire with a garden hose."[22] Indeed, the Gibson Committee fund was bankrupt, and no new campaign was planned. And for those fortunate families still on the rolls of the city's Home Relief Bureau, aid had been reduced to two dollars and sixty-seven cents a week.[23]

Only a year before, on February 27, 1931, social workers had held their first mass meeting, calling for municipal participation in the battle against unemployment. On April 28, 1932, they held a second mass demonstration, demanding that the city ap-

69

propriate an additional twenty million dollars for its public relief budget.[24] This time, however, they expected to link those public funds to appropriations from the federal government as well as from the state's TERA.

There are a number of reasons why New Yorkers took the lead in fighting for public funding. Certainly they were no more socially conscious, more sympathetic to the unemployed, or more devoted to reform than social workers elsewhere. Nor were New York's problems particularly worse than elsewhere. New York City, however, was the center of a national network of social-work communication. Several of its leaders headed national organizations which were concerned with deteriorating conditions throughout the country. The New Yorkers also constituted a community of action. They were a prideful lot, and candidly expressed their desire to keep New York in the forefront of social innovation. But more important than pride, they moved as a unit—their mass demonstrations, petitions, and letter-writing campaigns gave ample evidence of that—perhaps because they shared such a personalized network of professional associations. Their perceptions of changing conditions and of needs for new reforms harmonized, so one leader often spoke for many. By the close of 1931, New Yorkers spoke with a single voice about the public's duty in funding unemployment relief, and outsiders began to listen when they took their ideas to Congress late in December.

The drive for federal relief began uncertainly and inconspicuously during early fall of 1931. On October 13, a meeting to discuss relief prospects was convened by the National Social Work Council, a New York-based organization whose function was to coordinate the national activities of charitable organizations such as the Community Chests and the Red Cross. At that meeting, social workers found themselves divided; most agreed that something needed to be done about the funding of relief, but they disagreed about what, and no united position materialized.[25] Six days later, however, the NSWC's secretary, David Holbrook, along with Linton Swift and Walter West, began to plan a steering com-

70

mittee on federal action. It was to serve as a lobbying agency, developing a specific social work program for relief and bringing bills before both state and federal legislatures.[26] The combination of Holbrook, Swift, and West posed a striking variation on the theme of personal associations among New York's social work leaders: each came from the twin cities of Minneapolis-St. Paul, where their social service careers began during the period of the First World War, and all arrived in New York during the 1920s—Holbrook to head the NSWC, Swift to direct the Family Welfare Association of America, and West to lead the American Association of Social Workers. Soon these steering committee founders were joined by another former Twin Cities welfare leader, William Hodson, who was executive director of the Welfare Council of New York City. Other New Yorkers, including the TERA's Harry Hopkins, filled the majority of places on the steering committee, while the remaining positions were occupied by social workers from nearby northeastern cities. Even though one New York member in their number hoped that "other groups in other sections of the country will get together as [an] offset to [the] Atlantic Seaboard character of this movement,"[27] New Yorkers had established a new group that would carry them and their cause to Washington before New Year's Day, 1932.

Speaking as an individual rather than a representative of the group (but after his initial involvement with the steering committee), William Hodson published an open letter to President Hoover in the *New York Times* late in October. Cautious in his remarks, he mentioned a "growing feeling" and a "possibility that local funds may not be adequate" for the winter. He pointed out that public revenues already carried the burden of welfare services in most cities and states across the nation. "In the long run," Hodson asserted, without flatly calling for immediate federal action, "private philanthropy can only supplement taxation—it cannot be substituted for public funds as a source of revenue for unemployment relief."[28] Hodson's indirect assault on private charity as the major defense against the ravages of joblessness was taken up by Linton Swift and Walter West, who

71

were invited to Washington during November to meet with several senators and with the President's Committee on Unemployment Relief. They were "not advocating Federal aid" yet, but they began to do the spadework for what social workers could regard as an adequate federal bill.[29] Indeed, the steering committee had just given itself a name, the Social Work Conference on Federal Action, and as late as December 13 it had not harmonized into one voice.[30] Members generally agreed that federal help was needed in "certain localities" and in "resourceless areas," but they stood divided, some arguing for new federal public works and others for direct federal relief. A few still opposed any kind of federal unemployment program—probably because they feared the chicanery of politicians—thinking it "unwise to urge such a program and fasten the evils of such a system upon the country."[31]

At nearly the same moment, however, relief programs in New York City began to crumble, which stimulated interest in new funding. So when Senators Robert M. La Follette of Wisconsin and Edward P. Costigan of Colorado asked Walter West to line up social workers for testimony at public hearings to be held by the Senate Subcommittee on Manufactures, the response was eager.[32] On December 28 the hearings began. Among the New Yorkers who testified were West, Swift, Hodson, Paul Kellogg, Allen Burns, the executive vice president of the Community Chests and Councils, and Joanna Colcord of the Russell Sage Foundation. By the time of their appearance, it was clear that local and state resources would not be adequate for the winter, even in the rich Empire State. Hesitancy disappeared when West declared, "The relief problem has ceased to be a local one. It is national in origin, national in scope, and beyond the capacity of the local communities." Caution was swept aside when Swift called relief "a direct responsibility of the federal government."[33] Kellogg summarized their testimony, including his own, in *Survey Graphic*: "They showed how relief standards had shrunk below tolerable levels; how municipalities are hard pressed and how the fabric of voluntary social work is threatened; how the relief budgets embedded in the sums raised by the community campaigns last fall will not of themselves last the winter out." By the end of December 1931, the need for federal assistance in unemployment relief could no longer be denied. "[W]e are in the midst of an emergency, now in its third and cumulative winter," Kellogg argued, "and when industry has failed to take time by the forelock and where private charitable help falls short, the general public cannot dodge its responsibility to act through government." [34]

The steering committee now became the lobbying agent it was founded to be. It created a plan drawn explicitly from "the experience of the New York State Commission," the TERA. [35] It was presented at the subcommittee hearings and introduced in the Senate as the La Follette-Costigan bill on January 15, 1932. The great majority of senators, however, remained fearful of a federal dole and rejected both that bill and another proposed by New York's Robert F. Wagner, which promised $375,000,000 in loans to the states. The fortunes of federal relief finally changed during May 1932, when both Congress and President Hoover began to respond to the crisis by setting forth new proposals. [36] New York's reformers appeared in Washington again, working feverishly to incorporate features from the defeated La Follette-Costigan bill into the new legislation. [37] But the Relief and Construction Act of July 21, 1932, which offered loans to the states in support of relief programs, fell far short of their hopes. Unlike New York's TERA, which provided matching grants that increased local public spending and safeguarded how the money was spent, the new federal act ignored such fiscal incentives and did nothing to improve "standards of [welfare] administration in local communities." [38] Social workers had won the war, but not the battle. They would have to wait for Franklin Roosevelt's New Deal to see the TERA methods they favored adopted by the nation.

During May 1932, while the fight for federal relief was heating up in Congress, America's social workers met for another annual national conference. Drawing upon the recent win-

73

ter's harsh experiences, the conferees overrode the caution that had prevailed the year before. In place of dependence upon private philanthropy stood "impatience with old ideology, old social patterns, old methodology." Infected by a "virus of economic awareness and action," they delved deeply into problems of ensuring economic security. At this 1932 Philadelphia meeting, Gertrude Springer reported to *Survey* readers, "unemployment loomed not as a transitory calamity but as a fault of social organization to be struck at boldly and with determination." A New York voice sounded the keynote, moreover, when William Hodson, the newly elected president of the National Conference of Social Work, declared, "My friends, federal relief is respectable. The time has come." After the brutal winter of 1931–1932, social workers embraced public relief—local, state, and federal—without hesitation.

Psychiatric casework and its theories fell victim to that winter's icy cold. At the 1932 conference, social workers "swung far away from individual therapy and fine points of techniques," Springer observed, "and far over toward the realities of economic leadership and community cohesion." Their task no longer centered in helping maladjusted individuals; it lay in aiding healthy, self-respecting men and women on the road back to self-sufficiency. Even psychiatric caseworkers admitted, in what Gertrude Springer called "confessions of error," that their methods often ignored or inadvertently accepted social and economic injustices. "What business have we raising orchids when we are so inadequate to the job of providing bread!" a prominent caseworker let out. Finally, the Great Depression had subordinated "the riddle of personalities" to the facts of "material realities."

As casework psychiatry faded, public welfare administration came into vogue. "Public social work has become so much the larger part of social work," Stanley P. Davies of New York noted during the conference, "that it must inevitably be our primary professional concern." Indeed, the professionalization of public welfare was the next major issue now that the methods of giving relief and the problem of funding it had been

addressed. Only two years before, at the Boston national conference, members of the American Public Welfare Association, a
weak affiliate of the National Conference of Social Work, had
gathered as "a little group off on the side-lines" of private philanthropy's big show. Now, however, in New York and in every
other state, they were coming into power.[39] Often their ways
were not the ways of professional social workers, because public
welfare administrators were usually the appointees and associates of politicians, or small-time politicians themselves. Yet while
private philanthropy's social workers feared utter devastation in
1932, their public services were flourishing. If social work as a
profession was to survive, and if professional social workers
were to serve the great mass of the nation's unemployed, then
professionalism was vital to the growth of public welfare.

**Embedding
professionalism
in
public
programs**

7

By the time of the Great Depression, New York's reformers had spent more than three decades contending with the patronage system of Tammany Hall and its "charitable" tradition of helping people in exchange for votes. In spite of personal attachments to some reform-minded Tammany leaders, such as Al Smith, social workers often found the political organization repulsive. In the social workers' estimation, patronage—the awarding of government jobs on the basis of party loyalty—bred incompetence in the administration of public welfare programs, while politically controlled charity—usually "hand-outs" to party followers—perpetuated dependency. Tammany Hall also posed in microcosm the failures of a larger society that allowed politicians to decide the destiny of public welfare programs. Speaking for the State Charities Aid Association in November 1931, Homer Folks characterized New York State's municipal welfare commissioners as "generally speaking, inexperienced, untrained . . . [and] considerably political," its county welfare commissioners as "generally selected for institutional management" rather than for their qualifications as social workers, and its town welfare officials as generally incapable.[1] Yet the inability of private businesses to stabilize employment and the inadequacy of private philanthropy to dispense enough relief forced Americans to seek help from public officials.

Instead of the dreary almshouse, the disorderly public relief station, and the ward heeler's basket of food, social workers envisioned a system of public welfare that would use their skills to raise people out of poverty. The SCAA's Homer Folks, an "old-timer" who arrived in New York during the depression of the 1890s, was the champion of social work's drive for professionalism in public services. A farm boy from Hanover, Michigan, Folks was educated at Harvard as well as Albion College. He became secretary of the SCAA in 1893, using that organization to bring the knowledge and methods of social work to bear upon public welfare programs. With passage of the Widows' Pension Act of 1915, which provided public aid to dependent women and their children, he scored an early victory in the movement for public outdoor relief. Outdoor relief offered help to people in their own homes instead of forcing them into institutions; the 1929 revision of New York's Public Welfare Law and its Old Age Pension Law of 1930 extended Folk's efforts to the elderly, enabling them to stay in their own neighborhoods among family and friends while receiving public aid. As chairman of the Welfare Council's executive committee, he also directed the fight for municipal unemployment relief during the spring of 1931, and the TERA, which he helped initiate, spread the net of public assistance state-wide.[2]

Bracing all of Homer Folks's efforts was a conviction that recipients of public aid should be allowed to live in their own homes and determine their own needs without constant supervision. With professional personnel, Folks argued again and again, public welfare programs could be run efficiently and effectively, outside institutions and without the threat of political corruption. Moreover, governmental programs offered the advantages of "speed, universality, uniformity," as well as abundant fiscal resources.[3] Even though private philanthropy had built social work into a profession, Folks was among the first to see that social work and public authority had to merge if the unemployment crisis of the 1930s was to be met successfully.

Folks's call for public relief in 1928 demonstrated his exceptional foresight. Two years later, during the harsh winter of 1930–1931, most social workers still expected the city to stay out of the business of relief. They accepted a municipal breadline and shelters for the homeless as necessities during an emergency, but when Tammany's mayor, Jimmy Walker, initiated a police canvass to "discover" the jobless, created a Mayor's Committee for the Relief of the Needy Unemployed, called upon city employees to donate to that committee's Mayor's Fund, and empowered precinct commanding officers to determine family need and dispense relief, social workers reacted furiously. The Welfare Council demanded that no "new, untried, and inexperienced societies" be allowed to grant assistance.[4] Walker's policy smacked of political charity, but there was really nothing that social workers could do to deter him, so private philanthropy and Tammany Hall worked different sides of the welfare street during that first winter of crisis. While social workers tried to build a system of privately-supported relief that applied uniformly to all needy New Yorkers, the police, using no uniform standards or methods, indulged in outright charity, distributing the Mayor's Fund in hit-or-miss fashion. It seemed to social workers that funds hit Tammany's voters more often than not, while missing people whose votes for the machine were not **78** secure.[5]

If anything, Mayor Walker's activities spurred the desire of New York's reformers to place qualified personnel in municipal welfare agencies. Homer Folks, who saw the growing unemployment emergency as a "chance to prove equal to [the] job," challenged his colleagues to use their brains, their courage, and a good press to influence the mayor's decisions; he also called for laws to guarantee competence in public welfare administration.[6] The relief crisis of February 1931, which inspired the social workers' first mass meeting and led to resolutions demanding

public action, drove city officials and social workers closer together. Folks and the Commissioner of Public Welfare, Frank
Taylor, forged agreements that promised coordination of private philanthropy's relief efforts and new city programs. The
legislature's emergency act of March 1931, however, had failed
to set explicit standards for the administration of public programs. Meanwhile, city officials independently decreed that only
citizens who had voted during the last two years qualified for
municipal aid. That proviso seemed rife with mischief; Tammany Hall could keep its appointees in positions of authority,
use public revenues to help its voting "regulars," and discrimi-
nate against anyone who could not or did not vote. Social workers, who had finally come to champion the cause of municipal
action, now shuddered at the prospect that public relief might
degenerate into a system of unrivalled political corruption. "We
now find," Folks observed in April 1931, "that we cannot found a
satisfactory welfare system . . . unless we can build it upon a rejuvenation, reform and rehabilitation of public welfare."[7] The
logical place to turn for such rejuvenation was the state capitol,
Albany.

The process of seeding professionalism in public service
began in September 1931, after Governor Roosevelt convened
the legislature in extraordinary session. In his special message,
FDR had called for a temporary emergency relief act that would
create an administrative agency independent of the state's existing Board of Social Welfare. Its function was to dispense twenty
million dollars in state relief to support local home and work relief programs. Its administrators were free to set rules for the
handling of state funds, but the precise measure of their authority over the state's public welfare services was left unclear.[8]
Even though Roosevelt had made a dramatic move in response
to social workers' recent pleas, he found himself confronted by
unexpectedly antagonistic critics—New York's social work reformers—who worried about the nonprofessional loopholes in
his proposals. Later, a stunned Roosevelt was to inform Homer
Folks in disapproving terms that he had endured "an exceed-

ingly disagreeable situation" prompted by a "wholly unnecessary row" that was instigated by Folks's SCAA.[9] Indeed, the two friends had found themselves at loggerheads.

The *temporary, emergency,* and *independent* character of Roosevelt's proposed TERA marked the major point of contention. Reformers wanted legislation that permanently upgraded the quality of public welfare administration, and they preferred to increase the powers of a permanent organization, the State Board of Social Welfare. By locating the TERA within the administrative structure of the Board, Homer Folks argued, the new agency could "avail itself fully of the accumulated experience and knowledge of the State Board of Welfare, itself an unpaid, nonpolitical body, and . . . utilize the facilities and connections of that Department."[10] FDR's plan left too much power in the hands of local public welfare officials who could continue to manipulate relief in political ways.

In addition, social workers demanded that work relief be administered separately from home relief. Their motive was obvious: since work relief received financial preference and paid cash wages, local public welfare officials would be left with the smaller home relief program and would probably be restricted to giving relief in kind. At the same time, appointed bodies of citizens—dominated presumably by professional social workers—would administer work relief programs and protect the public against the dole. Folks was scarcely this blunt with Roosevelt. Instead he couched his meaning in vague words, noting that the TERA proposal put "all its eggs of all kinds in the one basket of the local public welfare official." "For ordinary home relief," he continued, "this seems wise, but for the organization and carrying on of new measures, such as work relief operations, requiring a wide range of cooperation on the part of other officials and agencies, a separate authority would seem to me more promising."[11] Folks confronted a difficult situation. His own Bruere Committee report had pointed to the political chicanery involved in public welfare administration, yet he could

80

hardly charge a friendly governor with the possible intention of using relief for political purposes.

FDR's motives were not clear, and they became subordinate to a nasty struggle that pitted social workers, the SCAA, and the Republicans in the senate and assembly against his plan. Using the excuse of illness, Homer Folks stayed away from Albany during the battle; his position was taken by his assistant, Elsie Bond, who joined forces with Republican leaders to draft the Wicks Bill, a social workers' measure. Claiming that no "politics" existed in the SCAA's approach, Republicans promised to secure "permanent improvement of our public welfare system" by placing the TERA within the Board of Social Welfare and by creating independent emergency work bureaus throughout the state.[12] The Wicks Bill passed in the senate, at which point Roosevelt threatened a veto, promised to recall the legislature into extraordinary session if an acceptable proposal was not enacted, and offered to work out points of difference in a meeting of leaders.[13] He expressed his disdain for the SCAA's interference, however, by excluding Elsie Bond and other social workers from the final negotiations. At last, on September 19, 1931, he announced his compromise.

Even though FDR claimed that the final version of the TERA measure was consistent with his initial proposal, he triumphed only in keeping the new agency separate from the State Board of Social Welfare. On other points, he made substantial concessions, especially in allowing independent local work bureaus to be established. And some points went far beyond his original suggestions, especially in bringing social work professionalism directly to bear on the TERA's policies and practices. The TERA was granted powers, first, to utilize absolute authority in the distribution of work relief funds; second, to establish strict rules applying to the conduct of local public welfare officials; and third, to act on the qualifications of city and county welfare commissioners who used its funds for home relief.[14] In short, the TERA could substantially upgrade the standards of

81

relief administration. Except for the fine distinction that continued to exist between an agency that was temporary and one
that would be permanent, social work's reformers had, in fact,
tallied a major, stunning victory. Nonetheless, Folks wrote FDR
in a conciliatory tone, looking ahead to the appointment of the
TERA's commissioners and to the "unavoidably terrible job"
they would face, while Roosevelt responded in kind, expressing
his hope that Folks would soon "be able to take charge of things
again." [15] Each carefully avoided recriminations, thereby smooth-
ing the way for closer cooperation in the future.

Any worries about FDR's intentions toward the TERA
should have been swept aside when he appointed its administrative board. Jesse Isador Straus, its chairman, was a New York
City merchant and philanthropist; Douglas Falconer, a social
worker from Rochester; and Harry Hopkins, an executive member of the Welfare Council of New York City. This strongly pro-
professional group had the power to dispense state funds on the
basis of short-term, renewable matching grants, and it used the
grants to ensure the installation of professional social workers.
Whenever a city or county applied for or sought to renew a
TERA grant, its welfare personnel were subject to review by the
commissioners, who moved swiftly in establishing proper qualifications for local public welfare administrators. [16] Local politicians, of course, complained mightily to the governor about
encroachments upon their bailiwick. Straus and his fellow commissioners remained steadfastly committed, however, to the "im-
perative" need for "competent people, with experience and
training [in] public welfare administration," and defended their
policy of bringing social workers from "the private agencies . . .
to the aid of the public departments in this time of crisis." [17] Thus
the TERA built sturdy bridges on which social workers crossed
from private philanthropy to public services.

Political abuses were also curbed by TERA. The commissioners prohibited discrimination on the basis of race (or eth-
nic group), status as citizens, or political affiliation. They also
spelled out the proper techniques of investigation. Home relief,

for example, required extensive inquiry into an applicant's property and financial holdings; his last employer had to verify his good performance as a worker; and his relatives and friends had to be evaluated as possible sources of aid. If assistance was justified, then adequate relief had to be determined according to the budgeted needs of his family. Monthly follow-up investigations were necessary.[18] A procedure this precise required at least basic training in the techniques of social casework as practiced by the private agencies. Compliance with TERA rulings, therefore, brought trained investigators and caseworkers as well as professional supervisors into public welfare administration. The device of matching grants gave irate local politicians no recourse: they either accepted social workers or forfeited state support—a sacrifice they would be hard pressed to justify either to jobless constituents or to tax-paying voters.

Backed by TERA's authority, the Welfare Council again approached Tammany Hall's city officials in the fall of 1931, bargaining this time from a position of power. Homer Folks and Frank Taylor hammered out an agreement that created an interlocking directorate for private and public work relief programs and a joint advisory committee for home relief programs. The Council's Social Service Exchange was authorized to keep official records on all relief recipients. Two representatives from private philanthropy became the chief administrators of the city's relief programs: Cornelius Bliss of the COS served as chairman of the municipal emergency work bureau, and Mary Gibbons of the Catholic Charities directed the municipal home relief program. In addition, all of the latter's supervisory personnel were drawn from the city's professional social workers.[19] These and similar actions across the state drew immediate approval for the TERA's commissioners. "The principles and procedures they have adopted rest on sound social practice," *Survey* commented. "The organization they have assembled commands professional respect. The methods they are introducing promise to put forward by years the progress of public welfare administration in the state."[20] Gertrude Springer was more pointed, identifying

83

TERA's impact with "the acceptance of the leadership of the professional social worker" in every aspect of unemployment relief.[21]

During the fall of 1931 the East Twenty-second Street community turned its attention to the prospects for federal relief. The significance of the TERA was perceived immediately, and it became the social workers' model for a federal program. In his public letter to President Hoover, William Hodson proposed a "partnership" between the national government and the localities, in which the national government would stimulate local relief efforts by offering matching grants and use its fiscal leverage to ensure competent administration and professional standards of service.[22] When the social workers' new steering committee on federal action lobbied in Washington during November 1931 for "adequate administrative safeguards" in any proposed federal legislation, it too copied TERA.[23] Later, the La Follette-Costigan bill for federal relief (introduced in Congress on January 15, 1932) incorporated TERA's methods into a plan for national action.[24] After the La Follette-Costigan bill met defeat, New York's Senator Robert F. Wagner introduced a bill that discarded the matching grants principle and dropped guarantees for professional standards of service. Defending the TERA model, *Survey* described Wagner's proposal as "within speaking distance of being a $375,000,000 porkbarrel" because it would permit states to use federal loans in any manner they desired. "From the point of view of social workers this bill . . . would have little to recommend it," *Survey* concluded, "were it not for the bitter need . . . and the paucity of existing relief resources."[25] A revision of Wagner's proposal became the Relief and Construction Act of July 1932, and the Reconstruction Finance Corporation was authorized to loan federal funds to the states for unemployment relief; the act still offered no safeguards for professional relief services.[26] For the time being, the TERA model's insistence on professionalism in public welfare programs had been rejected.

Though temporarily defeated, the New York reformers

concentrated on making the best of the new federal program. Speaking for the American Association of Social Workers, Harry Lurie urged members "to use their utmost efforts to prevent the exploitation of these funds for political or similarly undesirable motives." The best strategy appeared to be "building up and improving the standards of administration in local communities," and Lurie reminded his colleagues of their "obligation to . . . bring the experience of social workers to bear upon the relief administration which will be developed" in each of the states.[27] Throughout the summer and fall, organizations like the Family Welfare Association of America and the American Public Welfare Association called for the "whole-hearted cooperation of social workers with public-welfare agencies" in setting up state relief machinery. AASW chapters even formed state committees to approach governors "with a proffer of cooperation and counsel."[28] All their labors might have proved vain, however, if help had not arrived from an unanticipated source, the Reconstruction Finance Corporation (RFC).

The RFC proved more conscientious in administering public funds than its legislation required. Frequently criticized for its policy of forcing governors to declare "poverty oaths" of state bankruptcy before granting relief loans, the RFC advanced cautiously, distributing its funds slowly and in small amounts. Yet its caution also served to advance professionalism in public welfare administration. To protect its program against corruption, the RFC judiciously examined loan applications from the states, and like the TERA, granted public funds on a short-term basis. Grant renewals required reviews that forced state-developed relief services to maintain acceptable practices. As a result, the RFC kept federal funds from becoming a "state grab-bag" and coerced most states to organize competent relief staffs.[29] After it expended the last of its appropriation in May 1933, Joanna Colcord of the Russell Sage Foundation happily surveyed the fruits of its labors: "All but four states have now some form of state-wide relief organization, more or less effectively developed; and social workers of training, experience and good professional standards have been brought into positions of influence in more than half of them."[30]

The reformers had not abandoned the La Follette-Costigan bill. New public hearings were held late in 1932, and social workers, again led by Walter West of the Committee on Federal Action on Unemployment, reappeared to testify on the bill's merits.[31] In February 1933, the American Association of Social Workers' Sub-Committee on Methods of Administration urged the creation of "a small appointive board of persons specially qualified" to head a new federal relief program that would "employ social workers and such trained specialists as are necessary." The sub-committee acknowledged that the RFC had helped improve state services, but noted the agency's lack of "specific authority to assist in the development of state administrative programs."[32] Soon thereafter, the AASW's executive committee endorsed the idea of a powerful federal board that could improve relief standards by "developing more effective and more humane methods of administration."[33] Clearly, the TERA model still held dominion over the minds of New Yorkers, who dominated all of those committees, and they persisted in their desire to make it the nation's model for action.

By the end of Herbert Hoover's presidential years, the policies of the TERA on a local level and of the RFC on a national level had advanced the cause of professionalism in public welfare. By drafting explicit rules controlling the use of public revenues and by subjecting public programs to periodic review, both agencies held local welfare officials accountable for their actions. Moreover, even though neither directly controlled local programs, each granted social workers substantial influence in the development of local and state relief policies. Their efforts had implemented Homer Folks's belief that public welfare services could be administered efficiently, fairly, and impartially.

Yet their triumph contained its ironies. The cause of social justice had ridden on an enormous wave of sympathy for jobless Americans, and of course the reformers wanted society to compensate the unemployed justly. The professional techniques of social work, however, derived from an understanding of the psychology of unemployment, not its economics, and promised psychological benefits rather than a reordering of the nation's capitalist economy. Social workers never resolved the tension between their professional aspirations and the cause of social justice; they never made a clear choice between saving productive individualism for a capitalist society and restructuring capitalism. Instead they tried to mix professional methodology and reform impulses. They now led their profession in a distinct, although subtle, shift from righting economic injustice toward the complexities of psychology and human morale. A just means to save productive individualism with all of its implied inequities had become their ambivalent goal.

The
President
out
in
the
cold:

Herbert
Hoover

8

Herbert Hoover never enjoyed the regard of New York's reformers. Even though he endorsed and signed the first law bringing federal relief to the states and localities, he failed to win their approval. Perhaps the passions generated by the 1928 campaign never cooled sufficiently; perhaps he was never forgiven for beating Al Smith. Clearly, Hoover was a do-something president. Large expenditures for public works, a record deficit budget, and a host of proposals and programs that prefigured many New Deal measures characterized the innovative contributions made by his administration in fighting the Great Depression.[1] Nonetheless, social work leaders always felt isolated from the Hoover administration.

The president demanded loyalty and confidentiality from those who served him; thus it was impossible for outsiders to know what was happening inside the White House. New Yorkers came to believe that their concerns were not being addressed there. Their sense of being ignored probably drew them more closely together, especially after December 1931, when they began to appeal for federal relief. Throughout 1932 they perceived an indifferent and callous adversary in Herbert Hoover; they vilified him and celebrated his defeat in the 1932 election. Yet his policies were often as advanced as theirs. New Yorkers never guessed that the Woods Committee had set forth a progressive program for federal action, and they never appreciated the distance that Hoover traveled in advancing his position to that point. But Hoover made it easy to misunderstand him. He failed to communicate with the reformers, and his apparent aloofness hurt their pride.

Social work reformers had adopted a wait-and-see attitude at the beginning of Hoover's presidency. His record as food administrator in the War Industries Board, administrator of relief in Europe, chairman of the 1921 President's Conference on Unemployment, and Secretary of Commerce augured leadership that would be progressive in both economics and human relations. Following the stock market crash, Paul Kellogg wrote presidential adviser Edward Eyre Hunt hopefully, reviewing the unemployment problem and suggesting that "a stroke by him [Hoover] would be ever so opportune."[2] When Hoover responded promptly, setting up business conferences in Washington at which he implored industrialists to retain employees and to maintain current wages, social servants praised his efforts. "There have been patches of silver lining to the winter's clouds," Kellogg commented in the May 1930 *Survey*, "the biggest at Washington, where President Hoover called business leaders together and got the country off on its right foot." In addition, the president had pleaded for increased private spending on home and business repairs and new construction, and had promised to increase federal public works programs. Kellogg perceived a move "to throw the lever forward" by "using the leadership of the federal government to focus great voluntary forces for revival."[3] A few months later, Kellogg wrote E. E. Hunt again, urging continued "federal leadership in stimulating voluntary action," anticipating by only a few days Hoover's appointment of the President's Emergency Committee for Employment.[4]

The PECE began its work late in October 1930. Arthur

Woods of New York was its chairman. Woods had been the city's Police Commissioner during Mayor Mitchel's administration, a member of the 1921 President's Conference on Unemployment, and a director of philanthropic foundations in the city during the 1920s.[5] In addition to administering an emergency appropriation of over one hundred million dollars for federal public works, his committee was to actuate the program of voluntary measures that Hoover had outlined the winter before. But the committee was given no direct means of aiding the unemployed.[6] Moreover, "prominent men were purposely not selected" for its staff, precisely because Hoover did not want to call unnecessary attention to the unemployment problem.[7] As a result, most members were obscure social and economic theorists. Among them, however, was a lone social worker, Porter R. Lee, the director of the New York School of Social Work and former president of the National Conference of Social Work. His appointment drew an enthusiastic response from New York's reformers. David Holbrook and Joanna Colcord hailed it as marking a new, innovative acceptance of social workers and their experience in the councils of government.[8] Their approval derived partly from knowledge that Lee was to work closely with the Welfare Council of New York City and other Gotham-based social service organizations in developing the PECE's functions.[9] With the strategic placement of Woods and Lee on the committee, New Yorkers appeared to have a sure foothold for influencing national unemployment policies.

90   The president's "no-name" committee hardly lacked ambition. By the end of November, its members had produced an agenda of suggestions that offered Hoover a broad program for federal action. Comparing joblessness "to the ravages of war or disease," they described the nation's industrial system as bogged down "in a grave, tragic, stupid and anomalous situation." Yet unemployment was "subject to human control," and their mission was "to see that all possible efforts are made to provide each unemployed person with work, for work rather than charity is not only their choice, but their right." Having embraced the kind

of rhetoric later associated with the New Deal, PECE members suggested similar emergency measures, including federal road building, rural electrification projects, and urban housing programs. In addition, the federal government could sponsor a national bureau for gathering unemployment statistics, "a nation-wide system of public employment offices," and a national plan for unemployment insurance.[10] If the PECE was looking ahead, however, it was also looking backwards to the recommendations of the 1921 President's Conference, which had been chaired by Herbert Hoover.

The relief issue could not be ignored in the winter of 1930–1931. Hoover stood firmly against any congressional attempts to institute a federal "dole system," but considered enlisting the Red Cross as a relief-granting agency.[11] The PECE supported such use of the Red Cross, because it could dispense relief more fairly and effectively than government. "Within our committee and in the minds of every group outside of whom [*sic*] I have conferred," Porter Lee reported to Arthur Woods, "the feeling is unanimous that the poor law machinery of states and local communities is [with "very few" exceptions] wholly inadequate for unemployment relief."[12] Yet most social work leaders still wanted neither a national philanthropic campaign nor federal involvement, fearing that either "would be fatal to local community money raising now under way,"[13] and the Red Cross itself was "very loathe to assume any general responsibility for unemployment relief."[14] Local resources still seemed adequate for the months ahead, but that perception began to change during January 1931. Porter Lee reported a "movement . . . from bad to worse" in some parts of the country and recommended that the Red Cross "assume responsibility for the unorganized smaller cities and rural sections" where voluntary relief programs did not exist. Many large cities had begun to experience serious difficulties in raising relief funds, and an emergency seemed at hand. "Unless the situation changes remarkably for the better soon," Lee observed, "it seems to me clear that the assumption of unemployment relief by the Red Cross may necessi-

91

tate a grant of federal funds." In his estimation, the time had come for a meeting of leaders from the Red Cross, Congress, and the administration.[15] In sum, the PECE was moving rapidly toward federal intervention. Its concern deepened when it learned that federal public works had progressed slowly, that emergency appropriations for new projects languished in Congress, and that state and local governments as well as private institutions had cut spending for new construction.[16]

By mid-winter of 1930–1931, PECE members were generating internal memoranda that contemplated radical departures from Hoover's policies of voluntarism and local responsibility. One of them reviewed possible "*work* projects offering the best immediate opportunity for a Federal work program," including the modernization of public buildings and conservation of United States forests.[17] Another debated the different theories separating local relief and federal action, noting the inadequacy of current measures and concluding that the federal government was "the most available agency through which funds can be provided promptly enough to meet the need."[18] In addition to enacting strong relief measures, the Hoover administration needed to tell the American public the truth, making "frank" statements on "the amount of unemployment" and "on the general situation."[19] Indeed, Arthur Woods and his colleagues were working themselves into a rebellious mood.

The PECE kept its deliberations confidential, as was appropriate for a committee directly responsible to the president. The American public, including its complement of New York social workers, did not know that the Woods Committee had jumped ahead of the president, the nation's governors, and even social welfare leaders. New York was still a month away from the crisis that finally brought municipal relief, and the first state action—New York's—lay more than six months in the future. Certainly no condition of general alarm existed yet, and Herbert Hoover advanced only as far as enlisting the aid of a reluctant Red Cross, "very quietly and unobtrusively," to relieve the distress of miners and other unemployed industrial workers in

92

West Virginia.[20] Yet faith in the president was beginning to dete-
riorate. "I note a new and critical air toward Hoover," the National Social Work Council's David Holbrook observed.[21]

At the end of the winter, the Woods Committee prepared its final reports in which it articulated its criticisms of
Hoover's policies. The members commented that they did "not
see any official or unofficial body" that was taking ideas about
fighting unemployment and turning them "into a comprehensive
and concrete proposal of national policy—both public and private." Charging that public agencies were "estopped by questions
of political expediency" and that private philanthropies went
amiss "because of conflict of opinion in their own ranks," committee members advanced to the core of their concerns: "Most of the
agencies,—whether public or private,—which are influential
enough to do anything of a fundamental character,—are un-
ready to face clearly and openly the deepest issues which often
run so counter to our traditional American habits of thought."
The country needed, they concluded, "more fundamental ap-
proaches" to the problem of solving unemployment and "a
national program." Their own recommendations included promoting employment through public works and through special
work relief programs "rather than charitable relief."[22]

The Woods Committee was on a collision course with
Herbert Hoover and his White House lieutenants. The decisive
confrontation occurred over one of three unemployment bills
introduced in the Senate by Robert F. Wagner. In 1928 and
again in 1930, the New Yorker had proposed measures to create   93
a national service for gathering unemployment statistics, to
organize a program of federal public works for emergency use,
and to establish a federal employment service. Each derived
from the recommendations of the 1921 President's Conference,
and social workers had always supported them. Paul Kellogg
had been quick to reprimand Hoover for not seeking such legislation himself upon becoming president,[23] and reformers were
soon organizing lobbying campaigns on behalf of Wagner's
three bills.[24] By the end of March 1930, the Senate had approved

all three, but the House passed only the statistics measure, which became law in June.[25] When the Woods Committee was created late in October, Hoover still opposed Wagner's two remaining bills.

The PECE and the administration shared an important doubt about the emergency public works bill—it did not "centralize planning and construction activities in a [single] department or bureau."[26] Even though it provided for a planning board, a PECE member pointed out, Wagner's bill left actual construction activities scattered throughout the rambling structure of government and put the president "in the position of Moses, with the responsibility for declaring the existence of an emergency and ordering acceleration [of public works], with no way provided for the orderly and prompt functioning of existing machinery."[27] Nonetheless, it seemed too late to draft an alternative, so the PECE advised Hoover to opt for expediency and offer some amendments to Wagner's bill. "This is a salvaging operation only," the committee admitted, pushing for the president's approval and opening the way for adoption of the Employment Stabilization Act of February 1931.[28] The need for fresh public works appropriations kept the PECE and the administration working in harness for the second of Wagner's bills.

The third proved the rub. Hoover's White House advisers objected to federal financing of a national employment service, and Hoover asked his Secretary of Labor to draft a new bill that would place the burden of funding on the states. Presidential secretary Edward Eyre Hunt volunteered the assistance of the PECE, only to discover that "all of them are firm in their advocacy of the Federal aid provision" as set forth in Wagner's bill.[29] Indeed, PECE members strongly defended the thinking behind the Senator's measure. Federal financing, they argued, could be used to elevate "the standards of efficiency of the state bureaus" and to "safeguard political interference, and maladministration generally."[30] In addition, a national service could not exist without the participation of the federal government; for "the employment service to be effective, [it] must not consist of 48 separate operating units."[31] By February 1931, members were calling the measure "indispensable."[32] They offered numerous reasons why Hoover should support Wagner's bill: he could use federal employment offices as the outlets for a national system of unemployment insurance; he could avoid political damage; he could treat the law as "an experiment" and use it as "the starting point for the development of a program" that would suit his objectives.[33] After the Wagner bill was passed by both Senate and House, Woods and his associates offered their final plea, telling Hoover "that his failure to approve the bill would be a 'tragedy.'"[34] On March 7, 1931, Hoover gave it his veto.

The Woods Committee was furious. The president had listed reasons for his veto, but the PECE rejected each as erroneous. Indeed, before the veto was delivered, the committee composed a memorandum, "placed personally in the President's hands," that refuted all of the objections later used in his veto message. Recalling that first memorandum and issuing a second two days after the veto, the committee repeated each of its arguments in stinging, point-by-point detail, comparing its conclusions to the president's quoted words and pinpointing every error in his contentions.[35] The best that could be said on Hoover's behalf was that he had been misled by "a counsel of perfection," the memorandum lamented. The PECE obviously felt that the president had ignored its far sounder counsel.[36]

The Woods Committee was about to die. Nearly all of its initiatives were rejected or ignored, either by the president or by his staff. In April 1931, Arthur Woods resigned as chairman, claiming poor health and the press of other obligations. Hoover had promised to renew the committee's budget, but some of its functions—especially those regarding the planning of federal public works—had been taken over by the new Federal Employment Stabilization Board, which was the offspring of Wagner's second unemployment bill.[37] The life of the PECE ended quietly during August, when Hoover appointed a new President's Organization on Unemployment Relief.

The PECE never embarrassed the president, because it kept its memoranda and recommendations confidential. Nor did its members use private channels of communication to express their discontent. It was speculation, therefore, when social work leaders interpreted Woods's "silence" following his resignation as an indication of protest. "There have been some rumors," Harry Lurie allowed, "that the [PECE's] findings and [its] conclusions . . . concerning necessary relief measures differed considerably from the program that the President was willing to sponsor."[38] But social work leaders were left in the dark. Only years later, after the PECE's papers ended up in the office of New Deal relief administrator Harry Hopkins, did that disagreement become public knowledge.[39] Even then, however, Hopkins did not reveal how close the Woods Committee had come to anticipating the New Deal's unemployment program for the nation.

The president's new committee, the President's Organization on Unemployment Relief (POUR), was less powerful than the PECE. Walter S. Gifford, another New Yorker and president of the Charity Organization Society, headed POUR. It was to conduct a national campaign in support of local relief programs, "[a]dhering to the dogma of the President," as Harry Lurie put it, "that the prior responsibility for such assistance is logically that of the individual states."[40] Like the PECE, Gifford's Committee was granted no federal funds for relief. That circumstance prompted humorist Will Rogers to describe Gifford's job as Christ-like and "remarkable"—he was to "feed the several million unemployed," but was given nothing "to do it with." *Survey* printed the joke for its readers, but without levity, referring to the committee's charge as raising "a grave question" about the adequacy of local action.[41] Soon social workers discovered that they had additional reasons for doubts. "Everything is chaotic" in the Gifford Committee, Allen Burns of the Community Chests reported after a Washington meeting in mid-September. In his estimation, Gifford's subordinates had "no conception, knowledge or interest in [the] work of social agencies as such" and "none of them know or care anything about social work itself."[42] That report marked an inauspicious beginning for the relief effort of 1931–1932; in fact, it marked the end of the reformers' tolerance of Herbert Hoover.

Survey had become openly critical of the president in February 1931, when the administration called upon the Red Cross to undertake drought relief. Some of Hoover's "friends [had] visualized the great organizer of European relief marshalling his countrymen in the conquest of domestic misery," Paul Kellogg suggested stingingly, but in this case, as in others of recent vintage, the president chose instead to defend the public treasury against "wholesale raids."[43] Then, after the veto of Wagner's employment service bill, *Survey* implicated Hoover in a failure during the 1920s to promote "either unemployment stabilization or employment reserves, or to encourage experimentation with the insurance principle in steadying work and earnings"; they also began to blame him for the nation's current economic problems.[44] In September, after Walter Gifford joined in the administration's attempt to paint a rosy picture of employment, Kellogg's journal printed an anecdote about a niggardly Scottish woman who called her husband to supper with a public announcement of "scones and kippered herring," when her intention was merely that of "fulin' the neighbors."[45]

Other New York reformers joined the chorus of criticism. Harry Lurie described Hoover as "the chief opponent of measures which would involve the government in a direct program of relief." "Relief does not deal with the causes of unemployment," he conceded, "but the refusal to aid the . . . unemployed through relief measures . . . adds the sin of inhumanity to the vices of social incompetence."[46] I. M. Rubinow posed his criticism in humorous fashion: "The little help which the National Government has offered has been (a) statistics— always optimistic, as to the past, present, and future; (b) some additional hullabaloo—radio speeches, pamphlets, etc. and (c) such constructive suggestions as meeting a national problem of vast proportion by advice to paint fences, repair stoops and can and pickle tomatoes."[47] Moreover, when social workers traveled to Washington to testify before the La Follette-Costigan committee at the close of 1931, federal officials were still unable to supply accurate statistics on unemployment; public works programs had yet to be adequately implemented; and the responsibility for helping the jobless find employment still remained with the states. Shortly thereafter Hoover created the Reconstruction Finance Corporation, an agency funded and designed to help business, but he initially withheld monies for relief. As Kellogg described his action, Hoover put "national backing behind the credit structure so as to help banks, railroads, farm organizations and business corporations to dig in their toes, but not toward reinforcing the footholds of unemployed wage-earners."[48] By mid-winter 1931–1932, social workers' frustration had grown into bitterness that was directed toward the president's person as well as his policies.

New York reformers never fathomed an apparent contradiction in Hoover's character: the conflict between his earlier successes as a humanitarian relief administrator and his reluctance to implement unemployment relief during America's Depression crisis. Again and again they recalled his accomplishments in Belgium, Russia, and even in Mississippi in 1927, hoping to spur him into action, while the president plodded ahead at his own gait, proving incapable, it seemed, of doing "sheer courageous affirmative things."[49] In fact, both social workers and Herbert Hoover had pursued the same logic in approaching the relief issue after 1929. Each chose to test the limits of conventional measures first, defending the principle of local self-help initially before launching new experiments. Each moved from there to a doctrine of state responsibility, allowing experience to reveal the inadequacy of earlier assumptions. In September 1931, both would have agreed on the merits of New York's new TERA, seeing state action as the next step in a logical progression. After that, however, social work leaders sprinted ahead, reaching the higher ground of federal relief first. Hoover lumbered steadily up the same slope, but a few months

98

behind social work's New York leaders. In the meantime, another winter of devastating unemployment had passed, and the first to reach the peak never forgave Hoover his tardiness. That chronological circumstance colored all of their thinking about the president. They underrated the importance of his early commitment to a national economic recovery program that included, eventually, federal aid for relief. They exaggerated the differences between their innovations and his by forgetting their own earlier faith in voluntarism, local self-help, and fiscal orthodoxy. They underestimated the complexity of Hoover's attempt to counteract the impact of a Depression psychology that threatened to grind business to a halt. Because he felt that he could neither admit the true extent of joblessness nor develop programs to deal directly with the problem without causing panic, he dragged his feet on relief.

Social workers were less worried about the troubled psyche of business than the psychological well-being of the American jobless. Hoover seemed indifferent to their needs. Certainly he was inattentive to the rapidly changing assessments of unemployment offered by social work observers. He also ignored initiatives posed by his own Woods Committee, which cost him the opportunity to launch an innovative federal unemployment program. Indeed, nothing in the committee's remaining files indicates that he took much interest in its work. His communications with the PECE were impersonal and routine.

Perhaps most important, New York's social work reformers knew little about the inner workings of the administration. They were not parties to the PECE's deliberations, even though Porter R. Lee probably brought much of their experience to bear on PECE recommendations. They also lacked intimate contact either with the president or with his executive officers. A "newsy" journal like *Survey*, therefore, gained no special insights into the workings of the Hoover administration and offered little sympathy for its actors. It cast its judgments from afar. There may have been justification for Paul Kellogg's perception that "Mr. Hoover has surrounded himself with political advisers who insulate, inhibit and short-circuit him"; in any event, social work reformers themselves lacked entree to his inner circle. In addition, when Hoover did act, he appeared to do so without seeking consultation and consent. "The thing that he missed in all those years he was off in China, Africa and elsewhere," Kellogg asserted to Frances Perkins, "was that very give and take among the rank and file of folk in a democratic society which is such a handicap to him now in acting as its chief." [50] At the same time, reformers were receiving a good hearing in Albany, where a Democratic candidate for the presidency was laying the groundwork for his 1932 campaign.

The Great Humanitarian's reputation as a benefactor of the needy was finally destroyed beyond recovery when federal troops drove the Bonus Army from Washington in the summer of 1932. "It was a violation of every modern social principle of dealing with human distress," *Survey* charged, adding a caustic comment: "Belgium refugees, eighteen years ago, fared better than they." [51] Displayed boldly on the contents page of that same issue was a boxed-in summary of the president's newest recommendations for relief. Once again, Hoover was asking for the mobilization of voluntary services, and the box bore the headline, "WANTED: LEADERSHIP." [52]

FDR:

**the
social
workers'
choice**

9

When Franklin D. Roosevelt first campaigned for governor in the shadow of the Smith-Hoover presidential fight of 1928, New York social workers did not suspect that he was a blue-chip prospect as a leader of welfare reforms. Shortly after issuing her public endorsement of Al Smith, Henry Street settlement's Lillian Wald composed a second letter, endorsing Herbert H. Lehman for the post of New York's lieutenant-governor; she praised him as one of the settlement's oldest friends, a devoted philanthropist, and a knowledgeable ally of social workers. Wald sent a draft of her letter to C. C. Burlingham, director of the COS, asking him if she should include an endorsement of Roosevelt. "Your tribute to Herbert L. is of such a nature," he replied, "that you can not couple F. Roosevelt with it. F.D.R. has had no such relation to social work . . . he has been a fine clean politician, but . . . his whole career has been political." Apparently agreeing, Wald left the gubernatorial nominee's name out of her letter, which was published in the *New York Times*.[1] Nor did Roosevelt enter the Governor's Mansion with an established coterie of social service advisers and supporters. In his first letter to the newly elected governor, Paul Kellogg confessed that he knew of Roosevelt's interest in social welfare only second-hand; the scanty information that he possessed came from his wife, who was acquainted with the governor's wife. In a gesture of hoped-for friendship, Kellogg promised to send FDR some back-issues of *Survey*, hoping that they would capture the governor's interest.[2] Soon after his inauguration, however, social work's reformers discovered that FDR's Albany was as receptive to them and their ideas as it had been during the governorship of their recently fallen hero, Al Smith.

Eleanor Roosevelt was the trump card sealing her husband's partnership with social workers. Her contacts with them spanned the 1920s, when her philanthropic activities made her a friend of the New York branches of both the Women's Trade Union League and the National Consumers' League.[3] Rose Schneiderman, the president of the WTUL, believed that Mrs. Roosevelt first opened the governor's eyes to the reformers' programs; after his election, "she began to bring in everyone, old friends and new acquaintances, who could share their experiences and their ideas with him."[4] During the election races, she had also enticed the NCL's president, Mary (Molly) Williams Dewson, into the contest, and the two women had campaigned together for Smith and FDR. After the election, Dewson decided "like a good social worker . . . to cash in on" her successful efforts. Eleanor arranged a meeting with FDR, to whom Dewson presented the legislative program of the Consumers' League.[5] Soon thereafter, she became one of Roosevelt's key political organizers, specializing in the women's vote and serving as a liaison with social service groups. Schneiderman and Dewson were only two of the extraordinary women Eleanor Roosevelt brought into the governor's circle; others included Lillian Wald and Mary Simkhovitch, two of the foremost figures in the settlement movement. Another woman leader, Frances Perkins, was a hold-over from the Smith administration. Once the executive secretary of the NCL, Perkins had served Governor Smith as a member of the state's Industrial Commission; Roosevelt named her to chair that body.

The new governor immediately picked up the loose ends of welfare programs that Al Smith had left untied. He promised a forty-eight hour week and a minimum wage for women and child workers, an extension of workmen's compensation to cover occupational diseases, a revision of the state's tenement housing law and continuation of its rent law, a bill governing the use of labor injunctions, and a commission to study a system of old-age pensions.[6] Although those proposals were "old stories" to *Survey*'s editors, they commended the governor for standing "squarely behind a program for social legislation."[7] In addition, Roosevelt's support secured the new Public Welfare Law of 1929, which raised professional standards within the state's welfare department. He also encouraged the efforts of Herbert Lehman to improve treatment of the insane and of criminals in state institutions. After enactment of a forty-eight hour bill in 1930, he gave explicit recognition to his social work allies, sending the pens with which he had signed that measure to Rose Schneiderman and Molly Dewson.[8] At the end of Roosevelt's first year in office, *Survey* struck a note of surprised pleasure in his accomplishments: "New York is having the happy experience of having two governors in succession who are really interested in the social development of the state."[9]

FDR's responsiveness to growing unemployment also won him ever-increasing support among social service leaders, forty-seven of whom endorsed his reelection in November 1930.[10] In March of that year, he had signed an Old Age Assistance Law, and had called for coordinated private and public relief programs, increased municipal and county public works, expanded public employment services, and local job campaigns. His own fiscal conservatism dampened his enthusiasm for an emergency program of state public works, but his reliance on business voluntarism for employment stabilization and on local relief programs accorded with the recommendations of the

Bruere Committee, which had been at work on an emergency economic plan for much of 1930. Indeed, as an indication of the significance of the committee's work for social service leaders, the campaign for Roosevelt's reelection was led by Lillian Wald, Henry Bruere's one-time boss at Henry Street settlement.[11]

After 1929 FDR took the initiative in publicizing the social workers' welfare proposals beyond New York's state boundaries. At a national governors' conference in June 1930, he advocated state systems of privately supported and publicly administered old-age assistance and unemployment insurance programs. In January 1931, he convened a regional governors' conference to hear experts such as William Leiserson testify on behalf of mandatory unemployment insurance. Then, at another governors' conference in June 1931, two months after he had signed the bill allowing local governments to grant public outdoor relief in New York, and about two months before he introduced a measure leading to the creation of the TERA, Roosevelt appealed to his fellow governors to lead their states in assuming responsibility for relief. In October 1931, he sent Industrial Commissioner Frances Perkins to England to study European systems of unemployment compensation; at the end of November he received her report supporting "an American system" of unemployment reserves maintained by private industry. In February 1932, his Interstate Commission on Unemployment Insurance also recommended the reserves scheme, which he subsequently endorsed in a special message to New York's legislature. All of this was followed carefully by *Survey* and *Survey Graphic*, which reported the governor's progress to their national audiences.

104

In the meantime, attention shifted to Washington, where the reformers were battling for federal relief. In 1932 FDR also turned his energies to national issues and presidential politics. "THIS DAY NEXT YEAR WILL BE INTERESTING," Frances Perkins telegrammed Roosevelt on March 4, 1932, anticipating by twelve months exactly the inauguration of the next American president. "I APPROVE YOUR FAITH," he telegraphed back.[12] In only three years, a gubernatorial candidate whose social thought was a mystery to social workers had become a presidential contender, and one of his major assets was the social welfare program in his home state. The work of the Bruere Committee had established FDR as a leader in efforts to promote business stabilization, while his early endorsement of unemployment insurance was daring for a political leader of that time. "Surely you don't want Franklin Roosevelt to march ahead of the Survey in the procession," I. M. Rubinow teased one of the magazine's editors, implying that the governor had preempted even *Survey* in publicizing the merits of unemployment compensation.[13] The TERA, too, as Rexford Tugwell remembered, "gave Roosevelt a claim to practical concern for the unemployed not matched by others."[14] Each of those policies enhanced FDR's reputation as an active, vigorous innovator in public policy and increased his support among social workers. Lillian Wald enthusiastically endorsed his presidential candidacy in 1932, and even Homer Folks deserted the Republicans and opted for Roosevelt. "I know that I may count on you for counsel and support in the future as I have in the past," a grateful president-elect wrote Folks later, suggesting that Washington would be very much like Albany.[15] Indeed, FDR's Albany years had set social work reformers on their way to Washington.

True, the reformers were scarcely novices in getting things done themselves; political scientist Belle Zeller, a contemporary, used the campaign in support of the 1929 Public Welfare Law as a textbook model in her study of pressure group tactics.[16] After the depression deepened, reformers used the same tactics—"building up popular support" and "breaking down specific sources of opposition"—in campaigns for public relief, old-age pensions, unemployment compensation, and other welfare measures. Two kinds of organizations kept up the pressure in Albany: independent, cause-oriented groups such as the New York Conference for Old Age Security, and the full-time lobbying groups such as the American Association for Labor Legislation. Later, professional social work groups like the United

Neighborhood Houses and the New York branch of the American Association of Social Workers, which had previously avoided political activities, joined these earlier activist groups.

The new activism contrasted sharply with the nonpartisanship of the mid-1920s and marked a distinct change in attitude. When it gave unemployment insurance an unprecedented public endorsement, the AASW chapter declared that "the old policy was one of safety and not of action"; a new policy was needed because "the time has come for the chapter to stand forth and bear witness." [17] In New York City, the Welfare Council also became a primary instigator of reform. Its Coordinating Committee on Unemployment, for example, used "conference and personal interviews, widespread publicity, frequent appearances before the Board of Estimate and Apportionment and the City Relief Administration, and the pressure exerted by [its] far flung membership" to get city officials to take action. [18] In addition, it used its house journals to publish appeals on behalf of pending legislation, printing names, addresses, and telephone numbers. These appeals precipitated waves of letters, telegrams, and telephone calls to public administrators and elected representatives. As Molly Dewson observed, pointing to well-practiced pressure tactics, "The proponents of progressive labor legislation were well organized in New York." [19]

But the reformers' success depended on a core of closely related leaders like Dewson who "kept hard and continuously on the job," and the Albany connection was essential to extending their personal network. [20] No central organization gave them cohesion, so they were guided of necessity by leaders who worked with several different groups simultaneously. Greenwich House settlement's Mary Simkhovitch, for example, was a vice president of the Conference for Old Age Security, a member of the executive committee of the Conference on Unemployment Insurance Legislation, a vice president of the Housing Association of New York, a member of the executive committee of the Welfare Council's Coordinating Committee on Unemployment, and

a member of the headworkers' committee of the United Neighborhood Houses. Social worker Florence Kelley once described
the reformers' personal interaction in terms of exchanges of
ideas "over the back fence," and her conception emphasized the
importance of the kind of person-to-person contacts that Simkhovitch's associations epitomized.[21] During the Smith and
Roosevelt years, such contacts were extended to Albany and occurred with such frequency that social workers dubbed the Empire State Express, a train that made the round trip between
New York and Albany each day, their own "Special." In Albany,
reformers infiltrated the offices of assemblymen and senators,
cornered legislative leaders in conferences, and besieged committee meetings and public hearings. After spending a full day
lobbying in the State House, some social work leaders also received invitations to join the Roosevelts "for tea or dinner or an
overnight stay."[22]

Excerpts from Homer Folks's daily calendars illustrate
the variety of contacts among social service leaders and also between them and public officials. On Monday, October 19, 1931,
he spent the morning in conference with Elsie Bond, his chief
assistant and the State Charities Aid Association's professional
lobbyist in Albany. He spent the afternoon with William Hodson
preparing for a meeting of the Welfare Council's executive committee, of which Folks was executive director. On Tuesday, he
met again with Bond, presided at the executive committee meeting, and conferred with Jesse Straus, the newly appointed chairman of the TERA. A week later, on Wednesday, October 28,
Folks held another morning conference with Bond, after which
"Mr. [Harry] Hopkins and Mr. [Douglas] Falconer lunched with
me." Hopkins and Falconer, of course, were the two newly appointed TERA commissioners. The following morning, Folks
"Went to Albany on Empire State" to attend a "Conference of
[TERA] Welfare Officials." He ate lunch with "Harry Hopkins,
Mr. Jesse Straus and Lt. Gov. Lehman." During the afternoon he
attended the conference, delivering an address. At 6:00 he

"called on Governor Roosevelt," and spent the rest of the evening at the Executive Mansion before returning to the city on
the Empire State Express.[23]

The dates of Folks's meetings are also significant; during
the month of October 1931, the TERA's commissioners formu-
lated their basic policies. His notes do not identify his personal
contributions to the decisions of state officials, but he could
scarcely avoid exerting influence. His conferences with Bond,
who was involved in the decision-making process, allowed him to
keep abreast of TERA developments.[24] Moreover, Folks was
probably responsible for the appointment of Harry Hopkins to
the TERA, after another intimate associate, William Hodson of
the Welfare Council, turned down an earlier invitation.[25] Undoubtedly, he also presented his ideas to political leaders like
Lehman and Roosevelt. The personal factor—the measure of respect, trust, and even affection that existed between reformer
and public official—was of incalculable albeit intangible importance. As Folks himself observed, "The difficult part is to get
understanding in a place of responsibility long enough to get results," and sustained personal contacts were as essential as expertise and organizational support in augmenting understanding.[26]

Eleanor Roosevelt was expert not only in helping others
gain access to her husband, but in forming new contacts herself.[27] As Paul Kellogg's brother, Arthur, discovered, "She is a
good bit of a social worker" herself and "completely social-
minded."[28] When jobless persons in New York City wrote re-
questing her help, she corresponded with Jane Hoey, the assistant director of the Welfare Council, and asked for help in
finding them assistance. Soon Hoey became a regular guest at
the Executive Mansion.[29] Years later, FDR appointed Hoey the
first director of the Bureau of Public Assistance in the Social Security Administration. *Survey*'s editors also came to enjoy a
unique alliance with Eleanor Roosevelt. She sent them countless
bits of information and statements of policy from the governor's
office, and they in turn sent news items and articles to her, implicitly hoping that these items would reach the governor's

desk.[30] Many of Mrs. Roosevelt's public speeches were also delivered in conjunction with the activities of social service societies, another indication of her closeness to social workers.[31] For their part, reformers were aware of the Roosevelts' national potential; *Survey's* Arthur Kellogg, for example, noted in August 1931 that Eleanor might "turn out to be the mistress of the White House."[32]

Frances Perkins was probably the reformers' most important link with Franklin Roosevelt. She and *Survey's* Paul Kellogg shared a warm friendship fortified by professional respect. "I find myself very weak on the names of people who ought to serve," she wrote him at a time when she was appointing a committee to study unemployment. "Will you fill in the names where you can?"[33] Kellogg, of course, was delighted to oblige. Since Roosevelt often left the details of welfare programs and policies in Perkins's hands, such consultations occurred frequently. She had "asked Paul Douglas, Henry Bruere, and Paul Kellogg to put their great minds on the agenda for the [regional] Governors' Conference" of 1931, she informed FDR, its host.[34] On another occasion, Perkins asked Kellogg "what the social workers think ought to be done about a relief program or about unemployment." This request came at an auspicious moment, because Roosevelt had just been elected president and Perkins wanted to convey his ideas for the coming winter to Congress. "Your job is to worry about details of this sort," she told Kellogg, probably with tongue in cheek, since theirs had always been a collaborative relationship. "I, naturally, will be willing to fill in anything you want."[35] In response, Kellogg outlined the program that he and his associates had presented to the La Follette-Costigan committee, adding his fervent hope that Perkins would be the nation's new Secretary of Labor. "That would mean more than I can say to the things a lot of us care about."[36]

Perkins always believed it her responsibility to bring social work reformers before FDR, and these meetings (among other things) helped achieve her long-term project "to educate the Governor" in up-to-date methods of social action.[37] Like Molly Dewson, she had cast her lot with FDR and government

109

service, and both women used that commitment to advance social work's professional standards and programs. "I am a social worker by intuition and desire and experience," Dewson confessed, "and here was my opportunity."[38] The opportunity was hardly one-sided, for "Roosevelt took advantage of long years of study, research and experimentation in labor legislation: and utilized those responsible for it."[39]

Franklin Roosevelt was not perfect, however, and Albany was not a reformer's paradise. Despite his growing reputation as an innovator, Roosevelt enacted only part of his promised program. Old-age assistance, a more efficient state employment service, and state unemployment relief stood as his major achievements. Most of the Bruere Committee's recommendations, on the other hand, died in a legislature that refused to implement them, usually by withholding appropriations. Unemployment compensation similarly languished, regardless of the headlines that FDR made as its champion. Conservatives dominated the legislature's special committee that investigated unemployment insurance, and they recommended a voluntary, company-sponsored compensation scheme. Efforts to secure a mandatory state program from the floor of the assembly met with repeated failures, and Roosevelt vetoed a bill that would have allowed private insurance companies to write commercial policies for industry. Nor did the governor meet with much success in securing minimum wage and maximum hours standards for industry. Finally, the state's old-age assistance program was never revised to suit his demands, and public works expanded too slowly, chiefly because the governor remained parsimonious with public revenues.

Reformers could not easily dismiss these failures as temporary or the result of political circumstances, because Roosevelt's nonsuccesses—and some of his successes as well—often revealed disagreements between them and him. His fiscal orthodoxy frequently affected his social policies. His reluctance to expand state public works, for example, derived from his desire to defend a balanced budget. Even the TERA was funded on a pay-as-you-go basis, drawing from current tax revenues during its first year and from a bond issue during its second. And FDR insisted, in Hoover-like fashion, that local communities pay what they could for relief.[40] Social work reformers were concerned that increased taxes took resources from a public already beset by economic hardship, and they believed that communities should get what they needed for relief, not what they could afford. Although the reformers themselves were fiscal conservatives by today's standards, they would have welcomed some short-term deficit spending in order to help the needy immediately. The governor also accepted state unemployment relief with great reluctance. He believed public relief threatened to put unworthy recipients on an endless "dole," and the prospect of cash relief struck him as too permissive. Roosevelt favored restrictive relief-in-kind when assistance was given to people in their homes; moreover, he wanted proof of need to be a mandatory feature of public relief programs. His preference for work relief stemmed from his belief that a "work test" was appropriate in measuring a recipient's worth.[41]

Such conceptions violated some of the new relief principles that social workers sought to establish. Roosevelt wanted to protect the state treasury and avoid giving anyone anything that was not deserved, while they desired relief methods that would allow the jobless to retain their psychological sense of independence. Again and again, Frances Perkins remembered, social workers had to "work around" FDR's fear of the dole.[42] His thinking about compensation programs also failed to accord exactly with reformers' ideas. For instance, he favored a system of contributions by both employees and employers, because that arrangement made programs a fiscally self-sustaining form of insurance, not an extension of the public dole.[43] FDR even objected to his own administration's Old Age Assistance Act of 1930, calling it a "stopgap" measure, because the "cost of the . . . law is to be borne half by the state itself and half by the counties of the state."[44] Many reformers agreed strongly with the self-help principle, but less for its economic benefits than for its psy-

111

chological advantages. Employee contributions would free the recipients "from the accumulation of stigma and loss of respect" associated with relief.[45] In addition, reformers worried because the governor's convictions inhibited the development of programs for needy people who could not find entry into industry's regular jobs—jobs that would allow them to make contributions to insurance plans.

Other episodes from Roosevelt's gubernatorial years aroused the reformers' suspicion. The bloody battle with the SCAA over the TERA pitted the governor's commitments to local self-help, community autonomy, and temporary state relief against the reformers' demands for state financial responsibility, centralized authority, and permanent relief services. Homer Folks and Elsie Bond were dumbfounded when Roosevelt did not consult them and thereby avoid a confrontation.[46] Other social workers experienced personal rebuffs. Perkins, Dewson, and Walter West, for instance, presented FDR with a public health message "directed toward helping the individual human being . . . along the lines of sound and progressive thought"; the governor seemed pleased, but opted for another, more orthodox message, without offering an explanation.[47] Because the governor's closest advisers were fellow politicians or political experts like Louis Howe, Jim Farley, and Ed Flynn, Frances Perkins sensed that she was regarded as "a do-gooder" and held somewhat in contempt, perhaps by Roosevelt too.[48] In other words, the mysterious and enigmatic FDR of later presidential years was already apparent during his tenure as governor. New York's reformers were never as comfortable with Roosevelt as they had been with Al Smith.[49]

Nonetheless, reformers usually approved of FDR. As Molly Dewson revealed later, "I liked his technique in attacking problems—almost always," and most social service leaders stuck with Roosevelt, becoming New Dealers themselves or avid New Deal supporters, because they believed with Dewson that they were "working for what I consider the up grade."[50] He won the allegiance of social workers because he appealed "to their moral

112

sense and their social feelings."[51] In addition, Roosevelt the politician proved receptive to social work's "educational effect." He learned that good welfare policies also made for appealing political strategies that built public support.[52] If FDR learned a good deal from social welfare leaders, he taught them much about politics. Reformers came to accept the fact that Roosevelt's early Depression programs "grew out of . . . emerging and necessary rescue actions" and fell short of perfection.[53] Although they were justifiably proud of the "part that welfare agencies and their central councils have played in forcing upon city and state governments the major responsibility for emergency relief," they had learned that it took time to create effective public programs. During Roosevelt's Albany years, social work reformers completed their apprenticeship in practical government. "I have no illusions about the fact that we have only made a beginning," the Welfare Council's William Hodson stated in *Survey* in June 1933, "and I recognize the delays and difficulties that lie ahead." Since social workers must realize that "we have no ideal choice" in programs, "our present reliance must be in experiment and adaptation."[54] With that message to the nation's social workers, New York's reformers heralded the recent arrival of FDR's New Deal.

Interlude:

waiting
out
the
longest
winter

10

"These being the unhappy times, so out of joint, in which we live," Homer Folks mused aloud in October 1932, "what is now the good life for us; whither does the path of duty lead; what is the new guiding star?"[1] On election day, November 8, 1932, a star appeared: president-elect Franklin D. Roosevelt. New York's reformers were inspired. Indeed, settlement head workers predicted "a renaissance of settlement influence" in politics, because their residents had "training in social participation" and a "leadership that is prepared."[2] Soon, a new mistress of the White House added her appeal, calling on social workers to demonstrate "a gift for politics" and charging them with the responsibility of creating a national unemployment program.[3] Yet four months—nearly an entire winter—lay between the November election and the March inauguration of Franklin D. Roosevelt.

During the winter of 1932–1933, social work leaders became acutely conscious of themselves as a group and of their potential for implementing permanent change in the nation's welfare system. Their campaign to have Frances Perkins selected as Secretary of Labor manifested this awareness, but they had been building toward that point for years.[4] Their various backgrounds and expertise on different issues might have led to disharmony, but their sense of themselves as a community of individuals in a common endeavor overwhelmed their differences. This sense of unity flowered in the winter of 1932–1933 and became a binding power that most of them acknowledged until their deaths years later. It was during this winter that their perception of the special needs of the able-bodied unemployed matured into a complete program to save productive individualism. By March 1933, they were demanding the psychological devices of cash relief, "real jobs" in work projects, and unemployment insurance for federal action.

In seeking to account for the success of reform movements, Porter R. Lee once attributed them less to the "inherent merit" of new programs than to "the magnetism of their proponents." Lee developed this insight in a paper entitled "Personality in Social Work," which he delivered at the 1926 National Conference. Lee scarcely knew at the time that he was explaining the influence that New York's reformers would enjoy during the New Deal. "Settled conviction, rooted prejudice, entrenched habit, established routine—these yield to a variety of influences," the director of the New York School of Social Work suggested, "but to none so readily as to the influence of man with man." In his judgment, "the tasks of social work demand in their performance something more than technical proficiency." They required skill in "the art of human relationships," and that skill depended on personality. Personality turned ideas into actions, and personality gave a holistic meaning to the many different activities in which social workers engaged.[5] Lee believed that personality put clout into reform movements, a conviction shared by his fellow New Yorkers. Indeed, they articulated a credo of personalism that attributed to individuals the power to identify common methods and goals and to provide a sense of unity for all.

Conversely, the personality of the group may serve as an instructive model for the individual. Early in February 1929, so-

115

cial workers held a luncheon honoring Frances Perkins as the newly appointed head of New York's Industrial Commission. Perkins responded by addressing her thanks to the group's common endeavor. "I take it," she began her remarks, "that we are gathered not so much to celebrate Frances Perkins as [to pay tribute to] the symbol of an idea. It is an idea that has been at work among us for many years—the idea that social justice is possible in a great industrial community." Enlarging on her conception of self as symbol, she added, "Not only do I think you are celebrating a symbol today but, in a peculiar way, I feel that I am the product of all of you and of all the effort that has gone into these ideas." She elaborated on this point: "There is hardly a person here today who has not contributed something to my equipment, to my knowledge, to my information, and to my character." She acknowledged her personal debts to "dear Mary Dreier," to "that mother of us all, Florence Kelley," and to others who had made social welfare in New York a vital concern. Perkins described them as a "cordial, interlocking group of minds" that met in an "inner conference" to bend the powers of the state to the needs of its people. "I am the product of that group's thought and hope," she confessed, "and all I have ever done is, after all, what they have done, too."[6] Such was the disposition of New York's reformers, who found in the lives of others an index to the meaning of their own.

Perkins's speech expressed sincere respect and devotion, not the self-serving flatteries and sentimental compliments so common to such occasions. It illustrated the mixture of personal and professional commitments that entered into every phase of the New Yorkers' thinking, work, and careers. Perkins's idealism so impressed Molly Dewson, a colleague and friend since the early days of the National Consumers' League, that she described the luncheon to Eleanor Roosevelt as "one of the great occasions of my life."[7] Others identified that unity in different ways. Lillian Wald referred frequently to a "Henry Street family," including not only the settlement's residents, but also labor leaders, politicians, philanthropists, educators, and a host of other reformers associated in one way or another with Henry Street's history.[8] On occasion, members and friends of the New York Consumers' League referred to themselves as "the faithful few."[9] Paul Kellogg adopted the term "creative pioneers" to identify the New York group.[10] Frances Perkins remembered that Mary Dreier once referred "to the twenty or thirty of us in New York who promoted labor legislation as the CHILDREN OF LIGHT."[11]

Perhaps no more than thirty men and women were always at the forefront of social welfare causes; the numbers of this "sincere minority" were never great.[12] Sometimes their introspection could be myopic; Paul Kellogg once confessed the "ignorance and the insulation among all of us here in New York" because he knew nothing about a welfare proposal made by social workers in another city.[13] Bruno Lasker expressed exasperation on several occasions because he was constantly asked to sign "general 'liberal' statements always signed by the same bunch of people"—his fellow New Yorkers.[14] Yet the cohesiveness of the New York group provided a valued antidote to the fragmented national ranks of the social work profession. By the time of FDR's election, the same men and women had been working together for as long as three decades, building attachments that would carry through the Depression years and beyond. They found in their own group, as Perkins once put it, "the personal contacts out of which the reality as well as the inspiration of our democratic daily life proceeds."[15]

But there was little time for the niceties of personal reflections as New Yorkers braced themselves for the fourth and worst winter of the Great Depression, the winter of 1932–1933. Yet not all the news was bad. In January, Herbert H. Lehman was to succeed FDR as governor of New York. In addition to his experience in business and government, Eleanor Roosevelt observed, Lehman possessed "a social welfare background, a background of sympathy and interest in the suffering of humanity, a background of real desire to serve those who need help."[16] In November, voters had also approved a thirty million dollar bond

117

issue, which revitalized the TERA. Harry Hopkins now stood at the helm of that organization. He and Frances Perkins had become the most powerful social workers in the state; before the winter was spent, they would work out a plan to coordinate the TERA program and the services of the state employment bureau, making it possible for work relief employees to by-pass conventional relief agencies in getting jobs.[17] New York City also had a new Emergency Work and Relief Administration (EWRA), which had grown out of a social workers' protest of mass resignations from the previous winter's organization.[18] Because it made the personnel and programs of private and public agencies more interdependent, the EWRA promised to reduce the inefficiency that had crippled its predecessor.

Help from Washington seemed a remote possibility for the city, however. The state did not apply for an RFC relief loan while FDR was governor. Nor did social workers expect anything new from a lame-duck president. In fact, a quixotically inclined Hoover had just created another national committee to stimulate voluntary giving. Nor had the president-elect provided impetus for fresh federal action. During the campaign, many of Roosevelt's speeches on unemployment sounded like copy from Hoover's desk; an irate adviser even chastized him for imitating the standing president in his address of October 13, 1932, and urged him to make "vigorous affirmative statements" that would "provide a refreshing contrast [to] the Hoover policies and pronouncements."[19] Yet FDR risked no vigorous statements, opting for minimal controversy and the safest road to victory. As election strategy, that worked well, but it left social work reformers with no leverage in Congress and no guidance during the dark winter ahead. Roosevelt's star went into temporary eclipse during the interregnum between his election and inauguration, leaving social workers to advance through the darkness on their own.

The winter of 1932–1933 began with at least one-third of the city's working population unemployed. In November 1932, when voters elected Roosevelt, New York spent nearly six

118

and one-half million dollars on relief, distributed among one hundred seventy-nine thousand families. That single month's allocation alone amounted to three-fifths of the total outdoor relief expenditure for 1929.[20] The new winter bore down harder on relief services than any before. "At no time has the whole program seemed to me to be so woefully inadequate and so full of suffering for the people directly affected," the EWB's William Matthews informed Governor Lehman shortly after the new year.[21] By February 1933, the TERA's fund was already giving out, although its thirty million dollars had been expected to last two years. New York negotiated a relief loan from the RFC that month.[22] Nonetheless, public assistance offered only bare subsistence. A TERA investigation confirmed that of five hundred randomly selected families, only ninety-five got adequate help. The rest suffered from delinquent rents, unpaid gas and electric bills, and a host of other debts and burdens.[23] "We have substituted to a considerable extent a relief economy for an industrial economy," the Welfare Council's William Hodson confessed from the depths of the winter's crisis, "with the result that standards of living have fallen and we find ourselves struggling at every point to meet the creature necessities of life." There were, of course, thousands of additional needy families who were receiving no assistance at all. In spite of their prodigious efforts, Hodson admitted, social workers had found it impossible "to substitute charity for the pay envelope."[24]

In March 1933, when FDR finally became president, the city's relief load had grown by an additional ninety-one thousand cases. Private philanthropy's Emergency Work Bureau closed its doors for the last time, thus concluding the history of an innovative agency that had provided twenty-eight million dollars in work relief. Other private services, including the Red Cross's food and clothing program, were staggering along on their last legs.[25] Speaking for the Welfare Council, Solomon Lowenstein complained, "This complete and utter inadequacy of relief, due to insufficient appropriations, is indefensible as a matter of right and justice to those who are in need and it is

119

shocking to the humane instincts of this community."[26] A more lurid reality lurked behind the grim statistics, because the United Neighborhood Houses soon discovered that public relief services were intolerably bad: delays in receiving relief ran into weeks; applicants were often left ignorant about their status; men who were dropped from work projects were not transferred automatically to home relief; discrimination against minorities, particularly blacks, abounded; childless couples and single women received the barest assistance; single men received no help at all; and relief remained contaminated by political favoritism.[27] Facts like those drove Porter Lee to the ominous conclusion that the Depression had disclosed "the wilderness aspect of the world in which we work."[28]

The Great Depression had by this time completely shattered the old theory that individual communities could meet their own needs. Between 1929 and 1932, private philanthropy in New York increased its annual expenditures for relief over seven-fold, from two and one-half to nineteen million dollars. Public outdoor relief expenditures increased eight-fold, from ten million to over eighty million dollars.[29] Those figures concealed some shifting of funds from other programs into relief as well as the state's contribution through the TERA, but it remained obvious that New York City had given more and more, both through private philanthropy and public taxes, to a program that never achieved adequacy. Looking back across four icy winters of constant struggle, William Hodson disconsolately admitted that "the minimum needs of large numbers of unemployed people have not yet been met."[30] The old theory of community responsibility had not been a bad theory; it just failed to hold before the relentless onslaught of suffering. The traditions of private philanthropy had provided social workers with a proud heritage, but bitter experience taught them that government alone had the potential to ameliorate mass unemployment.

Yet government had met neither the material nor psychological needs of the unemployed. The very proliferation of public assistance programs raised the problem of how to respond to needs in a simple, direct way. New York City's Department of Public Welfare offered eight different types of aid, all governed by different laws and embedded in a maze of organizational confusion. "If you are a veteran you qualify under one law," Hodson observed; "if blind, under another; if aged and dependent, under another; if unemployed under still another; if you are the mother of dependent children yet another law governs."[31] The sundry services offered by private agencies compounded that complexity. "We have had two and a half years now of passing people around from one agency to another," William Matthews wrote a colleague in 1933, "and the results for those passed around are not very pleasant."[32] In addition, conflict between social work professionals and local politicians continued unabated. In March 1933, social workers resigned as a body from the Emergency Work and Relief Administration, protesting corruption, political chicanery, and the city's refusal to appropriate sufficient funds for relief.[33] Another city commission was created, of course, but the usual annual juggling of philanthropists, social workers, and city officials merely demonstrated how difficult it was to keep politics out of public programs.

The massive scale of unemployment and the rush to build government programs had also exhausted the supply of professional social workers. Overwhelmed by requests for trained personnel, the School of Social Work lowered its entrance requirements and abbreviated its course of study, but to little avail. The city's Home Relief Bureau, for example, employed only one hundred sixty-five trained social workers, who were responsible for supervising five thousand assistants—mostly drawn from relief rolls—who dealt, in turn, with over two hundred thousand relief families. The only preparation offered those assistants was a short lecture series that featured speakers such as the TERA's Harry Hopkins.[34] Gertrude Springer, alias "Miss Bailey," who wrote a series of *Survey* articles that taught practical social work lessons, probably educated more of the Depression's generation of novice public welfare workers than professional schools of social work.[35] The Depression had propelled social workers into the top ranks of social welfare, but high quality service for the needy remained an elusive dream.[36] There were too few trained people to help men and women who needed psychiatric care, who needed recreational programs, educational programs, or special medical services to treat prolonged illnesses—who needed, in short, personalized professional services.

In the face of those chilling circumstances, reformers questioned the value of maintaining vast relief organizations. Why should the jobless be subjected to amateur caseworkers, intimidating procedures, rigidly structured bureaucratic routines, and the persistent stigma of charity? "[T]he trouble with so much of our relief work now," the EWB's William Matthews complained, "is that we compel people to fit into programs rather than . . . fitting programs into men's desires and wants."[37] Addressing the same issue in a 1933 *Survey* article entitled "Social Workers: Pioneers Again," Porter R. Lee urged his social work colleagues to use their "pioneer spirit" to develop public programs that were responsive to the needs of individuals.[38] Meanwhile, the machinery of public relief grew both more depersonalized and less adequate to the job at hand. Public welfare pioneer Homer Folks sketched a possible solution in notes jotted down late in 1933: "Must build new, smaller, permanent house on site of present improvised huge temporary shelter, living in it meanwhile, and using its timbers so far as fit."[39]

The administration of relief certainly led to new questions. From the beginning of their Depression labors, reformers had been guided by the principle of adjusting society's resources to fit the needs of jobless Americans in a manner that would be both conservative—in the sense of conserving psychological values—and just. Yet they were never satisfied that their relief programs offered adequate means to aid the unemployed. Work relief came close to implementing their principle. Nonetheless, work projects absorbed relatively few of the jobless. Nor could reformers candidly support the illusion that work relief duplicated the normal job situation. Recipients were still investigated and placed on relief rolls, from which they were drawn for work. Moreover, their wages were not really wages, because they were paid according to a "budgetary deficiency" standard instituted by the TERA: casework investigators geared their earnings to estimates of each family's needs.[40] Their working conditions, including their hours of work, also remained below standards set in private industry, and the work they did frequently lacked social usefulness. More importantly, the less adequate program of home relief continued to bear the greater burden of alleviating suffering. Because a minority of the unemployed drew work relief earnings at a rate of assistance nearly double that received by the vast majority who were on home relief, social workers knew that the unemployed were not being served equally and fairly.[41] And since relief in kind, the only form allowed under home relief, treated the Great Depression's unemployed and permanent "unemployables" similarly, no claim could be made that most of the Depression's jobless New Yorkers were receiving treatment appropriate to their needs.

Indeed, it had become impossible to differentiate the unemployed from unemployables, and it verged on the ludicrous to suggest that such a distinction was being maintained through the differing policies of work and home relief. "The time has come to consider the whole question of relief as one problem," William Hodson declared in his 1933 annual report to the Welfare Council, "and to determine whether special categories and classifications are no longer needed, leading as they inevitably do to differences in treatment of persons who have the same fundamental claim on the community for assistance."[42] As William Matthews put it, "It is impossible to act on the merits of individual cases when the merit is need and all are needy."[43] A major shift in social workers' thinking occurred in 1933. They demanded universal cash relief in order to "preserve the dignity and morale of the family."[44] Members of the Welfare Council's Coordinating Committee on Unemployment agreed that the jobless should retain the right to manage their own lives whether on work or home relief, even if some succumbed to dependency on the dole. They wanted relief to be increased to approximate levels of family need, and they asked that funds be allocated on a long-term basis, so relief would be steady and services planned months in advance.

Underlying these reassessments was the persistent doubt about the value of relief in any form. "A dole is a dole whether given in cash or in kind," Linton Swift, the general director of the Family Welfare Association of America, had testified before the Senate Subcommittee on Manufactures in December 1931.[45] Early in 1932 New York's Senator Wagner echoed this conviction: "Charity, whether public or private, should be the last resort and not the first choice in dealing with the economic problem of the wage-earners for whom we fail to supply work."[46] Relief could never transcend the stigma of charity. Nor could it provide the positive incentives toward renewed self-sufficiency that reformers regarded as the acid test of successful welfare programs. In fact, it threatened to weaken "the footholds of democracy" by forcing "down into a common mass of uncertainty and insecurity, the great body of capable, self-respecting, self-dependent producers," who wanted no charity.[47] Moreover, relief did "nothing for prevention and little for cure" of the Depression, because it scarcely attacked the causes of unemployment.[48] "Overwhelmed with the volume of relief need," Neva Deardorff observed at the 1933 National Conference of Social Work, "social agencies, both public and private, have resorted to mass measures, and inevitably there has grown up a revulsion against such forms of aid and an insistence that this vast need for relief must be prevented."[49] From the perspective of troubled reformers, jobless Americans wanted the respect, the independence, the pride, and the self-sufficiency that could be secured through only one means: the security of regular work and the dignity of "a real job."[50]

The black winter of 1932–1933 was a catalyst producing a fresh mixture of new ideas and old. Home relief remained a necessity, but it should rest on a new footing—cash instead of kind—that would annul much of its demeaning affect. Work relief continued to hold the reformers' favor, but it should go beyond its existing limitations to fulfill its promise as work and minimize its function as relief. Social work lacked the personnel to extend services to the unemployed, but its professional practitioners could build into public welfare programs the kinds of psychological devices—cash relief, "real work" and "real jobs," and insurance systems of protection—that would offer superior means to buoy up the morale of the jobless. The experiences of the black winter fashioned a readjusted agenda of action for reformers. During the fall of 1933, Mary Simkhovitch of Greenwich House settlement would lead an assault on political corruption in New York City by marshalling social workers in support of a reform candidate for mayor, Congressman Fiorello La Guardia. In the wake of La Guardia's triumph, William Hodson would resign as executive director of the Welfare Council to accept appointment as the city's new Commissioner of Public Welfare, overseeing the operation of the largest urban welfare program in the nation. Meanwhile, Governor Herbert Lehman launched his own "little New Deal," bringing cash relief, unemployment insurance, and a host of new state services to distressed New Yorkers.[51] But now the reformers' achievements began to take on more than local significance. Their focus shifted to Washington, where on March 4, 1933, the winter's dark clouds started to slip away as President Roosevelt initiated his 100 day spring.

**Jobs
for
Americans:**

**from
springtime
bliss
to
winter
blues**

11

"There are more than cherry blossoms at Washington," Paul Kellogg announced in a mid-April, 1933, radio broadcast. "There's the new administration, which says 'Let's try.'"[1] Indeed, the New Deal had advanced about one-third of its way into the Hundred Days by then, and its commitment to action was obvious. It created the Civilian Conservation Corps, the first work program for young men, and the more comprehensive Federal Emergency Relief Act was less than a month from passage in Congress. A few days after Kellogg's broadcast, Eleanor Roosevelt delivered a radio message that focused attention on the significance of federal work programs. Noting the example set by the CCC, she assigned to federal government "the responsibility not only of ministering to the material needs of the moment, but of trying to meet . . . the people's need of work." Pointing to the "mental distress" suffered by jobless Americans, she praised the CCC for its efforts "in restoring morale, which, after all, is just as important as anything else that the government can do for them." It was government's duty, she proclaimed, to move beyond the needs of food and shelter and "to see that wherever possible people are given work, and the feeling that they are actually doing something in return for what they are being paid."[2] No social work reformer of the day could have excelled the new First Lady in articulating the psychological rationale for work programs. Yet the New Deal would implement that rationale only briefly, in the Civil Works Administration of 1933–1934, and then turn backwards toward relief and the compromises of the Works Progress Administration.

In the meantime, the ascendency of New York's social work reformers in the national administration came quickly. Roosevelt's appointment of Frances Perkins as Secretary of Labor capped an intensive social workers' campaign led by Molly Dewson, Mary Simkhovitch, Jane Hoey, and Lillian Wald. They praised Perkins as a woman who could draw women's votes into the Democratic Party, an experienced administrator under governors Smith and Roosevelt, and a social worker who stood for the liberal point of view on welfare issues.[3] The subsequent appointment of Harry Hopkins as head of the new Federal Emergency Relief Administration (FERA) secured a second crucial position for New Yorkers. Within weeks after FDR's inauguration, dozens more became residents of the District of Columbia or frequent visitors on official business. Soon *Survey* was referring to a "Little Cabinet" of social workers and their allies who exercised unprecedented influence in shaping federal policies.[4] New Yorkers had awaited such developments anxiously. In March, J. Prentice Murphy, the president of the Child Welfare League of America, had written Hopkins about the relief problem, expressing his hope that the "standards which have been set by the State of New York . . . will have a far-reaching effect throughout the United States."[5] Shortly thereafter, Franklin Roosevelt indicated to Frances Perkins his intention "to incorporate some of New York's experience in handling relief," affording an inroad for Hopkins and his TERA associates.[6] Yet Roosevelt had not been ready to take those actions at the beginning of his administration.

FDR did not come into office with a blueprint of federal

127

relief plans in hand. Nor had he set his administrators, including Labor Secretary Frances Perkins, to the task of creating such plans before his inauguration.[7] In fact, he arrived in Washington fully prepared to cling to Hoover's old measures. No "Work Bill" was needed, he surmised, because the Reconstruction Finance Corporation was still operating within its budget in extending loans to the states for relief. Nor was a federal program of emergency public works necessary.[8] Looking backwards instead of forwards, he proposed a Hoover-like federal committee "to coordinate relief work with and among the several States & Territories and the District of Columbia." Nonetheless, Roosevelt opened reform's door a crack, suggesting in his own handwriting that "we can employ . . . individuals at once on work which does not in any way interfere with normal employment, confining immediate efforts to forestry, soil erosion and similar projects."[9] FDR sketched the outline of what soon became the CCC.[10] Though similar projects in conservation work had been tried in New York during his governorship, the president took obvious delight in the apparent novelty of his proposal; perhaps its composition loosed the wellsprings of his imagination, opening his mind to other possibilities, because he soon began to welcome the ideas of New Yorkers about a federal relief program.[11]

Frances Perkins remembered the creation of the Federal Emergency Relief Administration (FERA) as occurring quickly and spontaneously, the result of a personal meeting beneath a staircase at the Women's University Club in Washington that included herself, Harry Hopkins, and William Hodson.[12] Perhaps that collaboration happened as she described it—if so, it adds a daredevil touch to the administration's early actions—but the story denies the deliberate, step-by-step process that led to the FERA. On March 7, the AASW's Committee on Federal Action on Unemployment designated Hodson, Walter West, and Linton Swift, the triumvirate who had been lobbying for federal relief for over two years, to approach Perkins in order to enlist her help in their cause.[13] Within a week, FDR entered the scene, approving a meeting of Perkins, the Senate's three warhorses for

128

relief—Robert Wagner, Edward Costigan, and Robert La Follette—and his own New York relief chief, Hopkins.[14] By March 15 several cabinet members were recommending a new federal program of relief appropriations to the president.[15] Two days later, the Committee on Federal Action reported its collaboration with Perkins, the three senators, and brain truster Raymond Moley, as well as its assistance in drafting a relief bill to be introduced in Congress the following Monday.[16] In a Thursday evening meeting, Roosevelt approved the proposed bill, and Harry Hopkins was "fully understood to be slated for Administrator of Federal Relief." Indeed, his powers were to be so extensive that the Committee described him as "a virtual dictator."[17] Details do not deflate entirely the excitement that Frances Perkins associated with creation of the FERA, but the relief act that became law on May 12, 1933 was scarcely the product of a quick conference under a staircase.

The FERA was a carbon copy of the TERA, imitating the pattern of its New York exemplar in every detail—its temporary, emergency character, its system of matching grants, its reserve of "discretionary" funds, its provisions for assisting both home and work relief programs, and its powerful administrator. *Survey*'s Paul Kellogg saw the parallels clearly, as well as its "sequence in cast of characters" and "the shift in scene from state to nation."[18] Nothing different should have been expected. For over two years, the AASW had campaigned for the TERA model in Washington. Costigan and La Follette had served as its congressional champions, and Wagner could not obstruct a successful program launched in his own state, especially when his new president was responsible for it. Roosevelt's lieutenants, particularly Perkins, knew it well, and the president could draw upon the experience of a trusted subordinate, Hopkins. Social workers, too, would back it, using their network of contacts to ensure its implementation. It was appropriate that *Survey*'s editor joined members of the Committee on Federal Action in Hopkins's office the morning after his appointment as FERA chief.[19] Like the others, Kellogg was there to discuss details of the program.

129

Later, *Survey*'s chief reporter, Gertrude Springer, sat in regularly at FERA administrative conferences.[20]

Other early New Deal actions gained the support of New York's social workers. They were deeply involved in the Labor Department's efforts to shape the National Industrial Recovery bill to suit the needs of workers. Endowed with the same vision of business cooperation that had motivated the Bruere Committee, the National Recovery Administration was to empower industrial trade associations to write their own controlling business codes, while the NRA oversaw the codes' enforcement.[21] The thrust of Labor Department efforts was to help establish minimum labor standards—maximum hours, minimum wages, and the prohibition of child labor—within the rubric of the new federal program.[22] Frances Perkins along with Molly Dewson and Paul Kellogg urged the president to ensure "*mandatory* minima for the workers" in proposed codes; they objected to allowing production and price controls to help business unless employees were helped too.[23] Perkins became the reformers' champion of workers' rights, using her office to throw a "horizontal scheme of protection through the base of any vertical scheme of cooperative action, industry by industry," as Paul Kellogg put it.[24] In addition, Perkins championed federal labor and consumers' boards that would monitor the NRA's operations in order to protect both workers and consumers against potential business abuses. After the bill became law, she appointed several New Yorkers to two such boards, including Rose Schneiderman of the Women's Trade Union League and Molly Dewson of the National Consumers' League. The National Industrial Recovery Act also met another of the reformers' demands: its Section II established a new Public Works Administration (PWA) that was to stimulate economic recovery.[25]

One other measure of the 100 Days—the National Employment System Act of June 6, 1933—met with the social workers' approval; it fulfilled the third of Senator Wagner's bills, which had been turned back by Hoover's veto two years before. In addition to establishing the United States Employment Service (USES), it put into effect a morale-sustaining device that was used in conjunction with federal work programs as early as the fall of 1933. "There is a fine psychology, a wholesome morale-building quality, in a man getting a job through an employment agency, on his merits, and having a place where a record is maintained of his sufficiency and efficiency as a worker," W. Frank Persons, the new head of the USES once explained.[26] "The fact that the public employment office is one place where an unemployed man or woman may go without any feeling of loss of self-respect or of seeking for charitable aid," he also suggested, "is of inestimable value in maintaining [their] employ-ability."[27] Persons's appointment was another happy choice for New Yorkers: born in Brandon, Iowa and educated at that state's Cornell College, he had worked with the COS and was a founder of the Welfare Council of New York City. Persons became another important contact within the administration, one particularly sensitive to the psychological emphasis that social workers were giving to their unemployment programs.[28]

New Yorkers were contributing to the development of all New Deal programs aimed at joblessness in urban settings, and they were justifiably proud of their accomplishments. "Wherever men congregate [in Washington]," the Welfare Council's William Hodson observed, "they are discussing proposals for economic planning and industrial reorganization which a short while ago would have been regarded as visionary or worse." FDR and his administrators were "courageously leading the way toward a new dispensation," he argued, and praised programs that indicated "a real concern for the welfare of all the people."[29] Echoing Hodson's pleasure, the New York-based Conference on Governmental Objectives for Social Work (a new AASW committee) paid similar tribute "to the courageous and ingenious social thinking represented by [New Deal] programs." In the Conference's judgment, "The best traditions and experience of social work [had] been utilized" in building "for the first time a national system of aid to families and individuals."[30]

A rampantly optimistic spirit infiltrated the 1933 meet-

131

ing of the National Conference of Social Work, where the nation's social servants sensed a new "partnership in shaping a
changing order," as Gertrude Springer reported in *Survey*. Two
New Yorkers, Harry Hopkins and William Hodson, captured
the spotlight. The newly appointed FERA administrator "spoke
to the crowd that filled every nook within reach of the amplifiers
as simply and directly as he would have spoken to a friend,"
Springer related, alluding to a personalism that now reached beyond the confines of the New York group. "Here was no remote
person, but one of themselves, who had come up through experience comparable to theirs, who spoke their language and who
was as eager as they to do the immediate job [of relief] and to
get on to something better."[31] Hopkins's friend and colleague,
William Hodson, appeared before the Conference as its newly
elected president. "We have the will to make relief more decent
and more adequate," he told his vast audience, "but more than
that, we have a deep yearning for a better social order and the
determination to make ourselves and our first-hand knowledge
felt in bringing it about." The time had come, Hodson concluded, to "face the pragmatic test and [to] mobilize our wisdom,
intelligence, and courage to make the best contribution to the
New Deal of which we are capable."[32] In Gertrude Springer's
own estimation, "Social work sensed new strength in itself" at
the Detroit meeting. "Its function was assured, its leadership
was recognized and proved, its philosophy was a part and parcel
of the promised new social order."[33]

132   A federal system of relief, however, troubled some social
work reformers deeply, and the FERA remained just that—a relief system. Only a short time before, during the winter of
1932–1933, their thinking had moved beyond the limits of New
York's TERA, when they called for "real jobs," cash wages, and
access to jobs without proof of destitution. Yet the FERA was
bound to the TERA model; its relief apparatus was provided by
state and local public welfare offices and it depended on the
"budgetary deficiency" allowance that applied to all modes of
public assistance.[34] As necessary as the FERA had become, it now

marched out-of-step with the changing assessments of social workers, who wanted to elevate the psychological benefits of work by divorcing it from relief.[35] Once again the New Deal fulfilled the reformers' hopes, this time with the Civil Works Administration in November 1933.

Roosevelt personally created the CWA with an executive order. Faced by a brief economic boom that collapsed, by increasingly active expressions of popular discontent, and by the prospect that his first winter in office would see a record number of unemployed Americans, the president used his own authority to put four million people to work immediately.[36] The CWA drew its funds from unspent PWA appropriations, which had the legal effect of freeing the new agency from legislative restrictions. As a result, the CWA hired two million workers without requiring proof of need. Job-seekers simply submitted applications for CWA employment through the USES's National Re-Employment Service, which had been created to supply workers for the PWA. Two million additional workers were drawn from the nation's relief rolls, but they too were placed in CWA jobs by the Re-Employment Service. Since CWA projects were restricted to construction work, a smaller Civil Works Service was created for unemployed professional people. In general, Civil Works employees were paid cash wages at prevailing rates and worked a number of hours that approximated standards for normal employment. Thus their monthly incomes resembled those of fellow workers employed by private industry.[37]

A New Deal colleague, Robert Sherwood, later described the CWA as "a clean sweep for the Hopkins theories of work relief," suggesting that the new head of the CWA, Harry Hopkins, was the initiator of those innovations and implying that he personally maneuvered a radical departure from orthodox relief practices.[38] Hopkins certainly stood as the individual most responsible for the CWA, but he hardly acted alone. Once again, members of the AASW's Committee on Federal Action and of New York's TERA were at his side, offering their counsel at the meeting which produced the CWA's rules and regula-

133

tions.[39] In addition, Frances Perkins quickly became the cabinet's leading spokesman for the new agency's policies. "They are getting weekly pay envelopes with a living wage in them," she said of CWA employees. "Over and above this they have regained the self-respect and morale which was being so undermined by the buffetings of adversity."[40] Noting that CWA wage rates often exceeded minimum levels set for private industry in NRA codes, she defended the CWA as fulfilling a national interest by enhancing the consuming power of American workers.[41] New Yorkers again led the way, developing a real work program this time, and the city's reformers were delighted.

"Dear Harry," H. L. Lurie wrote Hopkins, "I am most enthusiastic concerning the Federal Civil Works Plan and . . . I consider it an enlightened and revolutionary departure from the antiquated theories of poor relief which have so far dominated our . . . measures for the unemployed." Lurie had served on the city's commissions for public relief, so he drew upon his own experience in praising the CWA for making "joblessness rather than destitution the basis for the service rendered," for setting "high standards of wages," and for developing "policies on hours and wage rates" that offered "normal employment."[42] Lurie also highlighted the CWA's merits before a joint congressional committee hearing in Washington: "Destitution as the basis of eligibility for unemployment assistance has been eliminated, a rate of wages approximating the normal wage rate . . . has been established, and the unemployed whom it serves are freed from the restraints of [relief] supervision and tutelage." His comments somewhat exaggerated the CWA's accomplishments, but his tone conveyed social workers' enthusiasm for the program. The reformers' concern, like Lurie's, was that "the Civil Works plan should be permanently retained."[43] Within weeks after the CWA began, however, the president announced its termination.

When the New Deal reversed course and abandoned the CWA, social workers joined many other Americans in protesting furiously. Demonstrations were organized, letters poured into the White House and Congress, congressional hearings were called, and a bill was introduced to extend the life of the agency indefinitely.[44] In lieu of a personal meeting with the president—a request that was inexplicably denied—the AASW's Committee on Federal Action composed a letter to Roosevelt, in which it protested "a radical departure from the social program which we have applauded during the past year." The "values of the old C. W. A. program should be preserved," committee members pleaded, "chief among these being the sense of dignity in work and of earning a decent subsistence thereby."[45] In April 1934, Harry Lurie returned to Washington again, speaking this time about "the waverings and uncertainties of an indecisive national policy" and estimating that relief assistance had fallen "by approximately 70 per cent" with the end of the CWA on April 1.[46] Their appeals for the CWA's renewal, however, met a deaf response. In the meantime, the Roosevelt administration secured passage of a dubiously named Civil Works Emergency Relief Act, which actually gave new life to the old FERA and to "less satisfactory public charity or work for relief," as Lurie put it.[47]

Why did FDR kill the CWA, an agency that Harry Hopkins later called "a precocious child"?[48] Political pressure always figured in the fate of New Deal relief programs. Recalcitrant taxpayers and budget-minded public officials often refused to support large expenditures for wages, materials, and equipment. Businessmen resisted government competition for surplus labor, while their employees feared that work relief would undermine private industry's jobs and wages.[49] In the case of the CWA, however, such adverse pressures seem to have been minimal. An effective conservative coalition had not yet formed in Congress; businessmen found little favor with the public; the popularity of work relief was at a peak; and what organized political pressure the New Deal did confront came from the left, which applauded the CWA and urged its continuation.[50] Yet FDR's motives for finishing the program were clear: he was influenced by a budget-conscious worry about the CWA's cost, and he feared that the program might "become a habit with the country."[51] In a joint biography of Roosevelt and Hopkins, Robert Sherwood implies that FDR's concerns were paramount, and suggests that Hopkins and other relief administrators obeyed "with utmost reluctance and deep disappointment."[52]

Hopkins certainly obeyed FDR's orders, but it is not clear that he and his New Deal associates did so with great reluctance.[53] Early in December 1933, CWA officials received complaints about CWA wage rates and earnings, and their response was an immediate reduction in weekly working hours, thereby reducing CWA earnings.[54] Then, in a December 6 meeting, Hopkins advised his staff "that Civil Works was set up purely as an emergency measure; that there is no implication in this of any permanent policy in the government." The most that might be expected was "a continuance of this thing through the middle of March, on a descending scale after that and out by the middle of May or the 1st of June."[55] Whether Hopkins knew that the CWA was a temporary measure all along, or simply pulled back from its innovations, remains unclear. He did not, however, try to change the president's mind; instead, he and his associates retreated quietly to the policies of the FERA, producing the first rift between New Dealers and their social work allies in New York.

In their letter of protest to Roosevelt, social workers had outlined two principles they believed essential to an effective work program: that persons be allowed to apply for work without "the necessity of first getting on the relief rolls," and that their work "be full time at the going rate of wages."[56] The new FERA rules, however, afforded work at less than prevailing wages and "with 24 hours a week maximum." A FERA worker's highest possible earnings would stand at about half of those of an old CWA worker, and he was "limited to six months employment during the year." Moreover, FERA workers were to be drawn from relief rolls exclusively.[57] The psychological principles embedded in the CWA had disappeared, making 1934 a grim year for reformers.

New Dealers had not wholly abandoned the goal of sustaining morale in the unemployed, but they had shifted directions. They were equally intent on defending public coffers and forcing work relief employees back into private industry. In April 1935, New Dealers made this change clear by phasing out the FERA and replacing it with the Works Progress Administration (WPA). Like the CWA, the WPA used the USES's Re-Employment Service to place people on work projects, but "at least 90% of the persons so employed [had to] be taken from the public relief rolls."[58] That provision by itself distressed New York's reformers. As a committee within the AASW phrased its response, "The manifest shortcomings of a plan which relates work opportunities to need make us reluctant to endorse it as a continuing method of unemployment relief." The committee advised WPA authorities to "resist attempts to make them responsible for investigating the needs of persons who apply solely for work."[59] The administration, however, had set its course: it was committed to maintaining a curious ambivalence, offering respectable work (through the Re-Employment Service[60]) only to people "certified as relief recipients."[61]

That ambivalence affected the WPA's wages and hours policies. Like the CWA, the WPA classified employees as unskilled, skilled, or professional, adopted a graduated wage scale for each category, and paid workers the prevailing local rates.[62] These measures were intended to preserve both occupational integrity and the status accorded different kinds of work in American society.[63] But WPA policy limited the number of hours a person could work at his prevailing wage, thereby assuring that he could not earn as much as his counterpart in private industry.[64] "I ask you," WPA administrator Harry Hopkins said of the agency's lower earnings policy, "is it reasonable to suppose that an American worker . . . will reject private employment to remain in such a situation?"[65] In this way WPA administrators essayed a delicate and precarious balancing act between work and relief.

Disillusioned reformers, including economists and others among the social workers' friends, were quick to exploit the

WPA's ambivalences, and the pages of *Survey* often became vehicles for their criticism.[66] The stringent application of means tests delayed WPA employment until destitution exposed the jobless to the demoralizing effects of advanced deprivation.[67] Moreover, the unemployed could hardly avoid perceiving themselves as "charity" cases, since they were subjected to tests, investigations, and often supervision.[68] Fundamentally, the critics observed, the New Deal did not offer employment in lieu of relief, because it did not guarantee work and jobs as rights afforded every American regardless of need.[69] WPA's wage-hour formula also provoked attack. Paying men high hourly wages while severely limiting their hours of work imposed unwarranted idleness upon workers. A mechanic, for example, earned his WPA "security wage" in one week, leaving him ineligible for work during the remainder of each month.[70] If it was work that maintained morale, critics argued, then this policy undercut its supposed intent.[71]

Social workers also questioned the suitability of WPA jobs. Since relief administrators could not start work projects in competition with private enterprise, the occupations of individuals such as druggists, assembly-line workers, and securities analysts were avoided by the WPA. Moreover, the WPA's categories of occupations were "jerry-built" classifications. Bank tellers, real estate agents, and other kinds of businessmen joined people like dentists, lawyers, and teachers in the professional category, which qualified them for jobs writing guidebooks, serving as nurses' aids, and supervising children's playground activities. The unskilled category amounted to a hodgepodge of individuals for whom manual labor was the only common denominator. As a result, barbers, shoemakers, and tailors, along with semi- and unskilled workers such as machine operatives, teamsters, and janitors, were directed to construction projects.[72] Indeed, much of the occupational dislocation that its critics associated with work relief derived from WPA's emphasis on construction.[73] The "very nature [of] the work . . . was outside the workers' experience, if they had any other than that of common laborers," according to a student of the WPA's program in Illinois.[74] In fact, a Pennsylvania study disclosed that sixty-one percent of WPA work assignments were different from the workers' usual occupations.[75] Did not inappropriate, unwieldy classifications and arbitrary work assignments destroy subtle distinctions associated with American conceptions of job status and demoralize workers? Was not a barber demeaned when he was classified as an unskilled worker and assigned a job as a cement finisher? Did not a sales manager lose self-respect when he became a playground attendant?[76] The WPA provided work, but was it "real" work and was it free of the stigma of relief?

In addition to questioning the quality of work provided by the New Deal, critics charged that work relief programs had always been economically inadequate. At no time did they employ more than one-third of the nation's jobless people.[77] The vast majority remained dependent on direct relief, which (after the termination of the FERA in August 1935) was provided by states and localities without the assistance of the federal government. In addition, initially high earning levels collapsed under the pressure of insufficient funding. Within three to four months after the beginning of both the CWA and WPA, monthly work relief incomes had fallen to the same level as direct relief, which meant that the man who worked for his relief received no more than the man who did not.[78] Moreover, seventy-five to eighty percent of WPA workers were employed as unskilled laborers and paid on the lowest wage scale.[79] This fact made the idea of graduated incomes to emphasize job status seem ludicrous, especially since many workers were neither pursuing their normal occupations nor earning incomes that supported their normal way of living. "The wage paid for [work relief] should be the same for all, irrespective of individual former standards of living or of former occupations," a dejected William Matthews of the old EWB protested.[80] Finally, in an economy already characterized by depressed wage levels and straitened personal incomes, the New Deal's policy of noncompetitive earnings relegated work relief recipients to the lowest of subsistence living, a fact

139

sufficient in itself to cause doubt that work relief did much to bolster morale.[81]

Work relief's New York pioneer, William Matthews, always believed that it represented "a gallant, humane effort to meet the urgencies of life by a method that gave the best promise of preserving the skill, the morale and self-respect of the unemployed."[82] By the late 1930s, however, he was typical of New York leaders who had become disillusioned with the New Deal's programs. In his autobiography he noted the continuing presence of an "army of the unemployed" managed by an "army of welfare workers" in spite of the New Deal's promises to return American workers to regular jobs and to eliminate the stigma of charity. Matthews also believed that years of being shuffled from one relief program to another tended to drain the unemployed of "the desire to plan and manage their own lives" and to accept "the role of dependency on government." As he viewed the situation, the New Deal had created a ubiquitous relief "mechanism" that stood "in the way of natural human relations." Between the unemployed man and his work relief earnings stood need tests and investigations that violated his privacy, "made work" that frequently did not utilize his skills, and a wage-hour formula that seldom gave him a decent income on which to live.[83] Matthews's conclusions were particularly bleak, but many social work observers generally concurred.[84]

It may be impossible to determine how well the New Deal served the psychological needs of those employed by its work relief programs, for as a New Yorker put it at that time, "It is . . . difficult to weigh such qualities as self-respect, morale, and the maintenance of skills."[85] Nonetheless, it is obvious that New Dealers made a sincere attempt. Even at poverty levels, jobs and cash wages did infuse the stream of relief with morale-preserving symbols of respectability. As Harry Hopkins said, "The unemployed themselves want work," and the New Deal did create jobs, millions of them.[86] In addition, New Dealers pointed to hundreds of new or refurbished buildings, thousands of miles of freshly paved roads, and countless paintings, plays, and books that showed how productive those jobs had been.

Yet the death of the CWA and the subsequent vacillations of both the FERA and WPA between the poles of work and relief split the ranks of New York's social work reformers. Both New Yorkers and New Dealers remained committed to work relief's morale-sustaining goals, but they differed on the methods of attaining them. New Dealers preferred stronger incentives to draw people to employment in private industry. After the CWA's death, New Yorkers moved leftward, but the New Dealers clung to the private enterprise system. New Yorkers detected a fundamental conservatism in their New Deal colleagues, a conservatism which they saw now as hindering America's ability to solve its unemployment problem. The New Deal's WPA provided them with evidence for half of their indictment. Its program for unemployment insurance gave them the rest.

Better
half
a
Social
Security
Act
than
none

12

The laws creating both the WPA and a state-federal system of unemployment compensation passed Congress within four months of each other in 1935. Each grew out of frustrations in handling federal relief programs. Each attempted to answer the psychological as well as material needs of the unemployed. Each revealed the deference that New Dealers paid to the dictates of a business civilization. Finally, each propelled New York's reformers leftward, widening a breach opened by the CWA's demise. Between friends, disappointments and disagreements could be concealed. "For my part," Paul Kellogg wrote Harry Hopkins, "I think it was worthwhile [to recognize] the need for dovetailing the works program with the unemployment compensation coverage of the Wagner-Lewis bill, so that there will be protection for the worker whose compensation is exhausted—an underpinning that won't throw him into the hopper of relief if there is no [other] job at hand." [1] Kellogg genuinely believed in linking the WPA to the Social Security Act, but he was also hiding his bitterness at having lost a personal fight for a better unemployment compensation proposal. Insurance against joblessness had be-

come Kellogg's favorite issue. His disappointment was another
sign of the deep discouragement that many of New York's social
workers felt in spite of Roosevelt's "Second New Deal" of 1935.

By the early thirties, *Survey* was championing a public
system of unemployment compensation. Confronted by falling
demand for their products, private employers could no longer
be counted upon to adopt compensation plans; moreover, mass
unemployment had rendered such voluntary measures meaning-
less. "Private insurance, by industries or private carriers, is not
enough," Paul Kellogg proclaimed late in 1931. "The coverage
must be more universal to effect a social solution to the problem
of security."[2] Senator Robert F. Wagner, who had introduced an
unemployment compensation bill in Congress as early as 1930,
was even more emphatic: "To advocate insurance with sincerity
is to advocate compulsory insurance."[3] Mandatory compensation promised many advantages. It would shift "back onto industry some of the cost of its broken work which is now burying
our social agencies," Kellogg argued.[4] It would also be a useful
economic tool that would "sustain a minimum [of] purchasing
and providing power" when business recessions struck in the future; indeed, it would act "as a brake at the very outset of that
turn of the spiral," Kellogg explained.[5] Yet the most compelling
arguments centered on the psychological benefits to be gained
from unemployment compensation.

During 1931, *Survey* made note of a loud outcry for
compensation "as a more adequate, self-respecting and certain
measure of security for wage-earners than our present 'dole' of
public and private charity."[6] A study committee of the American
Association of Social Workers was envisioning compensation as
"a great social machine," which in addition to its other functions,
could be "so organized that the independence and self-respect
of the worker will be preserved and his efficiency maintained."[7]
Contributions by both employers and employees (through de-
ductions from wages) deepened the sense of a right to benefits.
As Frances Perkins once put it, compensation systems made
benefits "a right that has been bought and paid for," and nur-

143

tured the idea of providing for one's self.[8] Reformers admitted
that they had no precise way to measure morale, but agreed that
the new system meant a qualitative as well as quantitative difference.[9] Paul Kellogg enlarged on that point in a letter to William
Matthews, "Under unemployment insurance workers out of a
job who stood ready to work would be on a different footing
from people who were in trouble because of something other
than the economic factor." No longer would the temporarily jobless have to accept handouts, grocery tickets, emergency jobs, or
public relief. "My feeling has been that it makes a lot of difference to a worker out of a job, who wants work and is ready to
work," Kellogg continued, "to feel that he is still part of our
going industrial life; and that the benefit he gets is part of his
status as a member of that going life."[10]

Yet an American compensation system had to pay for itself, reformers agreed, in order to avoid the stigma of charity.
Therefore contributions and benefits had to be kept in balance,
and to protect funds against unlimited drains, reformers incorporated devices such as waiting periods, benefit ceilings, and
restricted periods of coverage. In addition, they tied the distribution of benefits to public employment bureaus, where the
unemployed would have to stand ready to accept suitable employment if it arose. Reformers justified each of those restrictive
devices. Since contributions provided a fixed income and public
support was prohibited, unemployment compensation could not
become a cornucopia of lavish benefits. In fact, reformers never
promoted it as a panacea for the ravages of joblessness. Waiting
periods were long enough (usually a few weeks) to devour some
savings or to force needy families into debt; benefits were aimed
at a level of survival (never at more than one-half of normal
earnings and usually much less); and periods of coverage were
short (often ten to sixteen weeks only), after which recipients
faced the prospect of going on relief.

"It must be borne in mind," Paul Kellogg noted, "that
under any system of unemployment insurance . . . the heavy
end of any wage losses . . . still is borne by the workers them-

selves."[11] Frances Perkins observed that "unemployment benefits represent a sharp drop in the amount of the wage-earner's usual income."[12] That admission tacitly pointed to another psychological feature of unemployment compensation: its deprivations would drive the unemployed to search for new work. In addition, the distribution of benefits through public employment bureaus put the jobless in the hands of officials who could coerce them into jobs or force them onto relief if they proved recalcitrant. Yet reformers rarely confessed that one of the purposes behind restrictive devices was to get compensation recipients back to work. Instead they talked about "standards," levels of support, and inducements to high morale.

John B. Andrews introduced his "reserves" scheme for unemployment compensation in 1930. Once the student of John R. Commons at the state university of his native Wisconsin, Andrews founded the New York City-based American Association for Labor Legislation in 1910. Like his mentor, he devoted his career to studying labor conditions, and his proposal represented nearly two decades of work on the issue of compensation. "Here is an attempt to meet an American situation with 'an American plan,'" he stated in his covering letter to fellow New York reformers. "As an American plan it is built out of two successful American practices," Andrews went on, "*First*, the accepted sound business policy of setting up in prosperous years a reserve fund . . . and *Second*, workmen's accident compensation laws which . . . furnish a stimulus to accident prevention." In order to avoid "the American dole system" of charity relief, he asserted, the "emphasis [of unemployment compensation] must be placed upon prevention" of joblessness.[13] The plan itself imposed nearly the entire cost of compensation on employers. Through a tax on payrolls, they either deposited funds into separate company accounts or contributed to pools organized by industrial groups. Every participating employer had to keep a set amount in reserve at all times, and he bore any compensation costs out of that reserve. If his reserve dipped below a minimum level required per employee, then he had to either renew or increase his contributions. At most, government assumed the minimal cost of state administration, while employees contributed nothing. Unemployment benefits were to be distributed "as the condition of the fund will permit." Under the guidelines of Andrews's AALL plan, jobless people waited two weeks to collect their first benefits; the maximum benefit was ten dollars a week; and the duration of the benefit period was thirteen weeks. They also had to pass "a work test," which meant filing applications "through employment offices."[14]

Andrews's AALL design was the most influential plan and became the model for all of Franklin Roosevelt's gubernatorial proposals after 1930 and for the Wisconsin act of 1932, which established the first state unemployment compensation program. It did not go unchallenged, however. During 1931–1932, Ohio created a commission of its own, charging it with the responsibility of drafting another plan and naming William Leiserson its chairman. Though a professor at Antioch College, Leiserson was a close associate of New York's reformers. Before the First World War, when he lived in New York, he had drafted the state's workmen's compensation and public employment service bills.[15] Contacts established then remained firm over the years. During 1931 and 1932, he frequently advised Frances Perkins and Governor Roosevelt on unemployment issues, and also became a member of FDR's Interstate Commission on Unemployment Insurance. Leiserson also kept close friendships within the New York social work group. He and Paul Kellogg were in constant communication, and he appointed New York's Isaac M. Rubinow to the new Ohio Commission. Rubinow was also in league with Abraham Epstein of New York; they were the two theorists most critical of John Andrews and the AALL plan.[16]

The Ohio Commission on Unemployment Insurance offered its program for state action in 1932. An alternative to the AALL model, its plan rested on mutual contributions from employers' payrolls and employees' wages. Funds were collected in a state pool that diffused the risk of compensation costs across company and industrial lines. Once pooled funds had risen to adequate levels, a merit system took effect, allowing companies with good employment records to reduce their contributions. The Ohio plan was designed to be absolutely self-sustaining; government would never fund its operation. Unemployed workers had to wait three weeks for benefits to begin; one-half of a man's former weekly wages or a maximum of fifteen dollars was prescribed as the benefit; and coverage lasted sixteen weeks. The jobless applied for benefits through public employment bureaus.[17]

Leiserson pinpointed the major difference between the AALL and Ohio plans: "Is it [unemployment compensation] to provide some income for workers when they are unemployed, or is it to encourage industries to stabilize employment by burdening those which don't?" He noted that the "two purposes are not necessarily contradictory," and the AALL and Ohio plans spoke to each goal, but their emphasis was different.[18] According to compensation expert Paul H. Douglas, the AALL plan "saddled" the cost of benefits "upon the employers in the belief that if they are held financially liable for the payments, they will seek to reduce unemployment."[19] Through its "reserves" system, the AALL plan stressed improved management techniques within industry, but its small provision for reserves (only seventy-five dollars per employee) seemed inadequate to meet the needs of the jobless.[20] On the other hand, the Ohio plan called itself an "insurance" system and looked to employee contributions in order to increase benefits. "The Ohio bill . . . aims directly at relieving distress," Leiserson claimed, pointing to both higher benefits and longer periods of coverage.[21] In addition, employee contributions underscored "the feeling of self-help and self-respect that comes from paying in one's own insurance."[22] Thus the AALL's "reserves" approach emphasized employment stabilization, whereas the Ohio "insurance" approach emphasized worker morale.

The details of the two different plans assumed animating, vital force in the minds of New York's reformers, who began to contest their respective merits. During 1932, battle lines formed, and the advocates of reserves, led by Andrews, lined up against the advocates of insurance, led by Leiserson, Rubinow, and Epstein (and by a silent partner, Paul Kellogg).[23] In addition, another major actor, Frances Perkins, had quietly asserted her presence. During the fall of 1931, Governor Roosevelt sent her to England, where she studied Britain's compensation program. Her subsequent report reinforced several of her boss's views, including the need for "a sound actuarial principle" and tough standards to protect funds. She recommended that premiums "be paid wholly by the employer," however, whereas Roosevelt preferred matching contributions by employees. "The administration [of a program] should be kept impersonal," Perkins argued, shunning the "boost to morale" theory behind employees' contributions; on the other hand, she did recommend a statewide pool of funds instead of separate accounts. Unemployment "is a social as well as an industrial problem," she attested, "and the cost should be spread just as widely as possible."[24] Perkins's preference for the AALL plan was probably well known before her sojourn in England; indeed, she had influenced FDR's ideas already, because he used the AALL model in his recommendations to the Governors' Conference earlier in 1931. Later, Paul Kellogg became convinced that unemployment compensation was her "special bailiwick" in New Deal legislation.[25]

Perkins and Roosevelt achieved no compensation law while in Albany, but they set their sights on a national program in 1934. The Wagner-Lewis bill, which was drafted during that year and evolved to become the Social Security Act of 1935, came out of the offices of Perkins's Department of Labor.[26] The president probably gave Perkins a free hand to develop her own plan.[27] If so, he made a smart decision, because the Secretary of Labor possessed the determination needed to cut through a tangle of conflicting theories and personalities. The result was a program of modest proportions that eventually carried the vote of Congress. The Wagner-Lewis bill was a bare-bones proposal that provided a federal tax on employers' payrolls and a subsequent tax credit for employers whose states legislated their own unemployment compensation programs. In other words, the states had to create programs before their employers received credit for taxes imposed on them by the federal government. The advantages of that approach were twofold: states had a powerful inducement to take action, yet were free to select any program, including the AALL and Ohio models. The disadvantage was that the federal government set no standards for the programs.[28] Even though this first Wagner-Lewis bill died in a congressional committee by mid-1934, Perkins had set the framework for federal legislation. What she needed was momentum for federal action, not a new legislative proposal.

In preparing for the session of Congress that began in January 1935, Roosevelt created a study group, the Committee on Economic Security, composed of five members, four from his cabinet, including Perkins, plus relief administrator Harry Hopkins. The COES was to recommend a social security program to the president, and its labors were supplemented by an Advisory Council composed of representatives drawn from business, organized labor, and "the public." Among the "public" members appointed by Perkins were Paul Kellogg of *Survey*, Helen Hall, the new director of Henry Street settlement, Josephine Roche, a former social worker and current assistant secretary of the Treasury, Molly Dewson, another former social worker now with the Democratic National Committee, and Raymond Moley, one of FDR's former brain trusters. Indeed, the Advisory Council looked like another gathering of the New York crowd. Even business members and labor representatives were positively disposed toward compensation laws.[29] Among those notably omitted from the Council were the feuding experts—John Andrews, I. M. Rubinow, and Abraham Epstein (William Leiserson now worked within the New Deal). "Apparently all the experts who had taken pronounced positions were left out of the setup," Kellogg suspected, and Perkins confirmed his suspicion later in her memoirs: "We steered clear of people who were too theoretical."[30] Obviously, Frances Perkins was attempting to perpetrate a calculated ruse: get good publicity for a revived Wagner-Lewis bill by securing the endorsement of a council free of discord.[31] Unfortunately, she miscalculated, for she appointed some people who were truly interested in drafting a pristine law for unemployment compensation.

On November 14, 1934, a National Conference kicked off the drive for social security legislation. Held in Washington, its featured speakers included Perkins, Hopkins, and Roosevelt. During the next month the Advisory Council (which was chaired by Frank Graham, president of the University of North Carolina) as well as the COES met periodically to plot the course of the Wagner-Lewis bill. The Advisory Council, however, began to split on a number of issues: whether explicit standards should be written into the bill; whether the employers' payroll tax should be increased beyond 3 percent; whether employees should be obligated to make contributions; whether the federal government should add a contribution from general tax revenues; and whether the federal government should supervise the operation of state programs. The Council left fragmentary records of its deliberations, however, and administration efforts to hide dissent from public view obscured details of its proceedings.[32] To hold down its own costs, the business group usually supported funding measures such as employees' contributions and government supplements. The labor group sought to increase employers' responsibility through a higher payroll tax, while rejecting employee contributions and supplements from general taxes. On most questions the "public" group held the deciding vote, and it often divided between members who were closely attached to the New Deal and outsiders who felt less loyalty to the administration.

Paul Kellogg led opposition to the Wagner-Lewis bill.[33] "The old history of social reform is to get the nose of the camel under the tent," Kellogg was to write in January 1935. Instead of accepting minimal gains, as had often been the reformers' approach, he wanted an optimal unemployment compensation program that would be set in place "while interest is keen."[34] No dewy-eyed idealist, he probably sensed from the beginning that his fight against the Wagner-Lewis bill would involve an uphill battle against his old friend, Frances Perkins. Kellogg's first victory came when the Council recommended mandatory standards, including a four-week waiting period and fifteen weeks of coverage.[35] The Wagner-Lewis bill called for a 3 percent tax on payrolls, making employers the exclusive contributors to compensation funds. To enlarge the fund and make possible higher benefits, Kellogg led a fight to increase the payroll tax to 4 percent and to add an employees' contribution of 1 percent to it.[36] A tie vote was reached on the higher payroll tax, but labor representatives blocked employee contributions.[37] Kellogg also favored a federal contribution to increase benefits, challenging the principle of keeping public funds out of compensation programs. In this case he was beaten back by Edwin Witte, the Council's powerful executive director, who cited FDR's position against the use of tax revenues and drew a line against contradicting the president.[38] Each of Kellogg's proposals attempted to expand the pool of funds in a cumulative fashion by stretching contributions across the ranks of employers, employees, and the public.

The Council's other major battle focused on the issue of federal authority: since the Wagner-Lewis bill did not provide explicit means by which the federal government could force states to maintain adequate compensation programs, some members wanted a device that would allow federal supervision. The instrument they struck upon was called a "subsidy plan," whereby the federal government would return the monies collected through payroll taxes directly to the states in the form of "grants-in-aid," instead of using employers' tax credits as provided for in the Wagner measure.[39] The subsidy plan worked much like the old TERA-FERA matching grants, which tied the delivery of funds to approval by a higher governmental authority. Once again, Paul Kellogg led the struggle against the New Deal's position. He defended the subsidy plan "both from the standpoint of standards and of securing a greater leverage and competence in the federal authority at Washington." In his estimation, there had to be "a minimum coherence to the bottom level of provisions everywhere, leaving the states to experiment above that level."[40] On one occasion, his efforts were rewarded with a favorable vote within the Council.[41] "I have been having a hard time to appear impartial and judicially minded, and at the same time squelch the subsidy plan," reported Thomas Eliot, the appointed legal counsel to the Advisory Council. He was sticking up for the administration's desire to steer a conservative act around a conservative Supreme Court by avoiding a confrontation on the issue of federal versus state powers: "Adopt the subsidy plan and then have the tax thrown out on one of these grounds," Eliot complained—"A lot of good the state laws will do us!"[42] All issues raised within the Council, however, were left to the cabinet-level Committee on Economic Security, which made all final recommendations.

Paul Kellogg was to experience absolute frustration. As nearly as can be determined, all Council votes were close, with Kellogg winning a couple of points. Yet two of Frances Perkins's representatives in the Council—Edwin Witte, whom she appointed executive director, and Thomas Eliot, who served in her own Department of Labor—assisted by heavyweight New Dealers including Molly Dewson delivered knockout blows. With a bare majority of nine to eight, supporters of the Wagner-Lewis bill blocked the rebels from filing a minority report.[43] They could not block the writing of a supplementary report, however, which was allowed by a favorable Council resolution.[44] But a supplementary report was not an official document. Therefore the minority was not free to make the statement public, whereas the administration was free to suppress it, which it did.[45] In most respects, the struggle had grown pathetic, because the COES had decided long before that the Wagner-Lewis bill was the New Deal's final proposal.[46]

Kellogg had been in a difficult position throughout the Council's deliberations, particularly in regard to Frances Perkins, his close friend and strongest tie to the New Deal. He never confronted her directly, aiming his attacks instead upon

Edwin Witte. Kellogg emphasized two themes in the supplementary report—the need for standards and the need for federal authority—and attempted to appeal to Perkins as an impartial and open-minded final authority. "I cannot tell you how much some of us feel is at stake in the issue raised in this supplementary statement," he wrote. "Between the lines, I think you can gauge how serious it is; and our hope is that you will espouse the increased coverage not only with your fellow members of the Cabinet committee, but with the President himself."[47] He was more frank with Witte. "You always opposed this whole principle of laying down national standards," he asserted in February 1935. "President Graham and others of us always were for it; and we carried a majority with us."[48] Witte countered by reprimanding Kellogg for not seeking high standards in state legislation;[49] during February, he was also complaining about the interference of New York "high brows."[50] Later, after Kellogg and Helen Hall had founded an *ad hoc* committee of New York social workers to protest the Wagner-Lewis bill and after Witte had received a copy of that committee's letter of protest from Kellogg, Witte's ire peaked. "While I very much regret your attitude in so bitterly fighting this bill," he wrote, "I appreciate your curtesy [*sic?*] in sending me a copy of your statement."[51]

The COES never budged from the basic Wagner-Lewis bill. In its "First Tentative Draft" of a report to the president, it revealed its irritation with an "unauthorized" leak about the controversy in the Advisory Council. "What is needed at this stage is experimentation, not further debate and research," committee members claimed, setting forth their recommendations.[52] Even though a final report was never submitted, Roosevelt picked up their ideas in his winter 1935 call for legislation. He endorsed a 3 percent payroll tax, federal tax credits for participating employers, and an "additional credit" as an incentive to employers to maintain stable payrolls (if their states adopted rating systems). No standards were built into the administration's proposal; each state was free to legislate its own plan, but its compensation system did have to be administered through federal public employ-

153

ment offices.[53] During the winter of 1935, Frances Perkins touted the New Deal-blessed Wagner-Lewis measure as an "American Plan," noting its difference from European programs and claiming its suitability for American conditions.[54]

In the meantime, Paul Kellogg reflected upon his experiences with the Advisory Council. While he vented his anger at Edwin Witte, he confided in I. M. Rubinow. "The administration very obviously left you [and other backers of the Ohio plan] off the set-up," Kellogg wrote Rubinow, "and the Committee's officials tried to commit us to the Wagner-Lewis formula, to avoid standards, to cut down the tax, and to make sure the Wisconsin reserve scheme should be a permissible line of state action."[55] Even then, at the end of January 1935, Kellogg was still "trying to pry loose [Advisory Council] reports and the supplementary statements, which have not been given to the public," so Rubinow himself was "very much gratified to learn that there was a substantial minority on the Council which recognized the inadequacy of the standards of unemployment compensation suggested in the [COES] report and in Wagner's bill."[56] In his estimation, the Wagner-Lewis bill was "frankly only a measure of exercising pressure upon the employers to break down their opposition to state acts" and scarcely a national insurance program.[57] Yet Rubinow admitted that "there was little force to back us up as compared with the weight of the New Deal," implying the frustration that insurance experts like Abraham Epstein must have felt when they, too, were omitted from the Advisory Council.[58]

154   There was justification for the assumption that the New Deal was biased in favor of the AALL and Wisconsin approach to compensation. The administration's key figure, Frances Perkins, had always been committed to John Andrews's plan. Both Edwin Witte and Arthur Altmeyer, the Assistant Secretary of Labor who drafted the COES's organizational format, came from Wisconsin and were familiar with its reserves program, which was similar to that of the AALL. In addition, Thomas Eliot, who served as legal counsel to the COES, had been the

principal author of the early Wagner-Lewis bill. Perhaps the major motivation was practical: they wanted a program that would pass Congress and withstand review by the Supreme Court. Nonetheless, if the states conformed to the minimum that was required, as Kellogg and Rubinow anticipated, then employers' contributions and reserves schemes would become the standard pattern across the nation. The higher benefits obtainable through contributions by employees would be sacrificed, and the prevention device of penalizing employers with high rates of dismissal would stand as the principle undergirding unemployment compensation.

There was also justification for the belief that Roosevelt's measure had not advanced beyond what he proposed in June 1930, during "Hoover's days."[59] It emphasized employment stabilization, stressed businessmen's participation in a "business proposal," and left great freedom to the states. FDR's original insistence on employee contributions had disappeared, but that had also happened during his years as governor, when his "social work friends"—probably Perkins especially—were advising him against the Ohio approach.[60] The absence of employees' required contributions of course sacrificed some psychological benefits for unemployed Americans. Much was still retained under the reserves approach, for "A man losing his job receives automatically as a right, a weekly sum of money which bears a direct relation to the length and other conditions of his former employment, and to the amount which has been contributed on his account."[61] Reformers committed to the Ohio plan— New Yorkers the foremost among them—could only hope that the states would show greater sensitivity than federal law required of them.

Nearly lost amid the clamor over unemployment compensation was an old-age pension program that did rest on insurance principles. The Social Security Act of August 1935 imposed a mutual 3 percent tax on payrolls and individual earnings that was paid by both employers and employees. In addi-

155

tion, it set up federal administration for the program. Old-age pensions served as the New Deal's response to the Townsend plan and other "visionary schemes" of the mid-1930s that promised "impossibly large free pensions," as Frances Perkins characterized them, to elderly people. "Small, steady allowances built up by regular contributions during early and middle life," Perkins had promised in December 1934, "is a definite possibility for us."[62] Indeed, an administration that accepted a federal insurance program for old age in one part of the Social Security Act had rejected those principles when applied to unemployment compensation.[63] Reformers like Kellogg, who had fought so desperately for a federal unemployment insurance program, could scarcely have missed the irony in that situation.

The battle over unemployment compensation was a strange affair. On its surface, it pitted a Wisconsin law against an Ohio proposal. At its deeper levels, it involved a toe-to-toe confrontation between New Yorkers, with Perkins, John B. Andrews, and Roosevelt squaring off against Kellogg, I. M. Rubinow, and Abraham Epstein. Molly Dewson, Josephine Roche, Raymond Moley, and Helen Hall, who would become Paul Kellogg's wife in 1935, joined the battle in the meetings of the Advisory Council. William Leiserson played his own peculiar part. He had been appointed adviser to the Technical Board, which also advised the COES, and that board convinced COES members to accept a federal insurance program for old-age pensions, thus implementing the gist of the Ohio plan that Kellogg was trying to secure on the other side of the Social Security Act's ledger.[64]

156

All of the involved New Yorkers found the situation painful and confusing. The New Dealers among them fought for their "American plans." The non-New Dealers moved to the political left. Kellogg even broached the issue of introducing public subsidies, raising the possibility that high standards for benefits might be more important than the principle of a self-supporting system. That step brought him close to the English model of employer, employee, and public funding. The Social

Security Act's unemployment compensation program, however, remained as "American" as Perkins, Andrews, and Roosevelt had always wanted it. Like its sister program, the WPA, it offered material benefits (but not too much), it buoyed up morale (but not too high), and it retained incentives to urge the unemployed back into private industry.

**Harmonies
in
depression
counterpoint**

13

Through 1933 New York's reformers and their compatriots in the New Deal shared the belief that social betterment was possible in a capitalistic economy. Frances Perkins succinctly stated their creed in *People at Work* (1934): "There is not necessarily any divergence of interest between the industrialist, the wage-earner and the consumer . . . rather there is a real community of interest." She knew that American society possessed class differences, but she believed these differences malleable. Unlike Marxists, who saw capital and labor at loggerheads, reformers like Perkins put their faith in compromise. The institutional apparatus for the working of compromise was called the "conference method," and it allowed representatives of different interest groups—business, labor, and the social work "public"—to come together to participate in a democratic process of decision-making. The representational format used by the Welfare Council of New York City, New York's old Bruere Committee, the New Deal's National Recovery Administration, and the Advisory Council of the Committee on Economic Security exemplified a "partnership" that brought "all elements of the community into conference for the solution of any human problem." The conference method guaranteed "a balance where the concern of all is for the welfare of each," and its use converted government into "a service agency for these essential activities of human cooperation."[1]

During 1934, New York's reformers began to examine critically their commitment to a business culture. They had been particularly upset by Roosevelt's sudden withdrawal of the CWA. During April 1934, an *ad hoc* group of New York dissenters, led by Paul Kellogg and Edward T. Devine, produced a "confidential" memorandum to the president that defined the widening gap between them and the administration. "We believe," the dissenters told Roosevelt in a personal meeting recorded by Paul Kellogg, "that the acid test of . . . policies is their effect on the actual distribution of wealth and income; their effect in raising measurably the general standards of living, the purchasing power of the nation's workers—urban and rural." Alluding to the demise of the CWA, they reprimanded FDR indirectly: "We need to abandon our emergency attitude toward unemployment and . . . to build the Federal-State-City relief set-up into an orderly system of administration with elements of permanent planning." They also took critical measure of the NRA, calling for powerful labor and consumers' boards, for minimum wages tied to a rising cost of living, and for collective bargaining between independent labor unions and employers. Lamenting the fact that "nothing in the way of a system of permanent security has as yet come out of the depression," they also demanded insurance programs for the jobless, the elderly, and the sick, public **159** housing projects for the poor, and cooperative planning and control of "public interest" industries. All programs were to be financed through increased federal income and inheritance taxes.[2]

The dissenters' statement led to social work's first organized resistance to Roosevelt's policies. It was circulated for approval among social workers across the nation, and more than thirty New Yorkers endorsed it.[3] Much that the statement suggested was not new. Its criticisms derived from commonly observed weaknesses in programs such as the NRA, which had given few benefits to labor, and several of its recommendations could have been found in rudimentary legislative form at Senator Robert Wagner's office on Capitol Hill. Nonetheless, the statement was a visionary document that challenged the first-year record of the New Deal. "This is, as I see it, only a trial balloon," Paul Kellogg cautiously wrote his more conservative colleagues when seeking their support, but he confidently told his liberal associates that "the text . . . will stretch the tent-ropes of people's imaginations," offering them the opportunity to identify whole-heartedly with its contents.[4] Several social workers refused to endorse the statement, and attacked Kellogg for criticizing the New Deal.[5] On the other hand, Mary Van Kleeck of the Russell Sage Foundation reprimanded the *ad hoc* group for its conservatism.[6] She failed to see anything meaningful in supporting old-style reforms, and she soon commenced her own crusade against the social work profession as well as Roosevelt.

A year younger than the president, Mary Van Kleeck grew up in Roosevelt's own Dutchess County, New York. She graduated from Smith College in 1904, the year of FDR's Harvard graduation. By the age of twenty-six, Van Kleeck had become director of the Russell Sage Foundation's Department of Industrial Studies, and her credentials as a progressive reformer included service on Mayor Mitchel's New York Committee on Unemployment. In 1933 she served briefly as an appointed member of the Advisory Counsel to the United States Employment Service, resigning in protest because she opposed the NRA's stand against labor strikes.[7] By 1934 her opposition to the NRA had broadened to take in most New Deal programs, as she made very apparent at that year's national conference of social workers. Many welcomed her remarks. Gertrude Springer observed that the conferees were preoccupied with the recent CWA debacle, so the "glowing enthusiasm" generated for the New Deal a year before had grown "cold and dead."[8] Van Kleeck cut to the core of that disillusionment, charging the New Deal with failure on three counts: the NRA had given industrial control to employers; federal relief programs had not given adequate purchasing power to the unemployed; and the proposed social security bill threatened to worsen the plight of the nation by using payroll taxes to withhold earned income from workers, while allowing employers to pass their costs on to consumers in higher prices.[9] She treated the New Deal as if it were a butchered cow: "The girl is good at skinning," Springer wrote *Survey*'s Arthur Kellogg privately.[10] In *Survey* she reported that "the largest halls available would not hold the crowds following the proponents of new ideologies"; this was an implicit reference to Van Kleeck, who had called for public ownership of industry.[11]

Van Kleeck reserved some of her choicest criticism for the profession of social work. In their efforts to get federal action, social workers suffered "illusions about government." "The theory which has largely dominated the political programs of social work," she noted, "is that government stands above conflicting interests and . . . [can] decide between those conflicts and compel standards and policies which are in the public interest." But she believed that the struggle between capital and labor could not be ameliorated, that government offered no help because it was organized to protect private property. It followed that social workers were committed to "preservation of the status quo" because they "were helping the politicians to see just how far it was necessary to go in yielding to the demands of the needy in order to protect" capitalist institutions. Aiming her concluding salvo at the Progressive Movement as well as the New Deal, she charged the adherents of both with complicity in sustaining property: "Both have essentially tended to maintain economic privilege in power, yielding only so much as is necessary to prevent too strong a protest" from workers, the jobless, and the poor.[12]

With a few bold strokes Van Kleeck had tendered an explanation for the New Deal's failures. The interests of labor had been ignored; government stood on the side of capital and property; and social work reformers had played into the hand of conservatives who used New Deal programs to protect the *status quo*.

161

"Never in a long experience of conferences," Gertrude Springer acknowledged in *Survey*, "has this observer witnessed such a prolonged ovation as followed the concluding period of Miss Van Kleeck's . . . case for a break with our existing form of government into a collectivism shorn of the profit motive." [13]

Van Kleeck was not the only critic at the conference. The RSF's Joanna Colcord and the Division of Government and Social Work of the American Association of Social Workers were also ready to attack New Deal programs. "By adequate relief," the professionals declared, "we mean food, clothing, shelter, protection of health and care in illness, and above all the conservation of self-respect which keeps people employable." The last point deserved emphasis, so social workers reaffirmed their commitment to the kind of work program found in the old CWA: "Work relief is preferable to cash or kind, but honest jobs are better still, and there is no real substitute for genuine employment." [14] The New Deal's FERA, which offered little work and insufficient relief, represented everything they found inadequate in Roosevelt's relief policies. As Springer recalled the scene, their "plea for 'a work program broad and diversified enough to provide reasonably suitable jobs at all times for all employable people' . . . brought the kind of applause that denotes conviction." [15] During the conference the ranks of the New Deal's critics grew in number and in intensity of denunciation.

Two New Yorkers, Harry Hopkins and William Hodson, attempted to defend the New Deal against Van Kleeck and Colcord, their fellow New Yorkers and the New Deal's harshest critics. Gertrude Springer reported that conferees listened "respectfully" to Harry Hopkins's "qualified promises of a planned public welfare system," but his speech was brief and delivered "in generalities." "[W]e who serve the government," he remarked, "have no apologies to make." Springer described the address as a "low spot." The conferees' polite applause, she speculated, "must have sounded strangely tame to one who only a year before . . . had had the power to lift social workers off their feet." [16] A greater disappointment involved the address of

162

Hopkins's friend, William Hodson, who was the Commissioner of Public Welfare in New York City, a celebrated New Deal spokesman, and president of the 1934 conference. Hodson, however, "had not prepared a speech," which accounted in part for a presentation that was "far from the stature of a presidential address." [17] He rejected radicalism, insisting instead on the continuing modification of "the existing economic order in such fundamental ways as will serve the well-being of the people as a whole." He saw that approach as "the objective of the present national administration," and declared that "I, for one, am still willing to throw my lot with the [New Deal], reserving always the right to differ and to criticize as a friend and not as an enemy." [18] His final words "RAISED SHARP CONTROVERSY OVER ISSUE OF FREE SPEECH," Springer telegraphed *Survey* headquarters. "ALLEN BURNS INTRODUCED RESOLUTION CENSURING HODSON. ITS A BATTLE." [19] The conference's nightmarish quality, darkened by the internecine battles of New Yorkers, ended the harmony between social workers and New Dealers.

Mary Van Kleeck did not inspire a radicals' crusade. Most of New York's social work leaders remained what they had always been—reformers committed to working within a capitalistic and democratic order. Nonetheless, they took fresh inventory of their old positions, found them wanting in some particulars, and moved toward imposing greater collective responsibilities on the part of the federal government, toward creating more comprehensive public welfare programs, and toward the guarantee of rights for labor as well as the unemployed. That thrust became evident a few months after the 1934 national conference, when Paul Kellogg led the fight in the COES's Advisory Council for a federally controlled unemployment compensation program. The frustration that he and his backers experienced in that endeavor added fuel to their discontent, because it cast shadows upon the efficacy of a conference method that no longer involved genuine deliberation. During January 1935, the *ad hoc* group of New York's 1934 dissenters

163

organized themselves as the Social Policy Committee. Dedicated to "giving evidence of liberal support to affirmative moves, in opposition to some, and in striking out along bolder lines," the SPC fastened upon the deficiencies of the Wagner-Lewis bill for unemployment compensation.[20] In a February meeting, Henry Street settlement director and former Advisory Council member Helen Hall reported that federal standards and a higher payroll tax might still be secured in Washington; "Miss Hall felt," the SPC's minutes read, "that the only people who did not support the demand for standards, were people connected with the Administration," which gave a telling indication of the distance that now separated New York's leaders from old allies like Perkins and Hopkins.[21] The committee endorsed a statement prepared by Edward Devine and recommended its circulation throughout Washington. "The rights of workers out of work should be the very heart of unemployment compensation legislation," the statement argued, elaborating specific standards for the bill. "To turn back the federal payroll tax to the states without setting the standards below which no state shall go," it claimed, "is to make a hollow shell of the protection for which the money is collected." The SPC also recommended that the compensation fund be increased from 3 percent to 5 percent of total payrolls, and that the additional 2 percent come "from the federal Treasury so that all of us as income tax payers . . . will share in bringing stability and security into the industrial life of America."[22]

164   In the meantime, the Delegate Conference of the American Association of Social Workers held a February meeting in Washington. It too criticized the social security bill's lack of standards and minimal funding, but the delegates also focused on its provisions for categorical relief. The Wagner-Lewis scheme offered federal aid to the states for public assistance given to the blind, the crippled, dependent children, and other dependent groups, but it promised no help for the able-bodied unemployed or for needy families and individuals generally. Those people, delegates observed, would be utterly dependent on their states and localities for relief, a condition that the delegates denounced.

In addition, in its provisions for a Public Assistance Bureau within a Social Security Administration—a bureau that would oversee federal-state programs of categorical aid—the Wagner-Lewis bill posited no safeguards for professional personnel and standards of administration. As a result, delegates called for a "merit system" within civil service that would promote administrators on the basis of performance. Finally, the delegates took note of pending legislation that would create the Works Progress Administration, insisting with some apprehension that it should not become a "substitute" for federal programs of public relief.[23] Their fears were well founded, because the New Deal was about to initiate its retreat from comprehensive federal welfare programs.

New Yorkers always knew that Franklin Roosevelt and his subordinates disliked direct relief—giving aid to people without any provision for work as a means of qualification. As Russell Kurtz of the state's TERA had noted in 1933, "The Administration considers relief a miserable business, necessary to tide people over an emergency but not to be continued a moment longer than the unemployment situation requires."[24] By the end of 1934, the Committee on Economic Security, with the concurrence of FDR, decided that the moment for ending direct relief had arrived. The COES members believed that a proposed federal works program for jobless Americans plus the social security package provided adequate protection for the unemployed. The time had come to return responsibility for care of able-bodied "unemployables" to the states and localities. A federal-state system of categorical aid would offer assistance for dependents such as the indigent elderly and "families without breadwinners," but the relief of simple poverty would once again become the duty of communities.[25] The New Dealers devoted 1935 to cutting adrift many of the state and local relief programs they had funded since 1933.

Passage of the Emergency Relief Appropriation Act in April 1935 insured the August 1935 demise of the Federal Emergency Relief Administration. Though often maligned by

165

social workers after 1933, the FERA still drew on New York's TERA model, extending federal matching grants that allowed the states to grant direct relief to unemployed people, whether they were unemployables or able-bodied. True, the new WPA and Social Security Administration promised help for substantial numbers of able-bodied employables, but as New York's Joanna Colcord observed, the combination was "a patchwork of relief plus insurance measures . . . leaving many areas untouched."[26] In addition to excluding numerous Americans from insurance coverage, the SSA's unemployment compensation program (which depended on state action) would not begin operation until January 1, 1938, while its old-age pensions would not be available until 1942![27] Those conditions left the WPA alone bearing the enormous burden of unemployment. That agency shortly came under attack as its inadequacies became apparent.[28] Indeed, termination of the FERA made the WPA's work projects the only federal avenue for unemployment relief. As predicted, the reversion of direct relief to state and local programs brought chaos. Even an "insider" within Harry Hopkins's circle, former New Yorker Josephine Brown, admitted later that the "period of transition" from the FERA to the WPA "was a time of uncertainty, insecurity and even terror for the relief client who could not get a work relief job and who had no sure niche in the developing categorical programs" of the SSA. "Suffering was acute . . . [because] funds for general relief were inadequate or entirely lacking in state after state."[29] In fact, Brown personally experienced the bitterness of social workers at the 1936 national conference, where she had defended the New Deal's actions against its many critics.[30]

But with the end of the FERA, New Dealers accomplished their objective—getting the federal government out of "this business of relief," as FDR put it.[31] Moreover, they implemented a tacit suggestion of the COES to bind all federal unemployment programs to a "Willingness to Work Test."[32] To earn federal aid after 1935, a jobless American had to work for the WPA. To earn unemployment compensation, an American had to labor in private industry. To earn an old-age pension, an American had to hold jobs throughout much of his life. The requirement of work became the ultimate catalyst in the New Dealers' formula for addressing the material and psychological needs of unemployed Americans. Yet they achieved their goal at the cost of a "federal public welfare department empowered to assist the states and localities in developing integrated programs which would provide public assistance to all types of persons in need," as Josephine Brown confessed.[33] That deficiency was perceived as a gaping hole by social work reformers, who knew that millions of able-bodied, jobless Americans still depended on direct relief for survival.

The death of the FERA also destroyed the federal government's leverage on states to improve standards of public welfare administration. Reformers expected these federal powers to be increased; instead they were removed. Both the WPA and the Bureau of Public Assistance within the Social Security Board were reduced to seeking voluntary cooperation of state public welfare administrators, and that cooperation was not forthcoming.[34] Social work reformers once again confronted the specter of politicians manipulating welfare programs. In addition, the social work profession lost its hold on the official organization of public welfare administrators, the American Public Welfare Association. At the 1936 meetings, the APWA's director announced his group's separation from the National Conference of Social Work. A stunned Gertrude Springer attempted to decipher the APWA's motives for *Survey*'s readers; she identified several, including wrangling within the ranks of professional social workers, too much criticism of the New Deal, and too much radicalism. Indeed, the director's own remarks left the clear impression that social workers no longer held the respect of elected public welfare officials.[35]

In 1936, when Franklin Roosevelt ran for reelection, neither he nor his New Deal administration received the enthusiastic support of New York's social work leaders. There had been too much friction; too many disappointments. The battle

167

of rival ideologies, the deficiencies in the WPA's mode of work relief, the shortcomings of unemployment compensation and social security, the lost program of federal direct relief, the unfulfilled hope for a federally maintained welfare state, the new vulnerability of the social work profession, and the frustations of repeated failures to achieve a meeting of minds left New Yorkers disillusioned. Many of them—Paul Kellogg, Joanna Colcord, Mary Van Kleeck, William Matthews, Helen Hall, Gertrude Springer—criticized the administration harshly. Yet most never severed the personal bonds that tied them to New Dealers.

"This is an interesting time to be alive," Henry Street settlement's Lillian Wald wrote Governor Herbert Lehman in 1934. "My contact with the [Roosevelt] administration . . . makes for a renewal of belief in democracy."[36] In spite of deepening illness, she was inspired to begin a new volume of her autobiography; she intended "to show that the little Settlement groups do not limit the[ir] service or influence to neighborhoods," but achieve national recognition.[37] In December 1934, Wald visited the White House as an honored guest of the Roosevelts. "It was nice to see so many Henry Streeters in the Administration," she wrote Lehman, adding with pride that "at almost every turn Henry Street and devotion to it was expressed."[38] Two years later, at the thirty-fifth anniversary celebration of the United Neighborhood Houses, she happily noted how many former settlement residents were still being "properly exploited for the good of the country" by the New Deal.[39]

168

Paul Kellogg's relationships with New Dealers also continued to be friendly. "In the days of 'rugged individualism' nobody turned to us [*Survey*] for endorsement in seeking appointment at Washington," he wrote Harry Hopkins in 1935, "but that quickly changed with the New Deal."[40] Kellogg was once again engaged in the happy process of sending either Hopkins or Perkins a "who's who" letter of candidates for federal appointments. Such personal endorsements were a regular part of communication between Kellogg's office and Washington, and the New York affiliation shared by Kellogg, Hopkins, and Perkins remained a vital factor in their consideration. "No —not a New Yorker—, but Caroline McCready" of Illinois, Kellogg once exclaimed when offering an exception to their unspoken rule of advancing New Yorkers in a recommendation sent Frances Perkins.[41] Letters asking and offering advice continued as well, along with requests to bring new proposals to the attention of the president. "Will you act as our ambassador in the matter?" was a standard inquiry in Kellogg's letters to Hopkins and Perkins.[42]

Bonds of community were also maintained through the rituals of ceremonial celebration. Every annual meeting of the New York Conference of Social Work brought some New Dealers back into the fold; as featured speakers and recognized celebrities, they sought to strengthen bonds of affection, recalling earlier times and elaborating debts owed to fellow New Yorkers.[43] Anniversary celebrations also offered opportunities for renewing old attachments. At a 1936 luncheon commemorating the thirty-fifth anniversary of the United Neighborhood Houses, Harry Hopkins reviewed his service in the New York group and calculated his obligations to the people gathered before him. Perhaps all shared in the levity of the participants' discovery that they—the vicars of relief—had incurred a deficit of twenty-two dollars in honoring Hopkins, the bishop of relief![44] After the infirmities of old age began to diminish their activities, homages to leaders such as Lillian Wald and Homer Folks provided additional confirmation of old ties. William Hodson personally supervised the preparation of a massive scrapbook to honor Wald upon the occasion of the fortieth anniversary of Henry Street in 1933.[45] When Homer Folks celebrated his seventieth birthday in 1937, a host of New Yorkers and New Dealers turned out. Members of the committee sponsoring the festivities included the names Bruere, Dewson, Devine, Hodson, Kellogg, Lee, Wald, Lehman, and Wagner. Two former governors, Hughes and Smith, and a governor become president, Roosevelt, sent telegrams and personal notes.[46]

Whatever their disagreements, New York's reformers

169

and their New Deal colleagues had much to be proud of: a United States Employment Service, a WPA that provided work relief, a federally inspired, state-based scheme of unemployment compensation, a federal-state system of categorical assistance for dependent persons, and a federal insurance plan of old-age pensions. By 1936, the component parts of the New Deal's program to deal with urban, industrial joblessness had come together, fulfilling many of the expectations, although not all the dreams, of New York's social work leaders. It stood as a masterful accomplishment. Moreover, professional social workers from New York were in charge of that program: the USES's W. Frank Persons, the WPA's Harry Hopkins, the Department of Labor's Frances Perkins, the Social Security Board's Molly Dewson, and Jane Hoey, who left the Welfare Council of New York City to direct the SSA's Bureau of Public Assistance. "We have had, I think, a common objective in which we felt a moral purpose," Frances Perkins told Paul Kellogg when she retired from public office in 1945, "and the cooperative effort has therefore been of great constructive benefit." Thanking Kellogg for his years of service in that effort, she pledged herself anew to "any of the projects you may be carrying on in this common objective."[47] Kellogg responded by listing the achievements of their mutual enterprise and by noting the members of the New York group who contributed to their successes. "Surely, there's enough of them to keep you and Senator Wagner and Harry Hopkins and others who have borne such constructive parts busy the rest of your natural lives just counting them over like beads."[48] Wald, Folks, Hodson, Simkhovitch, Matthews, Devine, Dewson—the principle of personal as well as professional attachments was never stated more clearly; it possessed the authority of a religious mystique.

The
American
way
of
welfare

14

To claim that the experience of New Yorkers accounts for the welfare programs enacted by the New Deal is like asking a pyramid's tip to balance its base. Yet no other group of social workers held as many key leadership positions as New Yorkers. No other contributed as consistently to the reforms of that era. No other partook of historical circumstances that led as logically from city to state to nation. New Yorkers made substantive achievements at all three levels of government, and the terms "New Yorker," "social worker," "reformer," and "New Dealer" became nearly interchangeable in the lexicon of American welfare politics during the 1930s.[1] The New Yorkers who became New Dealers set in place a welfare state that perpetuated a dualism: it embraced collective institutions as the means of serving the needs of millions of people, while directing those institutions toward the end of keeping each individual employable and committed to a free enterprise economy.

Social workers won their war for the minds of America's unemployed millions. Yet no revolution marked the 1930s; no social upheaval brought the jobless masses to a higher estate. In fact, it is questionable that a war occurred at all. Certainly New York's social work leaders never feared the unemployed as potential revolutionaries. The social quiet of the Depression's early winters convinced them that the masses sought no class justice for themselves. They were leaderless, according to Lillian Wald, while Paul Kellogg thought them apathetic.[2] Like most intellectuals of their time, social workers detected an unwavering conservatism in the American people, including people without jobs.[3] Even though some political radicals organized protest marches and Unemployed Councils, most jobless Americans blamed themselves for their plight instead of assaulting capitalism for its failures.[4] Historians, too, have bent increasingly toward an interpretation that credits the New Deal's reforms as essentially conservative achievements.[5] Visions of state socialism and the rumblings of a "Red Decade" play only a small role in recent accounts of the Great Depression. Even leaders of business corporations are now perceived as significant contributors to the New Deal's welfare programs.[6] Having never been threatened, either by the masses or by the reformers, American capitalism could scarcely have been overthrown.

Social workers proposed modest changes for their society, but they were hardly conservatives. They were heirs of a social gospel movement who took to heart its new ethic of social justice. When leaders called for relief benefits that would sustain an adequate standard of living for the unemployed, they were demanding that society alter its ways. When they called upon businessmen to take responsibility for unemployment, they were demanding a changed economic order that would remove the burden of joblessness from the backs of helpless individuals. When they called upon society to use its power in legislating protective programs, they were renouncing piecemeal, voluntary actions. They were inheritors of the Progressive Movement, and they expected to create a different America from the ruggedly individualistic but also callous society of the nineteenth century.

Yet reformers were also descendants of a nineteenth-century middle class that valued autonomy in a community's

172

affairs, the holding of private property, an ethic of work, and individual enterprise. Like their parents, they believed each community should take care of its own. New Deal programs that offered matching grants as an inducement to increase community financing of relief services and which left decisions about the quality of those services in the hands of local officials underscored the reformers' commitment to preserve local prerogatives. Social workers also valued private property, as did their parents. New Deal programs funded through worker contributions *before* unemployment or retirement demonstrate the reformers' propensity to avoid direct taxes on property and income. Similarly, social workers trusted the work ethic; it was work that provided benefits in the form of earned wages, compensation, and pensions. Finally, social workers, like their parents before them, believed in individual enterprise. Most New Deal unemployment programs rested on the principle of self-help, and several used inducements to encourage jobless people to demonstrate their initiative by getting off relief rolls. Reformers saw their welfare programs as instruments to perpetuate productive individualism. There were dissenters, of course. In 1934 a splinter group of New York social workers founded a radical journal, *Social Work Today*, and demanded national programs administered by federal officials, funded by heavy taxes on wealth, and granted to all jobless Americans without regard to work or need.[7] Mary Van Kleeck and Harry Lurie joined this group as figureheads, but most New York leaders in social work stuck—sometimes reluctantly—with the New Deal's conservative ways.

Social workers were not chained culturally either by worship of their ancestors' values or by identification with the middle class. They rejected the Victorian world with its moral judgments of personal good and evil. Their New York City—which served as their laboratory for America—was less provincial and less given to assessments of moral right and wrong than the socially orthodox, Protestant communities from which they came. Nor did they submit to middle-class notions of success and failure: no measure of personal thrift, sobriety, industriousness, and respectability, they knew, could save the individual if the institutions in which his life was embedded collapsed. Every jobless person might be as worthy as his employed neighbor; the difference between them was a matter of circumstances that neither could control alone.

If the unemployed were judged no different than Americans who held jobs, what help did they need to survive the Great Depression? There were material needs, of course, but that was not all. Jobless Americans needed proof that their own middle-class ways were valued. Thus, the unemployed wanted work, some indicators of personal merit, and renewed opportunities for individual advancement. In dealing with morale, social workers moved beyond simple codes of middle-class morality and even transcended the old Progressive preoccupation with social justice.

As the titles of their articles and speeches demonstrated repeatedly, reformers were seeking a distinctive "American Way," "American Approach," or "American Idea" of welfare. Local fiscal responsibility and local administrative discretion were important: social workers hoped to retain a spirit of neighborly concern within the nation's communities, and they wanted local officials to be free in meeting peculiar welfare problems. Working within the limits of an ongoing capitalist economy was also important. Businessmen could not be expected to forego profits, but they could be induced to make their operations more efficient, especially if they had to pay part of the cost of the unemployment they caused. On the other hand, government could not interfere with free labor and free markets, so public programs could neither draw workers from the private sector nor produce goods and services that would compete with private enterprise. The "American Way" also implied something better than subsistence levels of material assistance. Americans required more than food, clothing, and shelter; they expected some protection of their property, some educational and recreational opportunities, and freedom to purchase some "luxuries" such as cigarettes, beer, and even pretty hats. Yet the unemployed must not become content with their lot.

The psychological context of welfare programs was crucial in stimulating the jobless individual's return to private enterprise. Reformers annexed the concerns of psychiatric caseworkers, who had campaigned for the mental health of the individual throughout the 1920s, but substituted their own *ad hoc* model of psychological health and embedded it in an institutional framework for action. They created welfare programs that reinforced notions of social status, competitive merit, and individual accomplishment. Thus, retired persons on social security pensions received benefits proportionate to their separate contributions as workers. Skilled mechanics on WPA projects earned more than their equally unemployed, but unskilled co-workers. Jobless people earning unemployment compensation received amounts commensurate with the value of their labor to their former employers.

The reformers' psychological model drew explicitly upon the male American's traditional role of family provider. If his function as worker was perpetuated, if his sense of status was preserved, and if his obligations to family were met, then his family's mental health would accompany his own. Women also worked, but the New Deal largely ignored them. Survivors' benefits for social security pensions were tacked on to that program in 1939, while work relief programs such as the WPA never absorbed a due portion of the nation's jobless female workers.[8] Eleanor Roosevelt justifiably lamented that women were often overlooked by relief administrators. "They are so apt to forget us," she wrote Harry Hopkins,[9] and there is justice to the recent charge that the New Deal pressed women back into the home and their "proper place" as subordinates to men.[10]

Hopkins always promised to return men who were employable to private industry. In fact, the reformers defined employability according to the requirements of modern industry. Since the beginnings of the industrial revolution, business managers had been struggling with the recalcitrant ways of rural

Americans and immigrants from peasant societies, none of whom were accustomed to the disciplines and routines of an industrial environment.[11] By taking over the terms of work as defined by private industry—the prescribed length of a working day and week, the division of labor into different levels of skill, the specialization of jobs, and the payment of prevailing wages for different kinds of work—New Deal work relief programs perpetuated the disciplining process begun by businessmen. Even the provisions of the Social Security Act, which depended on contributions made because of steady work in private companies, implicitly emphasized the requirements of a modern industrial order.

All labor was valuable to private employers, but not equally so. Both women and blacks endured the inequity of being "first fired and last hired," which limited their ability to qualify for unemployment compensation and old-age pension programs. Women faced special difficulties, perhaps because their labor was considered temporary and their earnings regarded as mere supplements to male income. Certainly the New Deal's reformers did not treat women as an integral part of the labor force. Minorities such as blacks were neglected in different ways. Black Americans in the South were still rooted in an agricultural economy, and elsewhere were minimally absorbed into the industrial economy. WPA projects in the southern states actually gave many blacks their first contact with industrial discipline, but that transition was marred by segregation and social discrimination. Often blacks neither worked alongside whites nor earned the same wages for the same work. Meanwhile, blacks in industrial states suffered from their low status in the labor force: New Deal work relief programs afforded them the most menial jobs and meanest pay because they were unskilled.[12] Regardless of the intentions of New Dealers, who wanted programs to operate equally, the impact of the New Deal was frequently discriminatory.

One group, moreover, the nation's unemployables, never received constructive attention from New Dealers. They were

176

perceived as different than employables, in some cases because they were unable to work physically and in other cases because they were unfit psychologically. The Social Security Act established special categories of programs for the blind, dependent children, and certain others, but the psychologically incapable were treated like a pariah class. New Dealers shunted paupers, beggars, and n'er-do-wells back to the states and the auspices of local services in 1935. Only because the demands of unemployment became so overwhelming did unemployables receive benefits such as the distribution of relief in cash. Otherwise they might have been utterly overlooked. Psychological illnesses, reformers apparently assumed, could not be cured by welfare programs designed for workers whose behavior conformed to middle-class, industrial expectations. If unemployables got lost in the shuffle, their plight was of no paramount concern to New Dealers, because the war for welfare was being waged to protect and preserve productive individualism.

The analogy of war was used freely during the Great Depression. Americans saw themselves as fighting a war against human misery, against a capitalist economic system gone awry, against a political system that had served the interests of property and wealth too extensively, and against dead values that no longer served current needs.[13] In measuring the success of the New Deal, historians ask: Did New Dealers ameliorate suffering? Did they restructure capitalism? Did they make politics more democratic? Did they posit new values? Even though their answers tend to be equivocal, historians usually emphasize the affirmative. Moreover, they tend to measure the easily measured. Obviously, the New Deal spent unprecedented sums on welfare programs, passed numerous laws to make capitalist institutions more responsive to human needs, brought new groups into the political process, and substituted collective for formerly individualistic values. Budgets, legislative records, election returns, and rhetoric demonstrate those results.[14] But the war that social workers saw themselves as fighting—the war for the psychological health of jobless Americans—does not easily yield to statistics and graphs. Nor can historians measure the effect of what might have happened, but did not: that is, an absolute collapse of morale. Even during the Depression's grimmest winters, Americans refused to yield faith in the nation's institutions and values. The unemployed revealed the tenacity of their faith by holding themselves responsible for their joblessness. Their very capacity to endure makes it impossible to assess how much the social workers actually achieved.

Social work reformers were not oblivious to issues other than the psychology of unemployment. They knew that the New Deal's actions offered a range of responses to the Depression. Frances Perkins favored an emphasis on economics, on the stimulation of economic activity by supporting consumers' incomes.[15] Molly Dewson immersed herself in the politics of the era, looking for new coalitions of interest groups that might advance desired legislation.[16] Harry Hopkins concentrated on the psychological dynamics of welfare programs until 1938, when he began to stress their economic impact as well.[17] Like their president, the New Deal's social workers assumed that "good politics" involved a combination of imperatives—good economics, good vote-getting, and good psychology. Social workers were compromisers, too. The "conference method" of which Perkins spoke so frequently suggested their willingness to achieve consensus with all groups and interests—businessmen, labor union organizers, the unemployed poor, consumers, the owners of property. Their conservatism derived, in part, from their belief that democracy depended upon consent for its vitality. Like Franklin Roosevelt, they did not believe in a politics of conflict and confrontation.

Was the New Deal conservative or liberal? In its welfare programs, it was usually both. As one historian put it, "America is a welfare state that has acquired a universal reputation as the arch-defender of the free enterprise system."[18] His statement was deliberately paradoxical, and it was intended to highlight the difference between America's welfare state and those elsewhere. Yet the observation is hardly as paradoxical as it first appears, because social workers elected to build their welfare state on the foundation of a free enterprise economy. "Our aim," Harry Hopkins frankly revealed, is "to supply to industry as many physically strong, mentally alert, skilled workers as we can." Government programs were never intended to be an exact "replica of the outside business world," because it was in that world that the unemployed had to reclaim their full measure of productive individualism.[19] In a balancing act characteristic of the New Deal Era, social workers tried "to live by contrasting rules of the game," as sociologist Robert S. Lynd put it in 1939.[20] Their goal—helping the individual retain his status in the nation's social and economic environment—was essentially conservative, but their means—the collective institutional instruments for attaining that goal—were liberal. Indeed, the commitment of government to programs that dealt with the state of mind of the American people represented a major institutional development of the Depression Era. If the accomplishments of social work leaders were streaked with ambivalence, it was an ambivalence that typified all the major reforms of their time.

179

Notes

Preface

1. Frances Perkins, *The Roosevelt I Knew* (New York, 1946), pp. 23, 26, 108, and *passim.*

2. "The Reminiscences of Frances Perkins," vol. 3 (1955), p. 132, in the Oral History Collection of Columbia University. Part 2 is rich in material about the social work group in New York.

3. Frances Perkins to Paul Kellogg, Aug. 2, 1945, Survey Papers (Social Welfare History Archives, Minneapolis).

4. Clarke A. Chambers, *Seedtime of Reform: American Social Service and Social Action, 1918–1933* (Minneapolis, 1963), pp. 260–261. See also Bernard Bellush, *Franklin D. Roosevelt as Governor of New York* (New York, 1955) and Frank Freidel, *Franklin D. Roosevelt: The Triumph* (Boston, 1956) for analysis of New York programs that influenced federal legislation during the New Deal era.

5. Thomas Bender, *Community and Social Change in America* (New Brunswick, 1978), pp. 121–123.

6. John F. McClymer, "The Study of Community and the 'New' Social History," *Journal of Urban History* 7 (Nov. 1980): 108.

1

1. For a detailed discussion of biographical data on the lives of fifty New York leaders see William W. Bremer, "New York City's Family of Social Servants and the Politics of Welfare: A Prelude to the New Deal, 1928–1933" (Ph. D. diss., Stanford University, 1973), pp. 18–38.

Scholars have disagreed in their assessments of social workers and their welfare reforms. Frances Piven and Richard Cloward, for example, imply that social workers were agents of the capitalist elite, who tried to "regulate the poor" by conceding just enough charity and state aid to quell violent disorder. Others describe them as humanitarians who reconstructed institutions in order to afford the poor greater economic security. John Buenker gives them credit for cooperative ventures undertaken with the elected representatives of the urban, immigrant working class that produced a responsible welfare state. The humanitarian aspects of reform have been emphasized in studies by Clarke Chambers, Robert Bremner, Allen Davis, and Walter Trattner. Roy Lubove integrates the dualism of social workers' careers when he uses the label "professional altruists" to identify both the authoritarian and humanitarian elements in their thoughts and actions. The views of each of these scholars have influenced the analysis put forth in this book.

See Frances Fox Piven and Richard A. Cloward, *Regulating the Poor: The Functions of Public Welfare* (New York, 1971), pp. 3–8, 22–41, 80–117. Their *Poor People's Movements: Why they Succeed, How they Fail* (New York, 1979), pp. 76–92, makes the same argument. John D. Buenker (*Urban Liberalism and Progressive Reform* [New York, 1973], pp. 198–239 and *passim*) draws on the work of his mentor, J. Joseph Huthmacher, the author of "Urban Liberalism and the Age of Reform," *Mississippi Valley Historical Review*, XLIX (Sept. 1962), pp. 231–241. See also Clarke A. Chambers, *Seedtime of Reform: American Social Service and Social Action, 1918–1933* (Minneapolis, 1963) and *Paul U. Kellogg and the Survey: Voices for Social Welfare and Social Justice* (Minneapolis, 1971); Robert H. Bremner, *From the Depths: The Discovery of Poverty in the United States* (New York, 1956): Allen F. Davis, *Spearheads for Reform: The Social Settlements and the Progressive Movement* (New York, 1967); Walter I. Trattner, *Homer Folks: Pioneer in Social Welfare* (New York, 1968) and *From Poor Law to Welfare State: A History of Social Welfare in America* (New York, 1974); and Roy Lubove, *The Professional Altruist: The Emergence of Social Work as a Career, 1880–1930* (Cambridge, 1965), pp. 18–19, 35, 84, 105–108, 116, 121–122, 157–158. Otis L. Graham, Jr., *An Encore for Reform: The Old Progressives and the New Deal* (New York, 1967), pp. 169–172, notes the continuity of social workers and welfare reforms that linked Progressivism to the New Deal.

2. "The Reminiscences of Bruno Lasker" (1956), p. 165, in the Oral History Collection of Columbia University.

3. The literature on progressivism and politics in New York is vast. A concise treatment of the accord reached between social workers and public officials is in Allen F. Davis, "Settlement Workers in Politics, 1890–1914," *The Review of Politics* 26 (1964): 505–517.

4. See Arnold S. Rosenberg, "The New York Reformers of 1914: A Profile," *New York History* 50 (1969): 187–206; and Donald A. Ritchie, "The Gary Committee: Businessmen, Progressives, and Unemployment in New York City, 1914–1915," *The New York Historical Society Quarterly* 57 (1973): 327–347. For a report on the plan see *Survey* 33 (1914): 329–330.

5. "The Reminiscences of Frances Perkins," vol. 3 (1955), p. 144, in the Oral History Collection of Columbia University.

6. See Hace Sorel Tishler, *Self-Reliance and Social Security, 1870–1917* (Port Washington, 1971), and Paul T. Ringenbach, *Tramps and Reformers, 1873–1916: The Discovery of Unemployment in New York* (Westport, 1973).

7. Bruno Lasker to Albert Kennedy, June 1, 1931, Notebooks, vol. 8 (1931), Bruno Lasker Papers (Columbia University Library, New York City).

8. Perkins, "Reminiscences," 3:132.

9. Josephine Goldmark, *Impatient Crusader: Florence Kelley's Life Story* (Urbana, 1953), pp. 68–69.

10. See Stuart D. Brandes, *American Welfare Capitalism, 1880–1940* (Chicago, 1976), pp. 135–141 and *passim*.

11. Paul Kellogg, "Pittsburgh, Essen and Manchester," *Survey Graphic* 63 (Nov. 1, 1929): 178.

12. William Hodson, "Community Planning for Social Welfare," National Conference of Social Work, *Proceedings*, 1929 (Chicago, 1930), p. 496.

13. William Hodson to Lillian Wald, March 30, 1926, Henry Street Settlement Papers (Columbia University Library).

14. William Hodson, "Is Social Work Professional? A Re-examination of the Question," National Conference of Social Work, *Proceedings*, 1925 (Chicago, 1925), p. 631.

15. Paul Kellogg and Mary Ross, "Social Work at the Golden Gate," *Survey* 63 (Aug. 15, 1929): 516.

16. William H. Matthews, *Adventures in Giving* (New York, 1939), p. 146.

17. See Paul Kellogg to Senator James Couzens, March 22, 1928, with attached memorandum, Survey Papers (Social Welfare History Archives, Minneapolis).

18. Homer Folks, "Social Engineering," Address, Nov. 7, 1928, MS, Homer Folks Papers (Columbia University School of Social Work Library, New York City).

2

1. See, for example, Mary Kingsbury Simkhovitch, *Here Is God's Plenty: Reflections on American Social Advance* (New York, 1949), pp. 141–142.

2. Review of Alfred E. Smith, *Up to Now: An Autobiography*, by Paul Kellogg, *Survey Graphic* 63 (Nov. 1, 1929): 159.

3. [Anne Geddes, secretary to Lillian Wald] to Henry Moskowitz, Oct. 19, 1926, Henry Street Settlement Papers (Columbia University Library, New York City). See also, Lillian Wald to Harold Riegelman, Nov. 19, 1926, Henry Street Papers.

4. Porter R. Lee, "The Future of Professional Social Work," [1926], in Porter R. Lee, *Social Work as Cause and Function and Other Papers* (New York, 1937), p. 142.

5. William Hodson, "Social Workers and Politics," *Survey* 63 (Nov. 15, 1929): 199. Italics mine.

6. Mary Simkhovitch, "Are Social-Settlers Debarred from Political Work?" Address, MS, Mary Simkhovitch Papers (Schlesinger Library, Cambridge).

7. *Ibid.*

8. Ralph Pumphrey has argued that the politics of social workers has not divided along ideological lines. Instead their different tendencies have mixed in practice, so "familiar dichotomies [such as] conservative and liberal, public and private, treatment and prevention, or services to individuals as against services to the community at large" have had little effect on political choices. The political behavior of New Yorkers from 1928 through 1936 confirms his thesis, even though some ideological divisions did appear. See Ralph E. Pumphrey, "Compassion and Protection: Dual Motivations in Social Welfare," *Social Service Review* 33 (March 1959); 23 and *passim*.

9. See below, Chapter 13.

10. "The Reminiscences of Lawson Purdy" (1948), p. 41, in the Oral History Collection of Columbia University.

11. Otis L. Graham, Jr., *An Encore for Reform: The Old Progressives and the New Deal* (New York, 1967), pp. 107, 109, 167–170, 197.

12. See Matthew and Hannah Josephson, *Al Smith: Hero of the Cities; A Political Portrait Drawing on the Papers of Frances Perkins* (Boston, 1969), pp. 1–7, 101–103, 113–144, 194–197, 203, 222–224, 237–239, 277–278, 287–288, 323–331, 352, 388–392, 415, for materials on Smith's relationship to social workers and on his welfare policies. Oscar Handlin, *Al Smith and His America* (Boston, 1958) is also useful.

13. Kellogg, Review of *Up to Now*, p. 159.

14. See Simkhovitch, *Here Is God's Plenty*, pp. 92–152.

15. Devine's statement is quoted by the *New York Times*, Sept. 9, 1928, 7:1.

16. Eleanor Roosevelt to Lillian Wald, Aug. 7, 1928, and [Anne Geddes, secretary to Lillian Wald] to Eleanor Roosevelt, Aug. 9, 1928, Lillian D. Wald Papers (New York Public Library, New York City).

17. Lillian Wald and John Elliott to Paul Kellogg, Sept. 29, 1928, Survey Papers (Social Welfare History Archives, Minneapolis).

18. The statement is quoted by Edward T. Devine, Address, Oct. 12, MS, Survey Papers.

19. Progressive League to Paul Kellogg, Sept. 15, 1928, and Paul Kellogg to Frederick Howe, Sept. 24, 1928, Survey Papers.

20. Mary Dewson, "An Aid to the End," vol. 1, pp. 4–7, MS, Mary Dewson Papers (Schlesinger Library).

21. Simkhovitch, *Here Is God's Plenty*, p. 142; Josephson, *Al Smith*, pp. 388–392.

22. Lillian Wald to Harry Hopkins, Oct. 4, 1928, Wald Papers.

23. Lillian Wald to Paul Kellogg, Oct. 31, 1928, Survey Papers.

24. D. M. McDonald to Lillian Wald, n.d., Wald Papers.

25. Mildred Duncan to Lillian Wald, Oct. 22, 1928, Wald Papers.

26. Lillian Wald to J. Ramsey MacDonald, Nov. 7, 1928, Wald Papers.

27. Republican National Committee, "Noted Social Worker Endorses Hoover," press release, Oct. 1928, Survey Papers.

28. Edward T. Devine, Address, Oct. 12, 1928, MS, Survey Papers.

29. Joanna Colcord to Lillian Wald, Oct. 4, 1928, Wald Papers.

30. For recent assessments of Hoover's progressive philosophy of government see Murray N. Rothbard, "The Hoover Myth," in James Weinstein and David Eakins, eds., *For a New America: Essays in History and Politics from "Studies on the Left," 1959–1967* (New York, 1970), pp. 162–179; Joan Hoff Wilson, *Herbert Hoover: Forgotten Progressive* (Boston, 1975), pp. 54–121; and David Burner, *The Politics of Provincialism: The Democratic Party in Transition, 1918–1932* (New York, 1968), pp. 193–197, and *Herbert Hoover: A Public Life* (New York, 1979).

31. Paul Kellogg to Frances Perkins, March 29, 1930, Survey Papers.

32. Lillian Wald to Mary Smith, Sept. 14, 1928, Wald Papers.

33. Lillian Wald to J. Ramsay MacDonald, Nov. 7, 1928, Waid Papers.

34. Fred Johnson to John Elliott, Oct. 2, 1928, Wald Papers.

35. Mrs. K. L. Van Wyck to Lillian Wald, Oct. 5, 1928, Wald Papers.

36. John Hall to John Elliott, Oct. 2, 1928, Wald Papers.

37. See Allan J. Lichtman, *Prejudice and the Old Politics: The Presidential Election of 1928* (Chapel Hill, 1979).

38. Lillian Wald to J. Ramsay MacDonald, Nov. 7, 1928, Wald Papers.

39. William Hodson, "Social Workers and Politics," p. 199.

40. See *Survey* 63 (Nov. 15, 1929): 193.

41. Paul Kellogg to Frances Perkins, March 29, 1930, Survey Papers. During the campaign, Eleanor Roosevelt stressed the same idea. See Eleanor Roosevelt, Untitled Speech, [1928], MS, Eleanor Roosevelt Papers (Franklin D. Roosevelt Library, Hyde Park).

42. Kellogg, Review of *Up to Now*, p. 159.

43. Paul Kellogg to Frances Perkins, March 29, 1930, Survey Papers.

44. See Burner, *Herbert Hoover*, pp. 72–95, 114–130, 193–194. Burner does not make this point part of his discussion, but he shows how Hoover and "his people" dominated relief efforts.

3

1. Lillian Wald, *Windows on Henry Street* (Boston, 1934), p. 227.

2. I. M. Rubinow, "Can Private Philanthropy Do It?" MS, Survey Papers (Social Welfare History Archives, Minneapolis).

3. Paul Kellogg to Arthur Kellogg, Nov. 23, 1928, and Arthur Kellogg to I. M. Rubinow, March 12, 1929, Survey Papers. Less than two years later, Rubinow wrote Arthur Kellogg that "everybody is now talking about public relief and the inadequacy of private philanthropy. Such is the fate of the prophet." I. M. Rubinow to Arthur Kellogg, Nov. 20, 1930, Survey Papers.

4. Welfare Council of New York City, Committee on the Emergency Financing of Social Work, "Report," July 8, 1932, Herbert H. Lehman Papers (Franklin D. Roosevelt Library, Hyde Park).

5. Homer Folks, "Social Engineering," Address, Nov. 7, 1928, MS, Homer Folks Papers (Columbia University School of Social Work Library, New York City).

6. Beulah Amidon to William Leiserson, Jan. 24, 1928, Survey Papers.

7. *Survey* 60 (Aug. 15, 1928): 506; *Survey* 62 (June 15, 1929): 352.

8. "The Reminiscences of Frances Perkins," vol. 2 (1955), p. 90, in the Oral History Collection of Columbia University.

9. Paul Kellogg to Jane Addams, April 17, 1928, Survey Papers.

10. Paul Kellogg to Louis D. Brandeis, March 12, 1928, Survey Papers.

11. William Leiserson, "Unemployment, 1929," *Survey Graphic* 62 (April 1, 1929): 9.

12. See John A. Fitch, "What to Read About Unemployment," *Survey Graphic* 62 (April 1, 1929): 70.

13. See Albert U. Romasco, *The Poverty of Abundance: Hoover, the Nation, the Depression* (New York, 1965), pp. 3–6 and *passim*.

14. *Survey* 60 (Aug. 15, 1928): 506; Welfare Council, Board of Directors, "Summary of Minutes," Jan. 28, 1929, Henry Street Settlement Papers (Columbia University Library, New York City).

15. *Survey Graphic* 61 (Jan. 1, 1929): 444–445.

16. Paul Kellogg to Porter Lee, Feb. 8, 1929, Survey Papers. See also Paul Kellogg, "Unemployment and Progress," National Conference of Social Work, *Proceedings*, 1929 (Chicago, 1930), pp. 80–102.

17. *Survey* 63 (Nov. 15, 1929): 195–196.

18. Stella Koenig to Herbert Lehman, Dec. 4, 1929, Lehman Papers (FDRL).

19. [William Matthews], "Report on Park Work," MS, William H. Matthews Papers (New York Public Library, New York City).

20. *Survey* 64 (June 15, 1930): 272.

21. *Survey Graphic* 63 (March 1, 1930): 609.

22. Fitch is quoted by Mary Ross and Paul Kellogg, "New Beacons in Boston: The Fifty-Seventh National Conference of Social Work," *Survey* 64 (July 15, 1930): 343.

23. Beulah Amidon, "Some Plans for Steady Work," *Survey* 65 (Nov. 15, 1930): 202, 204; E. E. H. [Edward Eyre Hunt], "The President's Committee for Employment," *Survey* 65 (Feb. 15, 1931): 542–543.

24. Gertrude Springer, "The Burden of Mass Relief," *Survey* 65 (Nov. 15, 1930): 199, 201–202.

25. A. W. McMillen, "Taxes and Private Relief Funds," *Survey* 65 (Nov. 15, 1930): 209.

26. See "The Reminiscences of Lawson Purdy" (1948), pp. 42–43, in the Oral History Collection of Columbia University.

27. *Survey* 65 (Nov. 15, 1930): 196–197; *Survey* 65 (Dec. 15, 1930): 351; Springer, "The Burden of Mass Relief," pp. 201–202; Welfare Council, Executive Committee, "Summary of Minutes," Nov. 24, 1930, Henry Street Papers. Copies of the guides can be found in the Henry Street Papers.

28. Gertrude Springer, "Well Advertised Breadlines," *Survey* 65 (Feb. 15, 1931): 545.

29. Karl Hesley to Lillian Wald, Feb. 28, 1931, Henry Street Papers.

30. Springer, "Well Advertised Breadlines," p. 545.

31. *Survey* 65 (Dec. 15, 1930): 351. See also Lower East Side Community Council, Unemployment Committee, "Minutes," Oct. 30, 1930, Henry Street Papers.

32. Frances Perkins, *People at Work* (New York, 1934), p. 44.

33. Henry Street Settlement, "Report," [Feb. 1931?], and Karl Hesley to William Deegan, Feb. 18, 1931, Henry Street Papers; Karl Hesley to Herbert Lehman, Jan. 21, 1931, and Karl Hesley, "Report on Social Activities," March 14, 1932, MS, Lehman Papers (FDRL).

34. Lillian Wald to J. Ramsay MacDonald, Jan. 30, 1931, Lillian D. Wald Papers (New York Public Library).

35. William Hodson to Herbert Lehman, Dec. 20, 1930, and attached Memorandum, Franklin D. Roosevelt Papers (Franklin D. Roosevelt Library).

36. Lawson Purdy to Porter R. Lee, Oct. 31, 1930, Herbert Hoover Papers (Franklin D. Roosevelt Library).

37. Welfare Council, Coordinating Committee on Unemployment, Executive Committee, "Summary of Minutes," Dec. 10, 1930, Lehman Papers (FDRL).

38. Lillian Wald to Mrs. Herbert Crowley, Jan. 30, 1931, Wald Papers.

39. *The Bulletin of the Welfare Council of New York City*, 4 (April 1931): 1, 3.

40. William Hodson to Franklin D. Roosevelt, March 2, 1931, Lehman Papers (FDRL).

41. Welfare Council, Coordinating Committee on Unemployment, Executive Committee, "Summary of Minutes," March 17, 1931, Henry Street Papers.

42. Frank Taylor to Joseph McKee, March 16, 1931, Lehman Papers (FDRL).

43. Editorial signed by William Hodson, *The Bulletin of the Welfare Council of New York City* 4 (April 1931): 4.

44. Homer Folks, "Planning Work Relief," Address, June 25, 1931, MS, Folks Papers.

45. Porter R. Lee, "What Can Social Work Do in the Face of Industrial Depression?" *The Bulletin of the Welfare Council of New York City* 4 (June 1931): 5–6.

46. See Winthrop Aldrich to George Case, June 22, 1931, Lehman Papers (FDRL).

47. *Survey* 16 (May 15, 1931): 236.

4

1. Louis Brandeis to Paul Kellogg, March 11, 1928, Survey Papers (Social Welfare History Archives, Minneapolis).

2. "Steady Work as an Asset," [1928?], MS, Survey Papers.

3. See George Martin, *Madam Secretary: Frances Perkins* (Boston, 1976),

pp. 214–230. Perkins articulated her philosophy of cooperation with business leaders in *People at Work* (New York, 1934), pp. 270–281, and in *The Roosevelt I Knew* (New York, 1946), pp. 22–23.

4. "Steady Work as an Asset."

5. *Survey Graphic* 64 (April 1, 1930): 3.

6. Frances Perkins, "My Job," *Survey* 61 (March 15, 1929): 773.

7. See Clarke A. Chambers, *Paul U. Kellogg and the Survey: Voices for Social Welfare and Social Justice* (Minneapolis, 1971), pp. 219–220.

8. Berle had been a resident at Henry Street settlement and was a frequent speaker and visitor there. He was well known among social workers and often mentioned in their reminiscences. Moley's contacts with social workers have not been as widely acknowledged, but he also was a speaker at Henry Street settlement, and a letter from the Welfare Council's Jane Hoey indicates his involvement with social workers and their organizations. See Jane M. Hoey to Raymond Moley, Sept. 9, 1931, Raymond Moley Papers (Hoover Institute, Stanford).

9. Perkins, "My Job," p. 773.

10. Paul Kellogg to C. M. Bookman, Feb. 28, 1930, Survey Papers.

11. Paul Kellogg, "The Spread of Employment Planning," Report of the Annual Meeting of the Industrial Relations Association of Chicago, Jan. 12, 1931, MS, Paul U. Kellogg Papers (Social Welfare History Archives). As early as December 1929, Kellogg was delivering speeches on business stabilization and community action programs. See Paul Kellogg to James Couzens, Jan. 8, 1930, Survey Papers. For articles on those subjects, see Beulah Amidon, "Ivorydale: A Payroll That Floats," *Survey Graphic* 64 (April 1, 1930): 18–22, 56–57, 61, 64; Paul Kellogg, "Dayton Plans for Work," *Survey* 64 (April 15, 1930): 71–72; and Paul Kellogg, "Outflanking Unemployment," *Survey Graphic* 64 (May 1, 1930): 146–147.

12. "The Reminiscences of Frances Perkins," vol. 3 (1955), pp. 142, 166, in the Oral History Collection of Columbia University.

13. "Profits from Well-Being," *Survey* 62 (Oct. 15, 1929): 105.

14. "Reminiscences of Frances Perkins," vol. 3, p. 144.

15. Perkins is quoted by Paul Kellogg, "Outflanking Unemployment," p. 147.

16. *Ibid.*

17. Henry Bruere *et al.*, "The First State Program for Employment: The Report of the New York Committee on Stabilization of Industry for the Prevention of Unemployment," *Survey Graphic* 65 (Dec. 1, 1930): 257–260, 290–295.

18. Paul Kellogg, "Security Next," *Survey Graphic* 67 (Dec. 1, 1931): 238.

19. Bruere *et al.*, "The First State Program," pp. 257, 290, 292–293.

20. Paul Kellogg to Frances Perkins, Feb. 13, 1931, Survey Papers.

21. Frank Freidel, *Franklin D. Roosevelt: The Triumph* (Boston, 1956), pp. 86–87, 139, 184.

22. Perkins, *The Roosevelt I Knew*, pp. 54–60, 90—94, 100–108.

23. See Albert U. Romasco, *The Poverty of Abundance: Hoover, the Nation, the Depression* (New York, 1965), pp. 133–142.

24. Mary Van Kleeck, "Planning to End Unemployment," *Survey Graphic* 67 (March 1, 1932): 639.

25. "Notes on economic planning," May 16, 1931, MS, Survey Papers.

26. "Speech of the Hon. Franklin D. Roosevelt, Governor of the State of New York at Governors' Conference," June 30, 1930, MS, Franklin D. Roosevelt Papers (Franklin D. Roosevelt Library, Hyde Park).

27. Franklin Roosevelt to G. Hall Roosevelt, Feb. 24, 1931, Roosevelt Papers.

28. Much of the discussion that follows derives from studies made by other historians and is noted accordingly. Chapter 12 offers a more detailed analysis of social security reforms enacted by the New Deal.

29. See Ellis W. Hawley, *The Great War and the Search for a Modern Order: A History of the American People and Their Institutions, 1917–1933* (New York, 1979), pp. 96–98. Compensation programs and similar measures also had the effect of reducing labor turnover and inhibiting strikes, because workers were tied more closely to their employers.

30. Robert M. Ball, "Social Insurance and the Right to Assistance," *Social Service Review* 21 (Sept. 1947): 338.

31. See Hace Sorel Tishler, *Self-Reliance and Social Security, 1870–1917* (Port Washington, 1971), pp. 89, 100–103; Daniel Nelson, *Unemployment Insurance: The American Experience, 1915–1935* (Madison, 1969), pp. 6–13, 22–24.

32. See Roy Lubove, *The Struggle for Social Security: 1900–1935* (Cambridge, 1968), pp. 45–65, 164–169: Tishler, *Self-Reliance and Social Security*, pp. 108–141.

33. John A. Garraty, *Unemployment in History: Economic Thought and Public Policy* (New York, 1978), pp. 147–149; Nelson, *Unemployment Insurance*, pp. 22–24.

34. Frances Perkins, "Unemployment Insurance: An American Plan to Protect Workers and Avoid the Dole," *Survey Graphic* 67 (Nov. 1, 1931): 119.

35. *Survey* 61 (Feb. 15, 1929): 669.

36. *Survey* 61 (March 15, 1929): 782.

37. *Survey* 62 (Oct. 15, 1929): 68.

38. William Matthews, "The Duty of the State to the Old," *Survey* 63 (March 15, 1930): 701.

39. *Survey* 63 (March 15, 1930): 691.

40. *Ibid.*, pp. 691–692.

41. *Survey* 64 (May 15, 1930): 180.

42. Eleanor Roosevelt is quoted by Clarke A. Chambers, *Seedtime of Reform: American Social Service and Social Action, 1918–1933* (Minneapolis, 1963), p. 167.

43. See Paul Kellogg, "The World—Tomorrow—What is Coming in Social Relations," Address, Nov. 24, 1932, MS, and Paul Kellogg to Samuel Fels, April 10, 1933, Kellogg Papers.

44. Paul Kellogg, "The Spread of Economic Planning," MS, Kellogg Papers.

45. Paul Kellogg to Lucius Eastman, June 30, 1932, Survey Papers.

46. Ronald Radosh, "The Myth of the New Deal," in Roland Radosh and Murray N. Rothbard, eds., *A New History of Leviathan: Essays on the Rise of*

the American Corporate State (New York, 1972), pp. 156–159. Radosh's essay, pp. 146–187, describes the close collaboration that often existed between New Dealers and business leaders on several different New Deal measures.

47. Paul Kellogg to James Couzens, May 21, 1928, Survey Papers.

5

1. Homer Folks, "Home Relief in New York City: A Look Forward and Backward," Address, Dec. 11, 1933, MS, Henry Street Settlement Papers (Columbia University Library, New York City).

2. See Hace Sorel Tishler, *Self-Reliance and Social Security, 1870–1917* (Port Washington, 1971), pp. 4, 34–45, 55–63, and *passim.*

3. *Better Times: The Welfare Magazine* (Jan. 4, 1932): 1; 13 (Feb. 22, 1932): 1.

4. Harry L. Hopkins, "The War on Distress," in Howard Zinn, ed., *New Deal Thought* (Indianapolis, 1966), p. 152.

5. Josephine Chapin Brown, *Public Relief, 1929–1939* (New York, 1940), p. 223.

6. William Matthews to Harvey Gibson, Sept. 16, 1932, William H. Matthews Papers (New York Public Library, New York City).

7. William Matthews to Paul Kellogg, Feb. 5, 1932, Survey Papers (Social Welfare History Archives, Minneapolis).

8. *Ibid.*

9. Mary Dewson, "Panel Discussion of New Deal Policies and Agencies," Address, July 31, 1935, MS, Mary W. Dewson Papers (Franklin D. Roosevelt Library, Hyde Park).

10. A revealing exchange of letters between an unemployed New Yorker, the Governor's office, and New York City relief officials illustrates this point. See Louis Stroll to Franklin Roosevelt, Feb. 1, 1932; Henrietta Buchman to Dorothy Kenney, Feb. 15, 1932; and Dorothy Kenney to Guernsey Cross, Feb. 19, 1932, Franklin D. Roosevelt Papers (Franklin D. Roosevelt Library).

11. William Matthews to the Editor of the New York *Daily News*, April 10, 1935, Matthews Papers.

12. Hopkins is quoted by Gertrude Springer and Helen Baker, "Social Workers View Their World," *Survey* 71 (July 15, 1935): 200–201.

13. William Matthews, *Adventures in Giving* (New York, 1939), p. 230.

14. Franklin D. Roosevelt, "Proclamation," [Jan. 1932], Roosevelt Papers. FDR's statement drew extensively from a draft of a speech sent him by Jesse Straus, who served on the Temporary Emergency Relief Administration. See Jesse Straus to Franklin Roosevelt, Jan. 5, 1932, Roosevelt Papers.

15. See, for example, Helen Hall and Irene Hickok Nelson, "How Unemployment Strikes Home," *Survey Graphic* 72 (April 1, 1929): 86; and Helen Hall, "Shall We Stick to the American Dole?" *Survey Graphic* 65 (Jan. 1, 1931): 403. In *Documentary Expression and Thirties America* (New York, 1973), pp. 145–148, 156–159, William Stott analyses the "middle classness" that appeared in social workers' studies of the unemployed.

16. Harry Lurie to Elwood Street, Sept. 1, 1933, Harry L. Lurie Papers (Social Welfare History Archives).

17. Lillian Wald, *Windows on Henry Street* (Boston, 1934), p. 231.

18. Paul Kellogg to Lawson Purdy, Feb. 12, 1931, Survey Papers.

19. William Hodson to Paul Starrett, Jan. 16, 1939, Harry L. Hopkins Papers (Franklin D. Roosevelt Library); Welfare Council of New York City, Vocational Guidance and Family Service Sections, "Report to the Coordinating Committee on Agreements Reached at Three Joint Conferences on Work Relief," Revised, Sept. 21, 1932, Henry Street Papers.

20. Harry Hopkins, Untitled Address, March 14, 1936, MS, United Neighborhood Houses Papers (Social Welfare History Archives).

21. Much of the information about Matthews' life is taken from his autobiography, *Adventures in Giving*.

22. See John A. Garraty, *Unemployment in History: Economic Thought and Public Policy* (New York, 1978), pp. 59–61, 117–121.

23. C. N. Bliss to William Matthews, Dec. 26, 1930; [William Matthews], "Report on Park Work," [1930], MS; and William Matthews to Harvey D. Gibson, Feb. 24, 1932, Matthews Papers.

24. William H. Matthews, "The Job-Line That Cost $28 Million," *Survey* 69 (Nov. 15, 1933): 372.

25. These three stratagems and the reasoning behind them were offered as justifications for the state's movement toward the Temporary Emergency Relief Administration. See State Board of Social Welfare and State Charities Aid Association, "A Memorandum on Work as a Means of Providing Unemployment Relief," June 1931, Herbert H. Lehman Papers (Franklin D. Roosevelt Library).

26. The William H. Matthews Papers, which constitute only one box of materials, offer a rich resource for tracing the development of the EWB and work relief policies. Volumes 13–14 of *Better Times: The Welfare Magazine* provide regular reports on changes in New York practices. In addition, see Welfare Council, Vocational Guidance and Family Service Sections, Memorandum, Nov. 16, 1931, Henry Street Papers; Gertrude Springer, "The Job Line," *Survey Graphic* 65 (Feb. 1, 1931): 496–497; Welfare Council, Vocational Guidance and Family Service Sections, "Report to the Coordinating Committee on Agreements Reached at Three Joint Conferences on Work Relief," Revised, Sept. 21, 1932, Henry Street Papers; Louis Resnick, "A Twenty-Million-Dollar Investment in Men—and Stones," *Better Times: The Welfare Magazine* 14 (Jan. 2, 1933): 16–20; Homer Folks, "Planning Work Relief," Address, June 25, 1931, MS, Homer Folks Papers (Columbia University School of Social Work Library, New York City); and Matthews, "The Job-Line," pp. 371–373.

191

27. William Matthews, "A Day in Conferences," Dec. 13, 1931, MS Matthews Papers.

28. William Matthews to Grace Gosselin, Oct. 24, 1931, United Neighborhood Houses Papers.

29. William Matthews, "A Day in Conferences."

30. American Association for Labor Legislation, "Standard Recommendations for the Relief and Prevention of Unemployment," Pamphlet, [1930?],

Survey Papers. The pamphlet refers explicitly and approvingly to recommendations that came out of "the unemployment situation of 1914–1915" and "the
President's Conference on Unemployment" of 1921. For the probusiness slant
that New York's reformers took toward work relief programs in 1914, see
Donald A. Ritchie, "The Gary Committee: Businessmen, Progressives, and Unemployment in New York City, 1914–1915," *New York Historical Society Quarterly*
57 (Oct. 1973): 327–347; and Paul T. Ringenbach, *Tramps and Reformers, 1873–
1916: The Discovery of Unemployment in New York* (Westport, 1973), pp. 173–178.

 31. See Harry L. Hopkins, *Spending to Save: The Complete Story of Relief*
(New York, 1936), p. 163; Harry L. Hopkins, "Social Planning for the Future,"
Social Service Reivew 8 (Sept. 1934): 403; Hopkins, "The War on Distress,"
pp. 157–158.

 32. Matthews, *Adventures in Giving*, p. 226.

6

 1. Gertrude Springer, "The Challenge of Hard Times," *Survey* 66 (July
15, 1931): 380–385; Billikopf is quoted by Springer, p. 381.

 2. Henry Bruere to Franklin Roosevelt, July 27, 1931, Franklin D.
Roosevelt Papers (Franklin D. Roosevelt Library, Hyde Park).

 3. Henry Bruere to Franklin Roosevelt, Aug. 7, 1831, Roosevelt Papers.

 4. The Joint Committee on Unemployment Relief of the State Board
of Social Welfare and the State Charities Aid Association [Homer Folks, chair-
man], "The Unemployment Relief Situation in Forty-five New York Cities, Summary," Aug. 11, 1931, Roosevelt Papers.

 5. Homer Folks to Franklin Roosevelt, Aug. 14, 1931, Roosevelt Papers.

 6. Elsie Bond to Franklin Roosevelt, Aug. 14, 1931, Roosevelt Papers.

 7. Franklin D. Roosevelt, Untitled Address "To the Legislature (In Extraordinary Session)," Aug. 28, 1931, Roosevelt Papers.

 8. Gertrude Springer, "Where Is the Money Coming From?" *Survey* 67
(Oct. 15, 1931): 73; Gertrude Springer, "The Lever of State Relief," *Survey* 67
(Jan. 15, 1932): 407–410.

 9. Welfare Council of New York City, Committee on the Emergency
192 Financing of Social Work, "Report," July 8, 1932, Herbert H. Lehman Papers
(Franklin D. Roosevelt Library); *Better Times: The Welfare Magazine* 13 (Oct. 19,
1931): 2; *Survey* 67 (Oct. 15, 1931): 91; *Survey* 67 (Nov. 15, 1931): 179; Welfare
Council (signed by William Hodson), "How New York City's Funds for Relief are
Being Spent," MS, attached to William Hodson to Herbert Lehman, Dec. 14,
1931, Lehman Papers (FDRL).

 10. Lillian Wald to [Kendall Mussey], Oct. 5, 1931, Lillian D. Wald Papers (New York Public Library, New York City); *Better Times: The Welfare Magazine* 13 (Nov. 23, 1931): 1; (Jan. 11, 1932): 1; (Jan. 25, 1932): 4; (March 21,
1932): 1; and 14 (Feb. 27, 1933): 2.

 11. Lillian Wald to [Kendall Mussey], Oct. 5, 1931, Wald Papers.

 12. Welfare council, "Report," July 8, 1932; *Better Times: The Welfare
Magazine* 13 (Dec. 7, 1931): 22.

13. Lillian Wald to Harvey Gibson, Dec. 3, 1931, Henry Street Settlement Papers (Columbia University Library, New York City).

14. Lillian Wald to Mrs. Alfred Liebmann, Oct. 20, 1931, Wald Papers; Stella Koenig to Herbert Lehman, Nov. 16, 1932, Lehman Papers (FDRL); Lillian Wald to Harvey Gibson, Dec. 3, 1931, Henry Street Papers.

15. "The Importance of Recreation to the Unemployed," *Better Times: The Welfare Magazine* 13 (Dec. 7, 1931): 15, and (Oct. 19, 1931): 1. See also Judith Ann Trolander, *Settlement Houses and the Great Depression* (Detroit, 1975), pp. 15–16, 29–31, 68–76, 149–151.

16. "The Importance of Recreation," p. 15.

17. Gertrude Springer, "The Burden of Mass Relief," *Survey* 65 (Nov. 15, 1930): 199.

18. *Survey* 67 (Feb. 15, 1932): 517; United Neighborhood Houses, Conference Meeting, Jan. 14, 1932, United Neighborhood Houses Papers (Social Welfare History Archives, Minneapolis); Mary L. Shipman, "Headlines of 1932," *Better Times: The Welfare Magazine* 14 (Jan. 2, 1933): 13–15.

19. Shipman, "Headlines of 1932," pp. 13–15; Welfare Council, "Unemployment Relief in New York City," April 28, 1932, New York Public Library Special Collections.

20. Welfare Council, Committee on the Emergency Financing of Social Work, "Report," July 8, 1932, Lehman Papers (FDRL).

21. Stella Koenig to Herbert Lehman, April 21, 1932, Lehman Papers (FDRL).

22. William Matthews to Robert F. Wagner, May 13, 1932, William H. Matthews Papers (New York Public Library).

23. *Better Times: The Welfare Magazine* 13 (April 18, 1932): 1, and (April 25, 1932): 2.

24. Shipman, "Headlines of 1932," p. 13.

25. D. H. Holbrook, Luncheon conversation with Helen M. Crosby, [Notes], Oct. 15, 1931, National Social Welfare Assembly Papers (Social Welfare History Archives). In 1945, the National Social Work Council became the National Social Welfare Assembly.

26. D. H. Holbrook, Luncheon conversation with L. B. Swift and B. Y. Landis, [Notes], Oct. 19, 1931, and David H. Holbrook, "Federal Action on Unemployment," Memorandum, March 18, 1933, NSWA Papers.

27. D. H. Holbrook, Phone conversation with J. C. Colcord, [Notes], Oct. 15, 1931, NSWA Papers.

28. William Hodson, "An Open Letter to the President on Federal Relief Appropriations," reprinted in *Survey Graphic* 67 (Nov. 1, 1931): 144–145.

29. Steering Committee of the Social Work Conference on Federal Action, "Minutes," Nov. 29, 1931, NSWA Papers.

30. Linton Swift, "The Social Work Conference on Federal Action," [Statement of Principles], Nov. 5, 1931, MS, Harry L. Lurie Papers (Social Welfare History Archives).

31. Steering Committee of the Social Work Conference on Federal Action, "Minutes," Dec. 13, 1931, Lurie Papers.

32. Steering Committee of the Social Work Conference on Federal Action, "Minutes," Dec. 23, 1931, Lurie Papers.

33. West and Swift are quoted in *Survey Graphic* 67 (Feb. 1, 1932): 463–464. By the time the social workers testified in Washington, the steering committee was affiliated with the American Association of Social Workers, calling itself now the Committee on Federal Action on Unemployment. The AASW's Walter West was the key figure in laying the groundwork for hearings before the subcommittee. See David Holbrook to George Rabinoff, Dec. 23, 1932, NSWA Papers.

34. Paul Kellogg, "Relief Needs; Relief Resources," *Survey Graphic* 67 (Feb. 1, 1932): 463–464.

35. [Joanna C. Colcord], "Preliminary Report to the Conference on Federal Relief, by the Sub-committee on Methods of Administration," [Nov. 1931], MS, Lurie Papers. See *Survey* 67 (Jan. 15, 1932): 425, and (Feb. 15, 1932): 516.

36. See Jordan A. Schwarz, *The Interregnum of Despair: Hoover, Congress, and the Depression* (Urbana, 1970), pp. 151–157, 161–162, and *passim*.

37. Joanna Colcord, "Social Work and the First Federal Relief Programs," National Conference of Social Work, *Proceedings*, 1943 (New York, 1943), pp. 390–391.

38. Harry L. Lurie, "Statement of the American Association of Social Workers: Operation of the Federal Relief Plan," [July 1932], MS, Lurie Papers.

39. Gertrude Springer, "The Fighting Spirit in Hard Times," *Survey* 68 (June 15, 1932): 260–271. Hodson, Grace Marcus, and Davies are quoted by Springer on pp. 263, 267, 268.

7

1. Homer Folks, "The Law and the Facts," Address, Nov. 5, 1931, MS, Homer Folks Papers (Columbia University School of Social Work Library, New York City).

2. See Walter I. Trattner, *Homer Folks: Pioneer in Social Welfare* (New York, 1968), pp. 1–38, 115–119, 228–240.

3. Homer Folks, "Public Outdoor Relief—Forecast and Retrospect," *Better Times: The Welfare Magazine* 13 (April 11, 1932): 1–2; Homer Folks, "Remarks," April 29, 1932, MS, Folks Papers.

4. *Survey* 65 (Oct. 15, 1930): 88; (Nov. 15, 1930): 196; (Dec. 15, 1930): 351; *The Bulletin of the Welfare Council of New York City* 4 (Jan. 1931): 1–2; Welfare Council of New York City, Coordinating Committee on Unemployment, "Release," [Nov. 1930], Henry Street Settlement Papers (Columbia University Library, New York City).

5. Lower East Side Community Council, Unemployment Committee, "Minutes," Oct. 30, 1930, and "Minutes," Nov. 10, 1930, Henry Street Papers.

6. Homer Folks, "Notes on Capes Course, Albany, N. Y.," Dec. 4, 1930, MS, Folks Papers.

7. P. F. Walsh to Jesse Straus, Nov. 2, 1931, Franklin D. Roosevelt Pa-

pers (Franklin D. Roosevelt Library, Hyde Park); "The Reminiscences of Lawson Purdy" (1948), pp. 44–45, in the Oral History Collection of Columbia University; Homer Folks, "Remarks on an Adequate Program for a State and Local Public Welfare Administration," Address, April 28, 1931, MS, Folks Papers.

8. Franklin D. Roosevelt, Untitled Address, "To the Legislature (In Extraordinary Session)," Aug. 28, 1931, Roosevelt Papers.

9. Franklin Roosevelt to Homer Folks, Sept. 29, 1931, Roosevelt Papers.

10. Homer Folks, Telephone Message to the Governor's Office, Sept. 14, 1931, Roosevelt Papers. See also "The Reminiscences of Homer Folks," (1949), p. 90, in the Oral History Collection of Columbia University; Elsie M. Bond to Herbert Lehman, Sept. 5, 1931, Herbert H. Lehman Papers (Columbia University Library).

11. Homer Folks, Telephone Message to the Governor's Office, Sept. 14, 1931, Roosevelt Papers.

12. "Statement by Hon. Russell G. Dunmore, Majority Leader of the Assembly, Relative to the Bill on Unemployment Introduced by Him, September 2, 1931," and Statement by Senator George R. Fearon, Sept. 17, 1931, Roosevelt Papers.

13. Franklin Roosevelt to George Fearon and Joseph McGinnies, Sept. 18, 1931, Roosevelt Papers.

14. [Office of Governor Franklin Roosevelt], Press Release, Sept. 19, 1931, Roosevelt Papers.

15. Homer Folks to Franklin Roosevelt, Sept. 22, 1931, and Franklin Roosevelt to Homer Folks, Sept. 29, 1931, Roosevelt Papers.

16. Exact TERA rulings remain obscure, because the commissioners seem to have established policies through a series of informal decisions that were seldom recorded as official acts. Several published articles, especially from *Survey*, are helpful in piecing together the TERA's policies, and the most informative among them are: Anon., [Report on TERA Policies], *Better Times: The Welfare Magazine* 13 (Oct. 19, 1931): 1; Gertrude Springer, "The Lever of State Relief," *Survey* 67 (Jan. 15, 1932): 407–410; Paul Kellogg, "Relief Needs; Relief Resources," *Survey Graphic* 67 (Feb. 1, 1932): 463–464; and Emma Lundberg, "The New York State Temporary Emergency Relief Administration," *Social Service Review* 6 (Dec. 1932): 547–566. The SCAA's Elsie Bond did work closely with Harry Hopkins and the other commissioners in developing TERA policies. See **195** David Holbrook, Phone conversation with Bradley Buell, [Notes], Nov. 19, 1931, National Social Welfare Assembly Papers (Social Welfare History Archives, Minneapolis).

17. Jesse Straus to Franklin Roosevelt, Feb. 19, 1932, and Douglas Falconer to Jesse Straus, Jan. 28, 1932, Roosevelt Papers.

18. Temporary Emergency Relief Administration, "Rules Concerning Home Relief," [Dec. 1931?], Roosevelt Papers.

19. Welfare Council, Coordinating Committee on Unemployment, Executive Committee, "Summary of Minutes," Oct. 27, 1931, and "Summary of Minutes," Nov. 25, 1931, Henry Street Papers; *Better Times: The Welfare Magazine* 13 (Oct. 5, 1931): 1; (Oct. 26, 1931): 1; (Dec. 14, 1931): 1; and (Dec. 28, 1931): 1.

20. Anon., "Spending Forty Millions," *Survey* 67 (Dec. 15, 1931): 291.

21. Springer, "The Lever of State Relief," p. 407.

22. William Hodson, "An Open Letter to the President on Federal Relief Appropriations," reprinted in *Survey Graphic*, 67 (Nov. 1, 1931): 144–145.

23. Steering Committee of the Social Work Conference on Federal Action, "Minutes," Nov. 29, 1931, NSWA Papers; [Joanna C. Colcord], "Preliminary Report to the Conference on Federal Relief, by the Sub-committee on Methods of Administration," [Nov. 1931], MS, Harry L. Lurie Papers (Social Welfare History Archives).

24. David H. Holbrook, "Federal Action on Unemployment," Memorandum, March 18, 1933, NSWA Papers.

25. *Survey* 67 (March 15, 1932): 659.

26. Gertrude Springer, "Getting the Most from Federal Relief," *Survey* 68 (July 15, 1932): 324.

27. Harry L. Lurie, "Statement of the American Association of Social Workers: Operation of the Federal Relief Plan," [July 1932], MS, Lurie Papers.

28. *Survey* 68 (Aug. 15, 1932): 369; Joanna Colcord, "Social Work and the First Federal Relief Programs," National Conference of Social Work, *Proceedings*, 1943 (New York, 1943), p. 392.

29. *Survey* 68 (Aug. 15, 1932): 370, and (Sept. 15, 1932): 418.

30. Joanna Colcord, "A New Relief Deal," *Survey* 69 (May 15, 1933); 181.

31. American Association of Social Workers, Committee on Federal Action on Unemployment, "Minutes," Dec. 15, 1932, and David Holbrook to George Rabinoff, Dec. 23, 1932, NSWA Papers.

32. American Association of Social Workers, Sub-committee on Methods of Administration, "Report," Feb. 4, 1933, NSWA Papers.

33. American Association of Social Workers, Executive Committee, "Resolution," [1933], NSWA Papers.

8

1. Reassessments of Hoover's presidency and reinterpretations of his policies have come rapidly since William Appleman Williams published his pioneering essay, "What This Country Needs . . ." in *The New York Review of Books*, Nov. 5, 1970, pp. 7–11. The "new view" of Hoover gives him credit for leading the way—for better or for worse—into the policies and programs of the New Deal. Murray N. Rothbard merits attention, because he outlined much of that new view before Williams, even though they did not share the same favorable perspective. See Murray N. Rothbard, "The Hoover Myth," in James Weinstein and David W. Eakins, eds., *For a New America: Essays in History and Politics from "Studies on the Left," 1959–1967* (New York, 1970), pp. 162–179, and "Herbert Hoover and the Myth of Laissez-Faire," in Ronald Radosh and Murray N. Rothbard, eds., *A New History of Leviathan: Essays on the Rise of the American Corporate State* (New York, 1972), pp. 111–145. Many of the new ideas about Hoover are summarized by another innovative researcher, Ellis W. Hawley, in *The Great War and the Search for a Modern Order: A History of the American People and Their Institu-*

tions, 1917–1933 (New York, 1979), which draws upon several of Hawley's published essays about Hoover. Joan Hoff Wilson, *Herbert Hoover: Forgotten Progressive* (Boston, 1975), offers a revised biographical interpretation, but the most thorough and informative new biography is David Burner, *Herbert Hoover: A Public Life* (New York, 1979). For the most part, I accept this reevaluation of Hoover, but his record on unemployment still falls short of his stature as a progressive on other issues.

2. Paul Kellogg to E. E. Hunt, Dec. 19, 1929, Survey Papers (Social Welfare History Archives, Minneapolis).

3. Paul Kellogg, "Outflanking Unemployment," *Survey Graphic* 64 (May 1, 1930): 146.

4. Paul Kellogg to E. E. Hunt, Oct. 15, 1930, Survey Papers.

5. Colonel Arthur Woods is an interesting historical figure, because his career touched closely upon the lives of both Franklin D. Roosevelt and Herbert Hoover. Woods was a teaching master at Groton School when FDR was a student there. Both served in the Secretary of War's office during the period of the First World War. And Woods became associated with business enterprises during the 1920s, such as the Consolidated Coal Company and the Colorado Fuel and Iron Company, that also involved Roosevelt. Indeed, his credentials appear much like those of a typical New York New Dealer, and his service to Hoover's administration provides a striking point of parallelism between the policies of Hoover and Roosevelt.

6. "Preliminary Report of the President's Emergency Committee for Employment," [November, 1930], Harry L. Hopkins Papers (Franklin D. Roosevelt Library, Hyde Park). The PECE papers in the Hopkins collection at the FDRL is a duplicate and complete set of papers also held by the Herbert Clark Hoover Library at West Branch. Contemporary descriptions of the PECE's work include Beulah Amidon, "Some Plans for Steady Work," *Survey* 65 (Nov. 15, 1930): 202, 204; E. E. H. [Edward Eyre Hunt], "The President's Committee for Employment," *Survey* 65 (Feb. 15, 1931): 542–543; and E. P. Hayes, *Activities of the President's Emergency Committee for Employment* (Concord, 1936).

7. "Formation of Committee," Interview—E. P. Hayes and E. L. Bernays, Feb. 26, 1931, Hopkins Papers.

8. David Holbrook, "Telephone conversation with Porter R. Lee," [Notes], Oct. 25, 1930, National Social Welfare Assembly Papers (Social Welfare History Archives); [Joanna Colcord], "Memorandum of a Possible Program of Study of Unemployment for the Russell Sage Foundation," Dec. 5, 1930, Hopkins Papers.

9. The President's Emergency Committee for Employment, Memorandum, Dec. 1, 1930, Hopkins Papers.

10. [PECE] to Herbert Hoover, "Suggestions on Unemployment," Memorandum, Nov. 21, 1930, Hopkins Papers.

11. David Holbrook, "Consultation by A. T. Burns and Homer Borst, at Hotel Commodore," [Notes], Oct. 24, 1930, NSWA Papers.

12. Porter Lee to Arthur Woods, "Suggestions in regard to relief," Memorandum, Jan. 14, 1931, Hopkins Papers.

13. David Holbrook, "Consultation by A. T. Burns and Homer Borst, at Hotel Commodore."

14. David Holbrook, "Conference with Robert E. Bondy and DeWitt Smith at 52 Gramercy Park," [Notes], Nov. 7, 1930, NSWA Papers.

15. Porter Lee to Arthur Woods, "Suggestions in regard to relief."

16. [PECE?], "Federal Government Millions Relieving Unemployment," n.d., Hopkins Papers. Arthur Woods is quoted in the document.

17. J. C. Lawrence to Arthur Woods, Memorandum, Jan. 23. 1931, Hopkins Papers.

18. Joseph Willits to Arthur Woods, Memorandum, Jan. 26, 1931, Hopkins Papers.

19. E. P. Hayes to Arthur Woods, "Conference with Economists," Memorandum, Feb. 2, 1931, Hopkins Papers. Woods is quoted in the document.

20. [Arthur Woods], Memorandum of Conversation with President Hoover and Judge Payne (Feb. 11, 1931), Feb. 16, 1931, Hopkins Papers.

21. [David Holbrook], "Notes on Visit at Red Cross Headquarters, Washington, D. C.," March 17, 1931, NSWA Papers.

22. [PECE], "Prevention of Unemployment," Memorandum, n.d., and Fred Croxton to Arthur Woods, "Program of the President's Emergency Committee for Employment," April 13, 1931, Hopkins Papers.

23. Paul Kellogg, "Outflanking Unemployment," pp. 146–147.

24. See, for example, a statement of support sent by social workers to George S. Graham, chairman, House Judiciary Committee, n.d., Paul U. Kellogg Papers (Social Welfare History Archives).

25. The history of Wagner's bills is traced in J. Joseph Huthmacher, *Senator Robert F. Wagner and the Rise of Urban Liberalism* (New York, 1968), pp. 60–63, 71–86, and in Jordan A. Schwarz, *The Interregnum of Despair: Hoover, Congress, and the Depression* (Urbana, 1970), pp. 23–44.

26. E. E. Hunt *et al.* to Arthur Woods, Dec. 12, 1930, Hopkins Papers.

27. J. C. Lawrence to Arthur Woods, Memorandum, Jan. 8, 1931, Hopkins Papers.

28. E. E. Hunt *et al.* to Arthur Woods.

29. E. E. Hunt to Arthur Woods, Dec. 23, 1930, Hopkins Papers.

30. Bryce M. Stewart to Arthur Woods, Memorandum, Dec. 19, 1930, Hopkins Papers.

31. Joseph Willits to Arthur Woods, Memorandum, Dec. 29, 1930, Hopkins Papers.

32. Bryce Stewart to Arthur Woods, Memorandum, Feb. 7, 1931, Hopkins Papers.

33. *Ibid.*; Joseph Willits to Secretary of Labor William N. Doak, Memorandum, Feb. 11, 1931, and J. C. Lawrence to Lawrence Rickey, secretary to the President, Memorandum, March 5, 1931, Hopkins Papers.

34. [PECE], "The Wagner Bill Veto," Memorandum, n.d., Hopkins Papers.

35. [PECE], "Analysis of the President's statement concerning the Wagner Bill for Employment offices," Memorandum, March 9, 1931, Hopkins Papers.

36. [PECE], "The Wagner Bill Veto," Memorandum, n.d., Hopkins Papers.

37. Herbert Hoover to Senator Wesley L. Jones, June 11, 1931, Hopkins Papers.

38. Harry L. Lurie, "The Place of Federal Aid in Unemployment Relief," Sept. 25, 1931, MS, Harry L. Lurie Papers (Social Welfare History Archives).

39. Harry L. Hopkins, *Spending to Save: The Complete Story of Relief* (New York, 1936), pp. 17–42.

40. Harry L. Lurie, "The Place of Federal Aid in Unemployment Relief."

41. Will Rogers, "Bacon & Beans & Limousines: A Radio Address for the President's Committee on Unemployment Relief," *Survey* 65 (Nov. 15, 1931): 185; *Survey* 65 (Sept. 15, 1931): 538.

42. D. H. Holbrook, Phone conversation with A. T. Burns, Sept. 14, 1931, NSWA Papers.

43. Paul Kellogg, "Drought and the Red Cross," *Survey* 65 (Feb. 15, 1931): 536.

44. *Survey* 65 (April 15, 1931): 115.

45. *Survey* 67 (Oct. 15, 1931): 67.

46. Harry L. Lurie, "The Place of Federal Aid in Unemployment Relief."

47. Isaac M. Rubinow, "The 'Versus' Complex," [Dec. 1931], MS, Lurie Papers.

48. Paul Kellogg, "Relief Needs; Relief Resources," *Survey Graphic* 67 (Feb. 1, 1932): 464.

49. Paul Kellogg to Frances Perkins, March 29, 1930, Survey Papers. Harry L. Lurie attempted a balanced analysis of Hoover's policies in "The Place of Federal Aid in Unemployment Relief."

50. *Ibid.*

51. *Survey* 68 (Sept. 15, 1932): 418.

52. *Survey* 68 (Sept. 15, 1932): 417.

9

1. Lillian Wald to Charles Burlingham, Oct. 16, 1928; Charles Burlingham to Lillian Wald, Oct. 16, 1928; and Lillian Wald to the Editor of the *New York Times*, Oct. 17, 1928, Lillian D. Wald Papers (New York Public Library, New York City).

2. Paul Kellogg to Franklin Roosevelt, Nov. 21, 1928, Survey Papers (Social Welfare History Archives, Minneapolis).

3. The importance of Eleanor Roosevelt's relationships with social workers has been assessed by Tamara K. Hareven, *Eleanor Roosevelt: An American Conscience* (Chicago, 1968), pp. 23–25, 37, 39, 56–90, and by Joseph P. Lash, *Eleanor and Franklin: The Story of Their Relationship, Based on Eleanor Roosevelt's Private Papers* (New York, 1971), pp. 236, 280–282, 310, 323–325, 328–329, 336, 345, and *passim*.

4. Rose Schneiderman, *All for One* (New York, 1967), p. 176.

5. Mary Dewson, "An Aid to the End," vol. 1, p. 7, MS, Mary W. Dewson Papers (Schlesinger Library, Cambridge).

6. This chapter's discussion of Roosevelt's gubernatorial policies and programs often relies on Frank Freidel, *Franklin D. Roosevelt: The Triumph* (Boston, 1956), and Bernard Bellush, *Franklin D. Roosevelt as Governor of New York* (New York, 1955).

7. *Survey* 61 (March 15, 1929): 782.

8. "CF" to Mary Dewson, May 12, 1930, Franklin D. Roosevelt Papers (Franklin D. Roosevelt Library, Hyde Park).

9. *Survey* 63 (Feb. 15, 1930): 564.

10. Democratic State Committee, press release, Oct. 19, 1930, Survey Papers.

11. *Ibid.*

12. Frances Perkins to Franklin Roosevelt, March 4, 1932, and Franklin Roosevelt to Frances Perkins, March 4, 1932, Roosevelt Papers.

13. I. M. Rubinow to Arthur Kellogg, Nov. 20, 1930, Survey Papers.

14. Rexford G. Tugwell, *The Brains Trust* (New York, 1968), p. 182.

15. Lillian Wald to Eleanor Roosevelt, Aug. 18, 1932, Wald Papers; Franklin Roosevelt to Homer Folks, Dec. 7, 1932, Homer Folks Papers (Columbia University School of Social Work Library, New York City).

16. Belle Zeller, *Pressure Politics in New York: A Study of Group Representation Before the Legislature* (New York, 1937), p. 153 and *passim.*

17. *Survey* 66 (April 15, 1931): 86.

18. William Hodson, "Social Welfare in the Crisis—From the Point of View of the Welfare Council," *Better Times: The Welfare Magazine* 14 (June 5, 1933): 4.

19. Mary Dewson, "An Aid to the End," vol. 1, p. 8.

20. *Ibid.*

21. Kelley is quoted by Bruno Lasker, "The Reminiscences of Bruno Lasker," (1956), pp. 180–181, in the Oral History Collection of Columbia University.

22. Mary Dewson, "An Aid to the End," vol. 1, p. 8.

23. Homer Folks, "Journal of Homer Folks, 1926–1931," MS, Folks Papers.

24. David Holbrook, Phone conversation with Bradley Buell, [Notes], Nov. 19, 1931, National Social Welfare Assembly Papers (Social Welfare History Archives).

25. "The Reminiscences of Frances Perkins," vol. 3, pp. 202–203; David H. Holbrook, Conference with Helen M. Crosby, [Notes], Nov. 23, 1931, NSWA Papers.

26. "The Reminiscences of Homer Folks" (1949), p. 63, in the Oral History Collection of Columbia University.

27. See, for example, Rose Schneiderman to Eleanor Roosevelt, Aug. 24, 1931, Roosevelt Papers.

28. Arthur Kellogg to Beulah Amidon, Aug. 30, 1931, Survey Papers.

29. See, for example, Jane Hoey to Eleanor Roosevelt, Nov. 20, 1930, and undated letter, Eleanor Roosevelt Papers (Franklin D. Roosevelt Library).

30. The Eleanor Roosevelt file in the Survey Papers contains numer-

ous examples of this kind of correspondence. A good indicator of the mutual understanding involved in the editors' relationship with ER occurred in 1934, when she noted that "I also gave it [an article] to the President to read." See Eleanor Roosevelt to Paul Kellogg, June 11, 1934, Survey Papers.

31. See, for example, Eleanor Roosevelt, "Radio Broadcast for Children's Aid Society," Jan. 10, 1932, Eleanor Roosevelt Papers.

32. Arthur Kellogg to Beulah Amidon, Aug. 30, 1931, Survey Papers.

33. Frances Perkins to Paul Kellogg, July 29, 1932, Survey Papers.

34. Frances Perkins to Franklin Roosevelt, Dec. 13, 1930, Roosevelt Papers.

35. Frances Perkins to Paul Kellogg, Nov. 23, 1932, Survey Papers.

36. Paul Kellogg to Frances Perkins, Nov. 28, 1932, Survey Papers.

37. "The Reminiscences of Frances Perkins," vol. 3, p. 166, and vol. 4, p. 478.

38. Mary Dewson to Katie Louchheim, Dec. 16, 1958, Mary W. Dewson Papers (Franklin D. Roosevelt Library).

39. Mary Dewson, "An Aid to the End," vol. 1, p. 17.

40. For discussion of Roosevelt's fiscal orthodoxy and his conservatism in general, see Freidel, *The Triumph*, pp. 139, 184, 192, 219–221, and *passim*.

41. William Matthews, *Adventures in Giving* (New York, 1939), pp. 215–216.

42. "The Reminiscences of Frances Perkins," vol. 3, pp. 175–176.

43. See George Martin, *Madame Secretary: Frances Perkins* (Boston, 1976), pp. 221–225.

44. "Speech of the Hon. Franklin D. Roosevelt, Governor of the State of New York at Governors' Conference," June 30, 1930, Roosevelt Papers.

45. "Mr. Folks' Address," *S. C. A. A. News: A Bulletin of Information for Committee Members* 18 (Feb. 1930): 5.

46. Homer Folks to Herbert Lehman, Sept. 28, 1931, Herbert H. Lehman Papers (Columbia University Library, New York City).

47. Mary Dewson, "An Aid to the End," vol. 1, p. 60.

48. Perkins is quoted by Matthew and Hannah Josephson, *Al Smith: Hero of the Cities, A Political Portrait Drawing on the Papers of Frances Perkins* (Boston, 1969), p. 428.

49. Tugwell, *The Brains Trust*, p. 282.

50. Mary Dewson, "An Aid to the End," vol. 1, p. 1; Mary Dewson to Family, Dec. 14, 1931, Dewson Papers (Roosevelt Library).

51. Frances Perkins, *The Roosevelt I Knew* (New York, 1946), p. 136.

52. Mary Dewson, "An Aid to the End," vol. 1, p. 16.

53. Perkins, *The Roosevelt I Knew*, p. 173.

54. William Hodson to the Editor, *Survey* 69 (June 15, 1933): 238.

10

1. Homer Folks, "The Good Life During a Depression," Address, Oct. 30, 1932, MS, Homer Folks Papers (Columbia University School of Social Work Library, New York City).

2. United Neighborhood Houses, Headworkers Meeting, "Minutes," Nov. 16, 1932, United Neighborhood Houses Papers (Social Welfare History Archives, Minneapolis).

3. Mrs. Franklin D. Roosevelt [Anna Eleanor Roosevelt], *It's Up to the Women* (New York, 1933), pp. 178–179, 184–185.

4. Mary Dewson, "An Aid to the End," vol. 1, MS, Mary W. Dewson Papers (Schlesinger Library, Cambridge) gives an account by a participant of the organizations and people who supported Perkins's appointment.

5. Porter R. Lee, "Personality in Social Work," National Conference of Social Work, *Proceedings*, 1926 (Chicago, 1926), pp. 19–20.

6. Frances Perkins, "My Job," *Survey* 61 (March 15, 1929): 773–774.

7. Mary Dewson to Eleanor Roosevelt, Feb. 7, 1929, Eleanor Roosevelt Papers (Franklin D. Roosevelt Library, Hyde Park).

8. Lillian Wald to Herbert Lehman, March 20, 1933, Herbert H. Lehman Papers (Columbia University Library, New York City).

9. Mary Dewson to Florence Kelley, Feb. 13, 1924, Mary W. Dewson Papers (Franklin D. Roosevelt Library).

10. Paul Kellogg to Frances Perkins, July 10, 1945, Survey Papers (Social Welfare History Archives).

11. Frances Perkins to Paul Kellogg, Aug. 2, 1945, Survey Papers.

12. Lillian Wald to Mary Smith, Feb. 11, 1932, Lillian D. Wald Papers (New York Public Library, New York City).

13. Paul Kellogg to Porter Lee, March 11, 1933, Survey Papers.

14. Bruno Lasker to Paul Kellogg, [May 1934?], Paul U. Kellogg Papers (Social Welfare History Archives).

15. Frances Perkins to Henry Street Settlement, Sept. 9, 1940, [on the occasion of Lillian Wald's death], National Federation of Settlements Papers (Social Welfare History Archives).

16. Eleanor Roosevelt, Untitled Speech, Oct. 26, 1932, Eleanor Roosevelt Papers.

17. Paul Kellogg to Frances Perkins, June 3, 1933, Survey Papers.

18. Harry Lurie to Cornelius Bliss, Jan. 11, 1932, Harry L. Lurie Papers (Social Welfare History Archives).

19. Anon., "Memorandum Concerning Position on Unemployment Relief," [Oct. 1932], Raymond Moley Papers (Hoover Institute, Stanford).

20. Welfare Council of New York City, Executive Committee, "Statement," [Sept. 29, 1932?], Henry Street Settlement Papers (Columbia University Library); Welfare Council, Research Bureau, "Outdoor Relief in New York City," Dec. 12, 1932, New York Public Library Special Collections.

21. William Matthews to Herbert Lehman, Jan. 17, 1933, Lehman Papers.

22. Homer Folks, "Public Relief as a Social Problem," National Conference of Social Work, *Proceedings*, 1933 (Chicago, 1933), pp. 44–45.

23. *Better Times: The Welfare Magazine* 14 (March 6, 1933): 20.

24. William Hodson, "Social Workers in a Changing World," *Survey* 69 (April 15, 1933): 148.

25. Welfare Council, Research Bureau, "Outdoor Relief in New York

City," April 1933, NYPL Special Collections; William H. Matthews, "The Job-Line That Cost $28 Million," *Survey* 69 (Nov. 15, 1933): 371–373.

26. Welfare Council, Coordinating Committee on Unemployment to the Board of Estimate and Apportionment of the City of New York, Sept. 23, 1933, Lehman Papers.

27. United Neighborhood Houses, Meeting of the Neighborhood Committee of the Unemployment Relief Committee, Nov. 1, 1933, UNH Papers.

28. Porter R. Lee, "Social Workers: Pioneers Again," *Survey* 69 (Sept. 15, 1933): 308.

29. Welfare Council, Research Bureau, "Expenditures for Outdoor Relief in New York City for the Calendar Years 1929, 1930, 1931, and 1932," and "Per Cent Distribution of Expenditures for Outdoor Relief . . . ," April 25, 1933, NYPL Special Collections.

30. William Hodson to the Board of Directors of the Welfare Council, April 5, 1933, Lehman Papers.

31. William Hodson, "Annual Report of the Executive Director of the Welfare Council of New York City," *Better Times: The Welfare Magazine* 14 (June 12, 1933): 1.

32. William Matthews to Robert Fechner, April 10, 1933, William H. Matthews Papers (New York Public Library).

33. Gertrude Springer, "Swapping Horses in a Flood," *Survey* 69 (April 15, 1933): 153; David Adie, "A State Handles Its Public Welfare Programs," National Conference of Social Work, *Proceedings*, 1933 (Chicago, 1933), pp. 516–533.

34. *Better Times: The Welfare Magazine* 14 (Nov. 14, 1932): 1, and (May 29, 1933): 2; Paul Kellogg to Porter Lee, Dec. 14, 1932, Survey Papers.

35. Clarke A. Chambers, *Paul U. Kellogg and the Survey: Voices for Social Welfare and Social Justice* (Minneapolis, 1971), pp. 144–145.

36. [TERA?], "Qualifications for new workers in emergency home relief bureaus of public welfare departments," Feb. 20, 1933, Lurie Papers.

37. William Matthews to Orbert Fechner, April 10, 1933, Matthews Papers.

38. Lee, "Social Workers: Pioneers Again," p. 311.

39. Homer Folks, "Outline: Trends of Home Relief in the Near Future," Dec. 11, 1933, Folks Papers.

40. [TERA?], "Memorandum Concerning Standards of Eligibility for Recipients of Work Relief and Suggestions for Procedure," Jan. 5, 1932, Lurie Papers.

41. Welfare Council, Committee on the Emergency Financing of Social Work, "Report," July 8, 1932, Herbert H. Lehman Papers (Franklin D. Roosevelt Library).

42. Hodson is quoted by *Better Times: The Welfare Magazine* 14 (June 12, 1933): 1.

43. Matthews is quoted by *Survey* 68 (June 15, 1932): 277.

44. Welfare Council, Coordinating Committee on Unemployment to the Board of Estimate and Apportionment of the City of New York, Sept. 23, 1933, Lehman Papers (Columbia).

45. Linton B. Swift, "Needs and Safeguards," *Survey Graphic* 67 (Feb. 1, 1932): 467.

46. Robert F. Wagner, "Rock-Bottom Responsibility," *Survey Graphic* 68 (June 1, 1932): 222.

47. Paul Kellogg, "Security Next," *Survey Graphic* 67 (Dec. 1, 1931): 240.

48. Gertrude Springer, "The Challenge of Hard Times," *Survey* 66 (July 15, 1931); 382.

49. Neva Deardorff, "Next Steps in Job Analysis," National Conference of Social Work, *Proceedings*, 1933 (Chicago, 1933), p. 623.

50. *Survey* 67 (Jan. 15, 1932): 427.

51. See Arthur Mann, *La Guardia Comes to Power, 1933* (Chicago, 1965); Charles Garrett, *The La Guardia Years: Machine and Reform Politics in New York City* (New Brunswick, 1961); Barbara Blumberg, *The New Deal and the Unemployed: The View from New York City* (Lewisburg, 1979); and Robert P. Ingalls, *Herbert H. Lehman and New York's Little New Deal* (New York, 1975).

11

1. Paul Kellogg, "Steps Toward Economic Recovery," Radio Address, April 14, 1933, MS, Henry Street Settlement Papers (Social Welfare History Archives, Minneapolis).

2. Eleanor Roosevelt, Untitled Radio Address, April 19, [1933], MS, Eleanor Roosevelt Papers (Franklin D. Roosevelt Library, Hyde Park).

3. See, for example, "Misc. Letters, 1932–1935" folder, Mary W. Dewson Papers (Franklin D. Roosevelt Library); United Neighborhood Houses, Executive Committee, "Minutes," Jan. 10, 1933, United Neighborhood Houses Papers (Social Welfare History Archives).

4. *Survey* 69 (May 15, 1933): 207–208.

5. J. Prentice Murphy to Harry Hopkins, March 13, 1933, Harry L. Hopkins Papers (Franklin D. Roosevelt Library).

6. Frances Perkins, *The Roosevelt I Knew* (New York, 1946), pp. 184–185.

7. "The Reminiscences of Frances Perkins," vol. 3 (1955), p. 573, in the Oral History Collection of Columbia University. For a detailed history of FDR's 100 Days, see Frank Freidel, *Franklin D. Roosevelt: Launching the New Deal* (Boston, 1973).

8. [Franklin D. Roosevelt], "Work Bill," Memorandum, [March 1933], Raymond Moley Papers (Hoover Institute, Stanford).

9. *Ibid.*

10. [Franklin D. Roosevelt], Untitled Memorandum, [March 1933?], Moley Papers.

11. Perkins, *The Roosevelt I Knew*, pp. 183–185.

12. *Ibid.*

13. American Association of Social Workers, Committee on Federal

Action on Unemployment, "Minutes," March 7, 1933, National Social Welfare Assembly Papers (Social Welfare History Archives).

14. Edward Costigan to Harry Hopkins, March 13, 1933, Hopkins Papers.

15. George Dern, Harold Ickes, Henry Wallace, and Frances Perkins, "Memorandum for the President," March 15, 1933, Moley Papers.

16. AASW, Committee on Federal Action on Unemployment, "Minutes," March 17, 1933, NSWA Papers.

17. AASW, Committee on Federal Action on Unemployment, "Notes on Meeting," March 17, 1933, NSWA Papers.

18. P. U. K. [Paul U. Kellogg], "Get Help Through," *Survey* 69 (June 15, 1933): 211.

19. Paul Kellogg to C. M. Bookman, May 26, 1933, Survey Papers (Social Welfare History Archives).

20. C. M. Bookman to Paul Kellogg, June 3, 1933, Survey Papers.

21. Perkins, *The Roosevelt I Knew*, pp. 103, 205–206, and *passim*; "Reminiscences of Frances Perkins," vol. 3, pp. 598–599.

22. "Reminiscences of Frances Perkins," vol. 3, p. 593.

23. Paul Kellogg to Frances Perkins, May 8, 1933, Survey Papers; Mary Dewson to Franklin Roosevelt, Feb. 1933, Mary W. Dewson Papers (Schlesinger Library, Cambridge).

24. Paul Kellogg to Frances Perkins, May 8, 1933, Survey Papers; see also Paul Kellogg to Samuel Fels, May 13, 1933, Survey Papers, for a report of a Washington meeting with Perkins.

25. See, for example, Rose Schneiderman to Eleanor Roosevelt, April 17, 1933, Eleanor Roosevelt Papers.

26. W. Frank Persons, Untitled Address, June 17, 1935, MS, Frances Perkins Papers (Franklin D. Roosevelt Library).

27. W. Frank Persons, "Public Employment Offices: Their Present Possibilities and Limitations," Address, Oct. 26, 1934, Perkins Papers.

28. Paul Kellogg to W. Frank Persons, June 13, 1933, Survey Papers.

29. William Hodson to the Editor, *Survey* 69 (June 15, 1933): 238.

30. The Conference's statement is quoted by Mary Van Kleeck, "Our Illusions Regarding Government," *Survey* 70 (June 15, 1934): 190. The dating of the statement was late 1933 or early 1934, because reference is made to "such programs as the NRA, the NRS, FERA, the CCC and the CWA." The last is most important, because it began late in 1933 and ties the Conference's appraisal to the New Deal's most advanced work program. See below.

31. Gertrude Springer, "Partners in a New Social Order," *Survey* 69 (July 15, 1933): 243, 245.

32. William Hodson, "Mobilize for the New Deal," *Survey* 69 (July 15, 1933): 245.

33. Springer, "Partners," pp. 243, 250.

34. Russell H. Kurtz, "Two Months of the New Deal in Federal Relief," *Survey* 69 (Aug. 15, 1933): 286, 289; Arthur E. Burns and Edward A. Williams, *Federal Work, Security, and Relief Programs* (Washington, 1941), pp. 26, 38.

35. See William W. Bremer, "Along the 'American Way': The New Deal's Work Relief Programs for the Unemployed," *Journal of American History* 62 (Dec. 1975): 636—652. My own emphasis on psychological values derives from the observations of several other scholars whose works are cited in this chapter, but I give particular credit to Alexander L. Radomski, *Work Relief in New York State, 1931–1935* (New York, 1947), pp. 55–57, 301, 319, for the benefit of his insight.

36. Forrest A. Walker, *The Civil Works Administration: An Experiment in Federal Work Relief, 1933–1934* (New York, 1979), pp. 29–38.

37. "Federal Civil Works Administration, Rules and Regulations, No. 1," Nov. 15, 1933, Frances Perkins Papers (Columbia University Library, New York City). See also William Hodson, "A Review of Public Relief—Federal, State, and Local—As It Affects New York City," Nov. 1933, Henry Street Settlement Papers (Columbia University Library); Harry L. Hopkins, "The War on Distress," in Howard Zinn, ed., *New Deal Thought* (Indianapolis, 1966), pp. 151–158; Jacob Baker, "Work Relief: The Program Broadens," *New York Times Magazine*, Nov. 11, 1934, pp. 6, 17.

38. Robert E. Sherwood, *Roosevelt and Hopkins: An Intimate History* (New York, 1948), p. 53.

39. AASW, Committee on Federal Action on Unemployment, "Minutes," Nov. 8, 1933, NSWA Papers; William Hodson to the Board of Directors of the Welfare Council of New York City, Nov. 16, 1933, Herbert H. Lehman Papers (Franklin D. Roosevelt Library).

40. Frances Perkins, Untitled Article, [1934?], MS, Perkins Papers (Roosevelt Library).

41. Frances Perkins, "Labor and the Modern State," [1934], MS, Perkins Papers (Roosevelt Library).

42. Harry Lurie to Harry Hopkins, Nov. 17, 1933, Harry L. Lurie Papers (Social Welfare History Archives).

43. Harry Lurie, "A Program for National Assistance," Address, Dec. 9, 1933, MS, Lurie Papers.

44. Russell Kurtz, "An End to Civil Works," *Survey* 70 (Feb. 15, 1934): 35; Sherwood, *Roosevelt and Hopkins*, pp. 50–57; Searle F. Charles, *Minister of Relief: Harry Hopkins and the Depression* (Syracuse, 1963), pp. 46–65.

45. AASW, Committee on Federal Action in Social Welfare, "Minutes," Feb. 18, 1934; Linton Swift to Members of the Committee on Federal Action, March 17, 1934; and AASW, Committee on Federal Action, "To the President," April 11, 1934, Lurie Papers.

46. Harry Lurie, "The Federal Program for the Relief of Unemployment," April 21, 1934, MS, Lurie Papers.

47. *Ibid.*

48. Harry L. Hopkins, *Spending to Save: The Complete Story of Relief* (New York, 1936), p. 124.

49. Nels Anderson, "The War for the Wage," *Survey* 71 (June 15, 1935): 164–165; Don D. Lescohier, "The Hybrid WPA," *Survey Midmonthly* 75 (June 15, 1939): 168. See also Walker, *Civil Works Administration*, pp. 149–150, 155–170.

50. James T. Patterson, "A Conservative Coalition Forms in Congress, 1933–1939," *Journal of American History* 52 (March 1966): 767; William E. Leuchtenburg, *Franklin D. Roosevelt and the New Deal: 1932–1940* (New York, 1963), pp. 91–94; Arthur M. Schlesinger, Jr., *The Coming of the New Deal* (Boston, 1958), pp. 273–277; Charles, *Minister of Relief*, pp. 60–61.

51. Walker, *Civil Works Administration*, pp. 137, 149–150; Roosevelt is quoted by Leuchtenburg, *Roosevelt and the New Deal*, p. 122. See also Peter Bachrach, "The Right to Work: Emergence of the Idea in the United States," *Social Service Review* 26 (June 1952): 153–164.

52. Sherwood, *Roosevelt and Hopkins*, p. 56. Walker takes the same position in *Civil Works Administration*, pp. 151–153.

53. In *Minister of Relief*, p. 61, Searle Charles argues convincingly that "Hopkins and other leading administration officials opposed the suggested expansion of CWA."

54. [CWA-FERA Staff]. "Meeting of Monday, Dec. 4, and Meeting of Tuesday, Dec. 5," [1933], [Minutes], Hopkins Papers; Walker, *Civil Works Administration*, p. 132.

55. [CWA-FERA Staff], "Meeting of Wednesday, Dec. 6" [1933], [Minutes], Hopkins Papers.

56. AASW, Committee on Federal Action in Social Welfare, "To the President," April 11, 1934, Lurie Papers.

57. Harry L. Lurie, "The Federal Program for the Relief of Unemployment," April 21, 1934, MS, Lurie Papers. See also "Program Inaugurated by FERA on Demobilization of CWA," MS, Frances Perkins Papers (Columbia University Library).

58. Frances Perkins, Untitled Address, [1935?], MS, Perkins Papers (Roosevelt Library).

59. AASW, "Report to Steering Committee from Committee on Current Relief Problems," May 1935, Lurie Papers.

60. "Address by W. Frank Persons Before Conference of State Administrators, Works Progress Administration," June 17, 1935, MS, Perkins Papers (Roosevelt Library).

61. Frances Perkins, Untitled Address, [1935?], MS, Perkins Papers (Roosevelt Library).

62. Hopkins, *Spending to Save*, pp. 164–165; "Wage Rates," *Survey* 71 (June 15, 1935): 176–177; Burns and Williams, *Federal Work, Security, and Relief Programs*, pp. 61–62.

63. Ewan Clague and Saya S. Schwartz, "Real Jobs—Or Relief?" *Survey Graphic* 24 (June 1, 1935): 293–295; Lescohier, "The Hybrid WPA," pp. 167–169.

64. Corrington Gill, *Wasted Manpower: The Challenge of Unemployment* (New York, 1939), p. 161; Baker, "Work Relief," p. 6.

65. Harry L. Hopkins, "Employment in America," *Vital Speeches of the Day* 3 (Dec. 1, 1936): 106.

66. See Clarke A. Chambers, *Paul U. Kellogg and the Survey: Voices for Social Welfare and Social Justice* (Minneapolis, 1971), pp. 158–162.

67. Lescohier, "The Hybrid WPA," p. 168.

68. William H. Matthews, "These Past Five Years," *Survey Midmonthly* 74 (March 15, 1938): 71–72.

69. Gertrude Springer and Ruth A. Lerrigo, "Social Work in the Public Scene," *Survey* 72 (June 15, 1936): 166–167; Dorothy C. Kahn, "Conserving Human Values in Public Welfare Programs," National Conference of Social Work, *Proceedings*, 1941 (New York, 1941), pp. 309, 312–313, 317–318.

70. Lescohier, "The Hybrid WPA," p. 168.

71. *Ibid.*, pp. 168–169; Maxine Davis, "On WPA, or Else . . ." *Survey Graphic* 27 (March 1, 1938): 165.

72. Grace Adams, *Workers on Relief* (New Haven, 1939), pp. 310–313, 327–328, 330–333.

73. Construction work made up 75 to 80 percent of all WPA projects. See Harry L. Hopkins, Radio Address, *Congressional Digest* 17 (June–July 1938): 177; Harry L. Hopkins, "The WPA Looks Forward: A Statement and a Forecast," *Survey Midmonthly* 74 (June 15, 1938): 198.

74. Davis, "On WPA, or Else," p. 166.

75. Howard M. Teaf, Jr., "Work Relief and the Workers," *Survey Midmonthly* 74 (June 15, 1938): 199.

76. Adams, *Workers on Relief*, pp. 273–285; Anderson, "War for the Wage," pp. 164–165.

77. Gertrude Springer, "Border Lines and Gaps," *Survey* 71 (Nov. 15, 1935): 332–333; Josephine Chapin Brown, *Public Relief, 1929–1939* (New York, 1940), pp. 169–170.

78. Joanna C. Colcord and Russell H. Kurtz, "Demobilization of CWA," *Survey* 70 (March 15, 1934): 91; Gertrude Springer, "X Equals?" *Survey Graphic* 23 (May 1, 1934): 249–250; Beulah Amidon, "WPA—Wages and Workers," *Survey Graphic* 24 (Oct. 1, 1935): 494.

79. "With the WPA," *Survey* 72 (May 15, 1936): 147; "WPA, RA, Drought," *Survey* 72 (Sept. 15, 1936): 272; Gertrude Springer, "You Can't Eat Morale," *Survey* 72 (March 15, 1936): 77.

80. William H. Matthews, "The Relief Issue: An Inside View," *New York Times Magazine*, Jan. 15, 1939, p. 20.

81. Springer, "You Can't Eat Morale," p. 76; "Relief Must Go On," *Survey Midmonthly* 74 (April 15, 1938): 112.

82. William H. Matthews, "These Past Five Years," pp. 70–71.

83. William H. Matthews, *Adventures in Giving* (New York, 1939), pp. 222–231, 238, 243.

84. See Kahn, "Conserving Human Values," pp. 309, 317–318.

85. Adams, *Workers on Relief*, p. viii.

86. Harry L. Hopkins, "Federal Emergency Relief," *Vital Speeches of the Day* 1 (Dec. 31, 1934): 211. The appeal that work relief had among the unemployed was indicated by a public opinion poll, which revealed that four out of five people on relief preferred work relief to direct cash relief. See Gertrude Springer, "This Business of Relief," *Survey Midmonthly* 74 (Feb. 15, 1938): 36.

1. Paul Kellogg to Harry Hopkins, Feb. 5, 1935, Survey Papers (Social Welfare History Archives, Minneapolis).

2. Paul Kellogg, "Security Next," *Survey Graphic* 67 (Dec. 1, 1931): 240.

3. Robert F. Wagner, "Rock-Bottom Responsibility," *Survey Graphic* 68 (June 1, 1932): 224.

4. Paul Kellogg, "Drought and the Red Cross," *Survey* 65 (Feb. 15, 1931): 576.

5. Kellogg, "Security Next," p. 240.

6. *Survey* 66 (June 15, 1931): 317.

7. "The Interest of Social Workers in Administration of Unemployment Insurance," MS submitted to American Association of Social Workers, Committee on Unemployment Insurance, June 1, 1931, National Social Welfare Assembly Papers (Social Welfare History Archives).

8. Frances Perkins, Untitled Radio Address, Dec. 14, 1934, Frances Perkins Papers (Franklin D. Roosevelt Library, Hyde Park).

9. "The Interest of Social Workers in Administration of Unemployment Insurance."

10. Paul Kellogg to William Matthews, Nov. 23, 1934, Survey Papers.

11. Kellogg, "Security Next," p. 239.

12. Frances Perkins, "Unemployment Insurance: An American Plan to Protect Workers and Avoid the Dole," *Survey Graphic* 67 (Nov. 1, 1931): 173.

13. John Andrews to Editor, The *Survey*, Dec. 17, 1930, Survey Papers.

14. "An American Plan for Unemployment Reserve Funds: Tentative Draft of An Act," Submitted as a Basis for State Legislation by the American Association for Labor Legislation, [1930], Survey Papers.

15. J. Michael Eisner, *William Morris Leiserson: A Biography* (Madison, 1967), p. 11.

16. Roy Lubove, "Economic Security and Social Conflict in America: The Early Twentieth Century, Part II," *Journal of Social History* 1 (Summer 1968): 337–350; Louis Leotta, "Abraham Epstein and the Movement for Old Age Security," *Labor History* 16 (Summer 1975): 359–377. See also Roy Lubove, *The Struggle for Social Security, 1900–1935* (Cambridge, 1968).

17. William Leiserson, "Ohio's Answer to Unemployment," *Survey Graphic* 68 (Dec. 1, 1932): 643–647, 650, 671–672.

18. *Ibid.*, p. 645.

19. Paul H. Douglas, "American Plans of Unemployment Insurance," *Survey Graphic* 65 (Feb. 1, 1931): 485.

20. Assessment made by the Interstate Commission on Unemployment Insurance as presented in Beulah Amidon, "Job Insurance Now," *Survey* 67 (March 15, 1932): 678.

21. Leiserson, "Ohio's Answer," p. 646.

22. *Ibid.*, p. 647.

23. Paul Douglas to Paul Kellogg, April 25, 1932, Survey Papers; Paul Kellogg to Herbert Lehman, March 15, 1933, Henry Street Settlement Papers (Social Welfare History Archives).

24. "Report of Industrial Commissioner Frances Perkins to Governor Franklin D. Roosevelt on Unemployment Insurance in England," Oct. 23, 1931, Franklin D. Roosevelt Papers (Franklin D. Roosevelt Library). See also, Perkins, "Unemployment Insurance: An American Plan," pp. 117–119, 173.

25. Paul Kellogg to I. M. Rubinow, Feb. 7, 1935, Survey Papers. Perkins acknowledged that she was a contact between John Andrews and Roosevelt. Frances Perkins to Raymond Moley, Jan. 28, 1933, Raymond Moley Papers (Hoover Institute, Stanford). Perkins's close work with Governor Roosevelt on compensation proposals is traced in George Martin, *Madam Secretary: Frances Perkins* (Boston, 1976), pp. 221–229.

26. J. Joseph Huthmacher, *Senator Robert F. Wagner and the Rise of Urban Liberalism* (New York, 1968), p. 175.

27. Martin, *Madam Secretary*, pp. 341–348.

28. Daniel Nelson, *Unemployment Insurance: The American Experience, 1915–1935* (Madison, 1969), pp. 198–200. The device for compliance involved consultation between the Secretary of Labor and the Secretary of Treasury. The former would inform the latter that a state maintained a satisfactory program and then the latter would approve tax credits. See "First Tentative Draft, Report of the Committee on Economic Security," Dec. 1934, Frances Perkins Papers (Columbia University Library, New York City).

29. "Advisory Council on Economic Security, Membership as of Nov. 6, 1934," Paul U. Kellogg Papers (Social Welfare History Archives). My emphasis on the Advisory Council and New Yorkers admittedly distorts the history of social security legislation by turning attention away from national politics and issues. Roosevelt, Perkins, Hopkins, and other New Yorkers serving in the administration had become national leaders who wanted to satisfy Congress and the Supreme Court. Similarly, Edwin Witte, who served as a liaison between the COES and the Advisory Council, was a compromiser: his efforts brought forth a mishmash of a proposal that successfully addressed political and constitutional concerns. Firsthand accounts include Edwin E. Witte, *The Development of the Social Security Act: A Memorandum on the History of the Committee on Economic Security and Drafting and Legislative History of the Social Security Act* (Madison, 1962); Arthur Altmeyer, *The Formative Years of Social Security* (Madison, 1968); Charles McKinley and Robert W. Frase, *Launching Social Security: A Capture-and-Record Account, 1935–1937* (Madison, 1970); J. Douglas Brown, *An American Philosophy of Social Security: Evolution and Issues* (Princeton, 1972). I am indebted to Clarke A. Chambers for calling my attention to this question of emphasis (Chambers to author, Sept. 14, 1981). In addition, his forthcoming paper, "Social Reform, Social Work, and Social Security: A Subject Revisited," offers a masterful commentary on the subject and its literature.

30. Paul Kellogg to I. M. Rubinow, Feb. 7, 1935, Survey Papers; Frances Perkins, *The Roosevelt I Knew* (New York, 1946), p. 285.

31. Kellogg was distressed about the absence of experts on the Council and hinted his own worries about its potential as a rubber stamp for the administration. See Paul Kellogg to Frances Perkins, Nov. 9, 1934, and Paul Kellogg to Edwin Witte, Nov. 12, 1934, Kellogg Papers.

32. In *Paul U. Kellogg and the Survey: Voices for Social Welfare and Social Justice* (Minneapolis, 1971), pp. 155–158, Clarke A. Chambers identifies the position that Kellogg took on the Advisory Council. Nelson, *Unemployment Insurance*, pp. 204–219, gives a detailed discussion of the Council's deliberations and the controversy growing out of them. Martin, *Madam Secretary*, pp. 342–356, tells Perkins's side of the story. I have drawn heavily on each of these sources.

33. Paul Kellogg, "Statement for *Christian Science Monitor*," Dec. 3, 1935, MS, Kellogg Papers.

34. Paul Kellogg to Samuel Lewisohn, Jan. 16, 1935, Kellogg Papers.

35. Paul Kellogg to Edwin Witte, Dec. 3, 1934, Kellogg Papers. Kellogg was disappointed that the waiting period was not shorter and the coverage period longer.

36. Paul Kellogg to Frances Perkins, Dec. 21, 1934, and Paul Kellogg to Belle Sherwin, Jan. 16, 1935, Kellogg Papers.

37. Kellogg to Perkins, *ibid.*; Frank P. Graham to Morris Leeds, Jan. 2, 1935, Moley Papers.

38. Edwin Witte to Paul Kellogg, Nov. 23, 1934, Edwin E. Witte Special Correspondence File (Social Welfare History Archives).

39. Frank P. Graham, "The Grant-in-Aid Type of Federal [-] State Co-operative Plan for Unemployment Compensation," [Supplementary Statement to COES], undated, Moley Papers.

40. Paul Kellogg to Edwin Witte, Dec. 3, 1934, Kellogg Papers.

41. Advisory Council of the Committee on Economic Security, Minutes of the Meeting of the Council on December 6–8, 1934, Mary W. Dewson Papers (Franklin D. Roosevelt Library).

42. Thomas Eliot to Mary Dewson, Nov. 30, 1934, Dewson Papers.

43. "Advisory Council on Economic Security, Membership as of Nov. 6, 1934," Kellogg Papers. Kellogg placed Xs next to the names of members who voted for a minority report. The count is my own.

44. Frank Graham to Morris Leeds, Jan. 2, 1935, Moley Papers.

45. Martin, *Madam Secretary*, p. 350; Paul Kellogg to I. M. Rubinow, Jan. 28, 1935, Survey Papers.

46. Nelson, *Unemployment Insurance*, p. 208.

47. Paul Kellogg to Frances Perkins, Dec. 21, 1934, Kellogg Papers.

48. Paul Kellogg to Edwin Witte, Feb. 7, 1935, Witte Correspondence File.

49. Edwin Witte to Paul Kellogg, Jan. 31, 1935, Kellogg Papers.

50. Witte is quoted by Nelson, *Unemployment Insurance*, p. 212.

51. Edwin Witte to Paul Kellogg, Feb. 25, 1935, Kellogg Papers.

52. "First Tentative Draft, Report of the Committee on Economic Security," MS, Perkins Papers (Columbia).

53. Nelson, *Unemployment Insurance*, p. 212.

54. See, for example, Frances Perkins, "Social Insurance for U. S.," Reprint of Radio Broadcast, Feb. 25, 1935, Perkins Papers (FDRL).

55. Paul Kellogg to I. M. Rubinow, Jan. 28, 1935, Survey Papers.

56. *Ibid.*; I. M. Rubinow to Paul Kellogg, Jan. 24, 1935, Survey Papers.

57. I. M. Rubinow to Paul Kellogg, Jan. 30, 1935, Survey Papers.

58. I. M. Rubinow to Paul Kellogg, Jan. 24, 1935, Survey Papers.

59. *Ibid.*

60. Roosevelt is quoted by Nelson, *Unemployment Insurance*, p. 201.

61. Frances Perkins, Untitled Radio Address, MS, Perkins Papers (FDRL).

62. *Ibid.*

63. *Ibid.* See also Martin, *Madam Secretary*, p. 348. Old age security drew great public attention and provoked much controversy in Congress, but its provisions prompted scant debate in the Committee on Economic Security, its Technical Board, and the Advisory Council. As Clarke Chambers says, those bodies "spent far more time and energy on the unemployment insurance titles" (Chambers, "Social Reform, Social Work, and Social Security," MS, p. 15).

64. Martin, *Madam Secretary*, p. 348.

13

1. Frances Perkins, *People at Work* (New York, 1934), pp. 141, 270, 273–274, 281, 286. See also Frances Perkins, "What is Worth Working for in America?" National Conference of Social Work, *Proceedings*, 1941 (New York, 1941), pp. 32, 37, 39.

2. Edward T. Devine, Untitled draft of statement, [April, 1934], MS, Paul U. Kellogg Papers (Social Welfare History Archives, Minneapolis); [Paul Kellogg *et al.*], "To the Honorable Franklin D. Roosevelt, President of the United States," [April 1934], Harry L. Hopkins Papers (Franklin D. Roosevelt Library, Hyde Park); Paul Kellogg, Memorandum, April 30, 1934, Kellogg Papers.

3. Press "Release," May 24, 1934, Kellogg Papers.

4. Paul Kellogg to Grace Abbott, May 14, 1934, and Paul Kellogg to Amos Pinchot, [n.d.], Kellogg Papers.

5. See, for example, Grace Abbott to Paul Kellogg, May 11, 1934, Kellogg Papers.

6. Mary Van Kleeck to Paul Kellogg, May 11, 1934, Kellogg Papers.

7. *Survey* 69 (Sept. 1, 1933): 322.

8. Gertrude Springer and Helen Cody Baker, "The National Conference at Work," *Survey* 70 (June 1, 1934): 179.

9. Mary Van Kleeck, "Our Illusions Regarding Government," *Survey* 70 (June 1, 1934): 190–193.

10. Gertrude Springer to Arthur Kellogg, [May, 1934], Survey Papers (Social Welfare History Archives).

11. Springer and Baker, "National Conference at Work," pp. 179–180.

12. Van Kleeck, "Our Illusions Regarding Government," pp. 190–193.

13. Springer and Baker, "National Conference at Work," p. 179.

14. Quoted in *ibid.*, p. 182.

15. *Ibid.*, p. 181.

16. *Ibid.*, p. 181; Gertrude Springer, "Rising to a New Challenge," *Survey* 70 (June 1, 1934): 180. Hopkins is quoted by Springer and Baker.

17. Gertrude Springer to Arthur Kellogg, [May 1934], Survey Papers.

18. William Hodson, "The President's Position," *Survey* 70 (June 1, 1934): 189.

19. Gertrude Springer to Arthur Kellogg, May 25, 1934, Survey Papers.

20. Social Policy Committee, "Minutes," Jan. 18, 1935, Kellogg Papers.

21. [Social Policy Committee, Minutes], Feb. 14, 1935, Kellogg Papers.

22. Edward T. Devine *et al.* to Hon. Pat Harrison, Feb. 20, 1935, Survey Papers.

23. American Association of Social Workers, Delegate Conference, "Report of the Conference," Feb. 17, 1935, Harry L. Lurie Papers (Social Welfare History Archives).

24. Russell H. Kurtz, "Two Months of the New Deal in Federal Relief," *Survey* 69 (Aug. 1, 1933): 284.

25. "First Tentative Draft, Report of the Committee on Economic Security," Dec. 1934, Frances Perkins Papers (Columbia University Library, New York City); William E. Leuchtenburg, *Franklin D. Roosevelt and the New Deal, 1932–1940* (New York, 1963), p. 124.

26. Quoted by Gertrude Springer and Ruth A. Lerrigo, "Social Work in the Public Scene," *Survey* 72 (June 1, 1936): 167.

27. Agricultural and domestic workers were explicitly excluded from the act's coverage, while payroll taxes were imposed on employers of eight or more workers, which left many small business employees without coverage. The act did provide federal aid for the indigent elderly, but a means test made that a relief provision. The blind were protected, but not the disabled.

28. Springer and Lerrigo, "Social Work in the Public Scene," p. 167.

29. Josephine Chapin Brown, *Public Relief, 1929–1939* (New York, 1940), p. 325.

30. Springer and Lerrigo, "Social Work in the Public Scene," pp. 165–166.

31. Quoted by Leuchtenburg, *Franklin D. Roosevelt*, p. 124.

32. "First Tentative Draft, Report of the Committee on Economic Security," Dec. 1934, Perkins Papers.

33. Brown, *Public Relief*, p. 170. See also Springer and Lerrigo, "Social Work in the Public Scene," p. 167.

34. Springer and Lerrigo, "Social Work in the Public Scene," p. 168; Agnes Van Driel, "Personnel in Social Security," *Social Service Review* 11 (Sept. 1937): 437.

213

35. Springer and Lerrigo, "Social Work in the Public Scene," pp. 167–168. See also Van Driel, "Personnel in Social Security," pp. 434–445.

36. Lillian Wald to Herbert Lehman, Jan. 22, 1934, Herbert H. Lehman Papers (Columbia University Library).

37. Lillian Wald to Lillie Peck, Feb. 10, 1934, National Federation of Settlements Papers (Social Welfare History Archives).

38. Lillian Wald to Herbert Lehman, Dec. 17, 1934, Lehman Papers.

39. Lillian Wald to Stanley Isaacs, March 13, 1936, United Neighborhood Houses Papers (Social Welfare History Archives).

40. Paul Kellogg to Harry Hopkins, May 6, 1935, Survey Papers.

41. Paul Kellogg to Frances Perkins, April 18, 1939. Survey Papers.

42. Paul Kellogg to Frances Perkins, Sept. 20, 1934, Survey Papers.

43. "The Harry L. Hopkins Dinner," June 22, 1933, Hopkins Papers; *Better Times: The Welfare Magazine* 14 (May 15, 1933): 1.

44. "35th Anniversary Luncheon," March 14, 1936, UNH Papers.

45. John Kingsbury to Lillian Wald, March 10, 1933, Henry Street Settlement Papers (Columbia University Library).

46. [Homer Folks's Celebration], Feb. 18, 1937, Homer Folks Papers (Columbia University School of Social Work Library, New York City).

47. Frances Perkins to Paul Kellogg, June 26, 1945, Survey Papers.

48. Paul Kellogg to Frances Perkins, July 10, 1945, Survey Papers.

14

1. "The Unofficial Observer," [John Franklin Carter], *The New Dealers* (New York, 1934). An interesting variation on this theme was provided by Elizabeth Dilling, who listed several New Yorkers in her book, *The Red Network: A "Who's Who" and Handbook of Radicalism for Patriots* (Kenilworth, Ill., 1934).

2. Lillian Wald to [Kendall K. Mussey], Oct. 5, 1931, Lillian D. Wald Papers (New York Public Library, New York City); Paul Kellogg, "The Spread of Employment Planning," Report of the Annual Meeting of the Industrial Relations Association of Chicago, Jan. 12, 1931, Paul U. Kellogg Papers (Social Welfare History Archives, Minneapolis).

3. Richard H. Pells, *Radical Visions and American Dreams: Culture and Social Thought in the Depression Years* (New York, 1973), pp. 87–88, 197—199, 319–326.

4. For an opposite view, see Frances Fox Piven and Richard A. Cloward, *Regulating the Poor: The Functions of Public Welfare* (New York, 1971), pp. 45–77.

5. Barton J. Bernstein, "The New Deal: The Conservative Achievements of Liberal Reform," in Barton J. Bernstein, ed., *Towards a New Past: Dissenting Essays in American History* (New York, 1968), pp. 263–288. I was unable to integrate James Patterson's ideas about poverty in America into my study. His new book offers several observations similar to my own. See James T. Patterson, *America's Struggle Against Poverty, 1900–1980* (Cambridge and London, 1981), pp. 37–77 and *passim*.

6. Edward Berkowitz and Kim McQuaid, *Creating the Welfare State: The Political Economy of Twentieth-Century Reform* (New York, 1980), pp. 78–116.

7. Jacob Fisher, *The Response of Social Work to the Depression* (Boston, 1980), pp. 119–121.

8. Lois Scharf, *To Work and to Wed: Female Employment, Feminism, and the Great Depression* (Westport, Conn., 1980), pp. 86–138. WPA Projects in New York City employed more women than was usual; see Barbara Blumberg, *The New Deal and the Unemployed: The View From New York City* (Lewisburg, 1979), pp. 77–78.

9. Eleanor Roosevelt to Harry Hopkins, Sept. 25, 1935, Eleanor Roosevelt Papers (Frankling D. Roosevelt Library, Hyde Park).

10. Sheila M. Rothman, *Woman's Proper Place: A History of Changing Ideals and Practices, 1870 to the Present* (New York, 1978), pp. 221–222.

11. See, Daniel T. Rodgers, *The Work Ethic in Industrial America, 1850– 1920* (Chicago, 1979) and Daniel Nelson, *Managers and Workers: Origins of the New Factory System in the United States, 1880–1920* (Madison, 1975).

12. See Bernard Sternsher, ed., *The Negro in Depression and War: Prelude to Revolution, 1930–1945* (Chicago, 1969).

13. William E. Leuchtenburg, "The New Deal and the Analogue of War," in John Braeman, Robert H. Bremner, and Everett Walters, eds., *Change and Continuity in Twentieth-Century America* (Columbus, 1964), pp. 81–143.

14. William E. Leuchtenburg, *Franklin D. Roosevelt and the New Deal, 1932–1940* (New York, 1963) remains the most authoritative single-volume text on the New Deal.

15. Frances Perkins, *People at Work* (Boston, 1934), p. 137 and *passim*.

16. Mary Dewson, "An Aid to the End," vol. 1, MS, Mary W. Dewson Papers (Schlesinger Library, Cambridge).

17. Harry Hopkins, "What is the 'American Way'?" [pamphlet], Works Progress Administration Publication of Address Delivered July 16, 1938.

18. Leonard Krieger, "The Idea of the Welfare State in Europe and the United States," *Journal of the History of Ideas* 24 (Oct.–Dec., 1963): 556.

19. Harry L. Hopkins, "Employment in America," *Vital Speeches of the Day* 3 (Dec. 1, 1936): 107. See also Peter Bachrach, "The Right to Work: Emergence of the Idea in the United States," *Social Service Review* 26 (June 1952): 153–164.

20. Robert S. Lynd, *Knowledge For What?, The Place of Social Science in American Culture* (Princeton, 1939), p. 59.

Leaders of social work in New York wrote voluminously. The archival collections of their labors often consume scores of linear feet of shelf space. No researcher can study all of it. Perhaps most useful for my purposes were the files of personal correspondence that figured importantly in every collection, for more than other materials these revealed patterns of interpersonal relationships. Selected memoranda, minutes of meetings, speeches, reports, and similar documents also helped flesh out the history that was recorded in contemporary as well as in later accounts by scholars.

The Social Welfare History Archives at the University of Minnesota in Minneapolis has become the nation's major center for the study of social work and welfare policy. Its guides, indexes, and folder-by-folder descriptions are more informative and useful than any others, though most archives offer helpful finding aids. Without question the SWHA's centerpiece collection is the Survey Papers, which gives access to the personal and professional ferment underlying the printed pages of a national publication, thereby revealing the concerns of social workers and their allies in government, business, and service professions.

Other SWHA collections also proved helpful. The Papers of the National Social Welfare Assembly (which had been the National Social Work Council during the 1930s) afford direct observation of the committees that sought federal action on relief after 1929. The Council's director, David Holbrook, made notes of lunch and telephone conversations that reveal many private thoughts otherwise unrecorded. Though a small collection, the Harry L. Lurie Papers give great insight into the labors of American Association of Social Workers committees on behalf of the unemployed. Lurie was a participating official in government programs and a perceptive critic. His unpublished speeches and drafts of papers disclose the thinking of a leader who, by 1934, had become a radical. The Paul U. Kellogg Papers contain many of the editor's speeches on community action, industry, and economic planning. Several folders detail Kellogg's disagreement with the administration's plans for social security; others document his leadership of dissenters in 1934 and of the dissenting Social Policy Committee thereafter. The Edwin W. Witte Special Correspondence File tells the Advisory Council's story from the perspective of its executive director, who defended the position taken by Franklin Roosevelt and Frances Perkins. A different perspective is revealed in the Papers of the United Neighborhood Houses of New York City, which depict the impact of unemployment in city neighborhoods. The SWHA also holds a large portion of Henry Street Settlement Papers, which begin in 1933 when Helen Hall succeeded Lillian Wald as resident director. My use of these was limited because they had not yet been indexed. The Papers of the National Federation of Settlements afforded me materials about the careers of Lillian Wald and Mary Simkhovitch.

The Franklin D. Roosevelt Library at Hyde Park, New York, houses a number of indispensable collections. The Franklin D. Roosevelt Papers include both the private papers and the public Records of the Governor of New York State

(1929–1932). Though essential, the Records of the Governor are difficult to use: they appear on microfilm, retain the format of the original filing system, and contain numerous cross-references. The Herbert H. Lehman Papers comprise the Records of the Lieutenant Governor of New York State (1929–1932). Beside supplementing the FDR Papers, the similarly microfilmed Records of the Lieutenant Governor offer material on other developments in New York City, since Lehman was a director of both the Welfare Council and Henry Street settlement. The Papers of Eleanor Roosevelt show her involvement in social welfare issues through speeches and radio broadcasts as well as private letters. Her correspondence with Perkins, Hopkins, and their government departments demonstrates the influence she exerted. The Harry L. Hopkins Papers include a complete set of documents from the President's Emergency Committee for Employment, which was a Hoover commission that disagreed with its president's reluctance to implement federal unemployment relief. Harry Hopkins's own work as administrator of the FERA, CWA, and WPA is detailed in minutes of committee meetings and memoranda of official rulings. A small file of Herbert Hoover Papers pertains to the president's communications with the PECE. Some material of Frances Perkins is located at the FDRL, and it is useful for its folders of speeches by W. Frank Persons as well as unpublished drafts of Perkins speeches, papers, and articles. The FDRL also holds a portion of the Mary W. Dewson Papers, including notes on her activities in politics and government and a valuable set of minutes from the meetings of the Advisory Council of the COES. The Papers of Samuel Rosenman do not contain material that is particularly revealing about welfare.

  The Rare Book and Manuscript Library at Columbia University possesses another collection of Henry Street Settlement Papers; here I found the fullest set of Welfare Council materials available, including minutes from executive committee meetings. The papers also provide minutes and reports generated by the Lower East Side Community Council, adding a neighborhood perspective to the Depression's impact on the city. The Papers of Bruno Lasker consist of notebooks; volumes V–IX (1928–1932) proved helpful in assessing changing attitudes during the Depression. Frances Perkins left still other papers to Columbia. This valuable group includes some hard-to-find copies of rules and regulations handed down by New Deal agencies (*e.g.* a memorandum describing the switch from CWA back to FERA) as well as a rare first (and only) draft of the report of the COES. The Columbia Library holds Herbert H. Lehman Papers as well, including another microfilmed set of the Records of the Lieutenant Governor. Its most worthwhile original documents are personal letters to and from social work leaders. I also read transcripts of interviews in the Columbia Oral History Collection; the more pertinent included those of Bruno Lasker, Lawson Purdy, Homer Folks, Henry Bruere, and especially Frances Perkins. Perkins's transcript runs to four volumes, of which the second and third are most telling in documenting the influence of New York reformers. The Columbia University School of Social Work possesses a valuable collection of Homer Folks Papers. I found them, however, crammed randomly into filing cabinets and boxes stored in a spare room. That was sad treatment, because the Folks material counts among the most valuable I examined. The School of Social Work has a folder of Porter R. Lee Papers too.

The Papers of Lillian D. Wald are located at the New York Public Library, as are the Papers of William H. Matthews. The Wald Papers proved very useful because her correspondence is arranged chronologically. That made it easier to understand her reaction to the Smith-Hoover election and to the deepening unemployment crisis. The Matthews Papers fill only one box, but they present a thought-provoking record of the development of work relief. The Special Collections Division of the NYPL holds complete sets of two Welfare Council publications, *The Bulletin of the Welfare Council of New York City* and *Better Times: The Welfare Magazine*. The former covers developments in the city through 1931, and the latter picks up the story after that.

Each was crucial to learning the chronology of changes in local welfare policies. They also reported speeches and other newsworthy items. Finally, several pamphlets, reports, and other Welfare Council materials are held in the NYPL's Special Collections Division.

The Arthur and Elizabeth Schlesinger Library on the History of Women in America at Radcliffe College in Cambridge, Massachusetts, has the Papers of Mary Simkhovitch as well as another group or Mary W. Dewson Papers. My research in the Simkhovitch Papers was not extensive, but her speeches articulate the relationship between social work and politics during the 1920s and 1930s. Molly Dewson's unpublished MS of a two-volume autobiography, "An Aid to the End," was especially helpful in drawing connections between social workers and government officials.

The Raymond Moley Papers are housed at the Hoover Institute on War, Revolution, and Peace in Stanford, California. Moley possessed a knack for keeping important documents, including memoranda on unemployment relief written in FDR's hand, and a copy of the supplementary report of the Advisory Council to the COES. The Moley Papers often filled in blanks left by research elsewhere.

Survey, Survey Graphic, and the *Midmonthly,* which replaced the *Graphic,* are indispensable periodicals for students of American social welfare. *Survey* was a journal for professionals, and it reported national as well as state and local changes in welfare policies. Survey publications, moreover, were never narrowly focused: Paul Kellogg and his associates wrote lively stories on a variety of topics, hoping to attract the attention of educated Americans everywhere to social issues. *The Social Service Review* is another professional journal that began publication in 1927; its articles manifest the latest thinking about welfare. The *Proceedings* of the National Conference of Social Work fill a similar function. *Survey,* the *Review,* and the *Proceedings* reveal what was happening in urban neighborhoods as well as in research libraries, classrooms, and offices.

My chapter notes contain references to other source materials, including published books, articles, and speeches, some newspaper stories, and a few autobiographies. I refer in addition to interpretive histories, monographic studies, biographies, scholars' articles, and other published accounts of social work history, the New Deal, and the American welfare state, and often indicate their usefulness to my study. My debt to these fellow scholars is very great, but their writings are voluminous, and I have not been able to credit everyone I have read.

AALL plan for unemployment compensation. *See* American Association for Labor Legislation

Able-bodied unemployed, 6–7, 54–57, 122–125, 174–176; and CWA, 132–134; and termination of FERA, 165–166; and unemployment compensation, 143–144; and USES, 130–131, 137; and Wagner-Lewis bill, 164; and WPA, 136–141

Advisory Council of Committee on Economic Security, 149–154, 156–157, 163. *See also* Kellogg, Paul U.; Perkins, Frances; Wagner-Lewis bill

American Association for Labor Legislation (AALL), 9, 39, 61 n, 105; AALL plan for unemployment compensation, 145–147; Wagner-Lewis bill, 148–155, 156. *See also* Andrews, John

American Association for Old Age Security (AAOAS), 9, 105. *See also* Epstein, Abraham

American Association of Social Workers (AASW), 8, 106, 143; and New Deal relief programs, 128–129, 131, 133–136, 137, 162, 164; and professional standards in public relief, 72 n, 85–86, 165. *See also*

Colcord, Joanna; Social Work Conference on Federal Action; West, Walter

American Public Welfare Association (APWA), 75, 85, 167

American Red Cross, 70, 91–93, 97, 119. *See also* President's Emergency Committee for Employment

Andrews, John, 9, 40, 49, 149; and AALL plan for unemployment compensation, 145–146; and favor of Frances Perkins, 148, 148n, 154, 156–157

Association for Improving the Condition of the Poor (AICP), 8, 29, 32, 51, 59. *See also* Hopkins, Harry L.; Matthews, William H.

Association of Community Chests and Councils, 9, 28, 67, 70. *See also* Burns, Allen T.

Berle, Adolph A., 7, 41, 41n

Bond, Elsie, 65; and TERA, 81, 82n, 107–108, 112

Brown, Josephine C., 166, 167

Bruere, Henry, 64, 109, 169; and Committee on Stabilization of Industry (Bruere Committee), 39, 43–46

Burns, Allen T., 9, 72, 96–97, 163

Charity Organization Society (COS), 8, 32. *See also* Devine, Edward T.; Gifford, Walter S.; Purdy, Lawson

Civil Works Administration (CWA), 127, 133–136, 159. *See also* Hopkins, Harry L.; Roosevelt, Franklin D.

Civilian Conservation Corps (CCC), 126–127, 128

Colcord, Joanna, 9, 21, 72, 85–86, 90; as critic of New Deal, 162, 166, 168

Committee on Economic Security (COES), 149–150, 152–154, 156, 165. *See also* Perkins, Frances; Roosevelt, Franklin D.; Wagner-Lewis bill

Committee on Stabilization of Industry (Bruere Committee), 39, 42–43, 64, 130, 158; and Franklin D. Roosevelt, 103–105, 110; report of, 43–46. *See also* Bruere, Henry; Kellogg, Paul U.; Perkins, Frances

Devine, Edward T., 3, 8, 9, 18–19, 20, 169; as critic of New Deal, 159, 164

Dewson, Mary (Molly), 9, 11,

224

19, 56, 106, 169; and
Frances Perkins, 9, 11, 19,
116, 127, 130, 149, 152;
and Franklin D. Roosevelt,
102, 103, 110, 112; in New
Deal, 130, 149, 152, 156,
170, 178
Douglas, Paul H., 40, 49,
109, 147
Dreier, Mary, 11, 116, 117

Eliot, Thomas, 152,
154–155
Elliott, John, 19, 20–22
Emergency Work Bureau
(EWB), 32, 35, 36, 58–61,
68, 119. *See also* Matthews,
William H.
Employment stabilization,
38–42, 105; and Commit-
tee for Stabilization of
Industry (Bruere Commit-
tee), 42–46; and
unemployment compensa-
tion, 145–147, 153, 155.
See also Bruere, Henry;
Kellogg, Paul U.; Perkins,
Frances
Epstein, Abraham, 3, 9; as
expert on unemployment
compensation, 11, 40, 49,
146, 148, 149, 154

Family Welfare Association
of America (FWAA), 8, 85.
See also Swift, Linton
Federal Emergency Relief

Administration (FERA),
127, 128–130, 132–133,
136, 162; termination of,
165–166, 167. *See also*
Hopkins, Harry L.;
Roosevelt, Franklin D.
Folks, Homer, 3, 9, 14, 54,
105, 114, 169; as leader of
social work profes-
sionalism in public relief,
76–83, 86, 112; and pub-
lic relief, 27, 35–36,
64–65, 122; and TERA,
79–82, 107–108. *See also*
Temporary Emergency
Relief Administration;
Welfare Council of New
York City

Gibson, Harvey D., 66–69
Gifford, Walter S., 96–97

Hall, Helen, 3, 149, 156; as
critic of New Deal, 153,
164, 168
Henry Street settlement,
4–5, 7–8, 29, 116–117,
168; Depression services
of, 33–34, 66–69. *See also*
Wald, Lillian
Hodson, William, 9, 108,
121, 169; as leader of
drive for public relief,
34–35, 36, 71–72, 74, 84,
128, 132; as president of
NCSW, 74, 132, 162–163;
and social work political

action, 16–17, 19, 22–23, 113, 125, 131, 132; and Welfare Council of New York City, 13, 58, 119, 120, 123. *See also* Welfare Council of New York City

Hoey, Jane, 3, 5, 127; in New Deal, 9–10, 11, 108, 170. *See also* Welfare Council of New York City

Holbrook, David, 70–71, 90, 93. *See also* National Social Work Council

Hoover, Herbert C., 31, 64–65, 73, 88, 88 n, 89, 96, 118; and PECE, 89–96; and social workers, 20–21, 23–24, 97–100

Hopkins, Harry L., 5, 7, 9, 19, 71, 121, 132, 150, 162, 169, 170, 175
—in New Deal: CWA, 133–136; FERA, 127, 128, 129; WPA, 137–141
—and TERA, 82–83, 108, 118; and William H. Matthews, 5, 9, 56, 59; on work relief, 55, 56, 58, 178, 179. *See also* Temporary Emergency Relief Administration

Kelley, Florence, 8, 11, 107, 116

Kellogg, Arthur, 7, 108, 109

Kellogg, Paul U., 7, 9, 12, 13–14, 27, 29, 44, 58, 72–73, 101–102, 117, 169, 172; and Al Smith, 15, 18, 19, 23; and employment stabilization, 40, 42, 42 n; and FDR's 100 Days, 126, 129, 130; and Frances Perkins, 39–40, 109, 152–153, 169, 170; on Herbert Hoover, 21, 23, 89, 93, 97, 98, 99–100; as New Deal dissenter, 153, 159, 160, 163–164, 168; and unemployment compensation, 39–40, 52–53, 142–145, 148, 149; and Wagner-Lewis bill, 150–154, 156

La Follette-Costigan bill, 73, 84, 86. *See also* La Follette-Costigan committee

La Follette-Costigan committee (Senate Subcommittee on Manufactures), 72–73, 84, 86, 109, 129. *See also* West, Walter

Lasker, Bruno, 4–5, 7–8, 117

Lee, Porter R., 9, 36–37, 115, 120, 122, 169; as member of PECE, 90–96, 99

Lehman, Herbert H., 103, 117, 125, 169

Leiserson, William, 27, 40, 49, 104, 149, 156; chairman of Ohio Commission on Unemployment Insurance, 146–147, 148
Lowenstein, Solomon, 10, 35, 119–120
Lurie, Harry, 3, 10, 85, 96, 97, 173; on work relief, 57, 134, 135. *See also* American Association of Social Workers

Matthews, William H., 5, 9, 11, 14, 69; as critic of New Deal, 139–140, 168; on Depression winter of 1932–1933, 119, 121, 122, 123; and Harry L. Hopkins, 5, 9, 56, 59; as leader of EWB, 32, 58–61; on work relief, 56, 60, 61. *See also* Emergency Work Bureau
Mayor's Committee on Unemployment, 5–6, 28, 43, 61, 61 n
Mitchel, Mayor John Purroy, 5–6, 43, 90. *See also* Mayor's Committee on Unemployment
Moley, Raymond, 7, 41, 41 n, 129, 149, 156

National Conference of Social Work: annual meeting of 1931, 63; of 1932, 73–75; of 1933, 131–132; of 1934, 160–163, 167. *See also* Springer, Gertrude
National Consumers' League (NCL), 9, 11, 117. *See also* Dewson, Mary (Molly)
National Recovery Administration (NRA), 130, 159–161. *See also* Perkins, Frances; Van Kleeck, Mary
National Social Work Council (NSWC), 70–73, 84–86. *See also* Holbrook, David
New York City Depression winters: of 1930–1931, 32–36; of 1931–1932, 66–70; of 1932–1933, 117–125. *See also* Hodson, William; Welfare Council of New York City
New York School of Social Work, 8, 9, 121. *See also* Lee, Porter R.

Ohio Commission on Unemployment Insurance, 146–147; and Ohio plan, 146–147, 154–156. *See also* Leiserson, William; Rubinow, Isaac M.
Ohio plan for unemployment compensation. *See* Ohio Commission on Unemployment Insurance

Old-age pensions, 50–52, 103–104, 110, 173, 175, 176; and Social Security Act, 155–156, 166

Perkins, Frances, ix, 5–6, 8, 9, 11, 33, 114–115, 116–117, 118, 170; and Al Smith, 18–19, 23; and employment stabilization, 39–40, 41, 42–45; and Franklin D. Roosevelt, 102–103, 104, 109, 111–112, 127, 148, 155; and Paul U. Kellogg, 27, 39–40, 109, 152–153, 170; as Secretary of Labor, 127–130, 134, 148–150, 156–157, 158–159, 178; and unemployment compensation, 39–40, 50, 104, 143–145, 148; and Wagner-Lewis bill, 148–155, 156–157

Persons, W. Frank, 9, 170; head of USES, 130

President's Committee on Unemployment Relief (POUR), 65, 72, 96–97. See also Gifford, Walter S.; Hoover, Herbert C.

President's Conference on Unemployment, 29, 89, 90, 91, 93. See also Hoover, Herbert C.

President's Emergency Committee for Employment (PECE), 31, 89–92, 99; rebellion against Herbert Hoover, 92–96. See also Hoover, Herbert C.; Lee, Porter R.; Woods, Arthur

Public relief, 26–27, 31, 34, 176–177; drive for city and state action, 34–36, 63–66, 68–70; drive for national action, 70–74, 118–124

—and New Deal: CWA, 133–135; FERA, 129, 132–133, 136

—termination of FERA, 165–166; Wagner-Lewis bill, 164; WPA, 136–141. See also Hodson, William; Hopkins, Harry L.; West, Walter

Purdy, Lawson, 11, 17, 34

Reconstruction Finance Corporation (RFC), 98; implements Relief and Construction Act, 85–86, 118, 128. See also Hoover, Herbert C.

Relief and Construction Act, 73, 84–86. See also Wagner, Robert F.; West, Walter

Roosevelt, Eleanor, 23 n, 52,

117, 126–127, 175; and
social workers, 11, 19, 102,
108–109, 109n, 114
Roosevelt, Franklin D., 10,
169, 178
—as governor: 25, 44–45,
51–52; and public relief,
36, 57, 64–65, 79–82;
and unemployment com-
pensation, 47–48, 104
—as president: 127–128,
178; and public relief,
127, 128–129; 133,
135–136, 165–166; and
Wagner-Lewis bill,
148–150, 153, 155, 157
—and social workers:
64–65, 101–102,
103–105, 107–113, 118,
134–135, 156–157,
159–160, 163–165,
167–168
Rubinow, Isaac M., 9, 11, 26,
26n, 97–98; as expert on
unemployment compensa-
tion, 11, 49, 105, 148, 149,
154, 156; and Ohio plan,
146–147

Schneiderman, Rose, 11,
130; and Eleanor and
Franklin D. Roosevelt,
102–103
Simkhovitch, Mary, 3, 9,
102; and social work po-

litical action, 17, 18–19,
35, 106–107, 125, 127
Smith, Alfred E., 32,
102–103, 169; and cam-
paign of 1928, 15, 17–19,
20, 22–24
Social Policy Committee
(SPC), 164. See also Hall,
Helen; Kellogg, Paul U.
Social Security Act, 142, 148,
154–157, 166, 175, 176,
177. See also Perkins,
Frances; Roosevelt, Franklin D.; Wagner-Lewis bill
Social Work Conference on
Federal Action, 70–73,
72 n. See also Hodson,
William; West, Walter
Social work professionalism,
76–78, 121–122; in city
and state relief programs,
78–84; in federal relief
programs, 84–86, 129,
132–133, 137–138, 140,
165–167. See also Ameri-
can Association of Social
Workers; Folks, Homer
Springer, Gertrude, 9, 31,
68, 83–84, 121, 130, 168;
reports NCSW annual
meetings of 1931, 63; of
1932, 74–75; of 1933,
131–132; of 1934,
160–163, 167
State Charities Aid Associa-

tion (SCAA), 8, 51, 64–65, 76–82. *See also* Bond, Elsie; Rolks, Homer

Straus, Jesse Isador, 57 n, 82, 107. *See also* Temporary Emergency Relief Administration

Swift, Linton, 9, 124; and drive for public relief, 70–72, 128. *See also* Social Work Conference on Federal Action

Tammany Hall, 18, 22, 82–84, 125; and politics in relief, 16, 33, 76, 78–79, 121. *See also* Smith, Alfred E.; Walker, Mayor James (Jimmy)

Temporary Emergency Relief Administration (TERA), 64, 65–66, 105, 107–108, 110–111, 118, 119, 120, 123; and FERA, 129, 166; and La Follette-Costigan bill, 73, 84, 86; and social work professionalism in public relief, 65–66, 79–86. *See also* Folks, Homer; Hopkins, Harry L.; Roosevelt, Franklin D.

Unemployed. *See* Able-bodied unemployed

Unemployment, 27–28; and Depression winters, 29, 30, 34–35, 66–70, 90–93, 118–120, 133

Unemployment compensation, 48–50, 143–145, 164, 166–167, 173, 175, 176; and AALL plan, 145–146; and COES and Advisory Council, 149–154; and Franklin D. Roosevelt, 47–48, 104–105, 110, 111–112, 148–149; and Ohio plan, 146–147; and Wagner-Lewis bill, 147–155. *See also* Kellogg, Paul U.; Perkins, Frances; Roosevelt, Franklin D.; Wagner-Lewis bill

United States Employment Service (USES), 130–131, 133, 137. *See also* Perkins, Frances; Persons, W. Frank

Van Kleeck, Mary, 9, 19, 46; revolt against New Deal, 160–162, 168, 173

Wagner, Robert F., 18, 93–95, 124, 130, 143, 169; and public relief, 73, 84, 129; and Wagner-Lewis bill, 148–155

Wagner-Lewis bill, 148–155, 164–165. *See also* Kellogg, Paul U.; Perkins, Frances; Roosevelt, Franklin D.

Wald, Lillian, 3, 7, 25, 34, 35, 57, 67–68, 127, 172; and Al Smith, 15, 17, 19–23; and Eleanor and Franklin D. Roosevelt, 101–102, 104, 105, 168; as settlement leader, 4–5, 7–8, 27, 116–117, 168, 169. *See also* Henry Street settlement; Welfare Council of New York City

Walker, Mayor James (Jimmy), 66, 69, 78–79. *See also* Tammany Hall

Welfare Council of New York City, 9, 13, 27, 28, 32, 77; as political action organization, 34–36, 66–70, 78–79, 83–84, 106. *See also* Folks, Homer; Hodson, William; Hoey, Jane

West, Walter, 9, 19, 112; and drive for public relief, 70–72, 72 n, 86, 128. *See also* American Association of Social Workers

Winter. *See* New York City Depression winters

Witte, Edwin, 151, 152–153, 154. *See also* Advisory

Council of Committee on Economic Security

Women's Trade Union League (WTUL), 11. *See also* Schneiderman, Rose

Woods, Arthur, 90 n; as chairman of PECE, 90–96

Work relief, 29, 56–58, 61–62, 111, 122–123, 162, 165, 173, 175–176, 179; and CWA, 132–136; and EWB, 60–61; and WPA, 136–141, 166. *See also* Hopkins, Harry L.; Matthews, William H.

Works Progress Administration (WPA), 136–141, 166, 167, 175, 176. *See also* Hopkins, Harry L.; Roosevelt, Franklin D.

A series edited by Allen F. Davis

Gospel Hymns and Social Religion: The Rhetoric of Nineteenth-Century Revivalism
    by Sandra S. Sizer
Social Darwinism: Science and Myth in Anglo-American Social Thought
    by Robert C. Bannister
Twentieth Century Limited: Industrial Design in America, 1925–1939
    by Jeffrey L. Meikle
Charlotte Perkins Gilman: The Making of a Radical Feminist, 1860–1896
    by Mary A. Hill
Inventing the American Way of Death, 1830–1920
    by James J. Farrell
Anarchist Women, 1870–1920
    by Margaret S. Marsh
Woman and Temperance: The Quest for Power and Liberty, 1873–1900
    by Ruth Bordin
Hearth and Home: Preserving a People's Culture
    by George W. McDaniel
The Education of Mrs. Henry Adams
    by Eugenia Kaledin
Class, Culture, and the Classroom: The Student Peace Movement in the Thirties
    by Eileen Eagan
Fathers and Sons: The Bingham Family and the American Mission
    by Char Miller
An American Odyssey: Elia Kazan and American Culture
    by Thomas H. Pauly
Silver Cities: The Photography of American Urbanization, 1839–1915
    by Peter Bacon Hales
Actors and American Culture, 1880–1920
    by Benjamin McArthur

Saving the Waifs: Reformers and Dependent Children, 1890–1917
  by LeRoy Ashby
A Woman's Ministry: Mary Collson's Search for Reform as a Unitarian Minister, a Hull House Social Worker, and a Christian Science Practitioner
  by Cynthia Grant Tucker
Depression Winters: New York Social Workers and the New Deal
  by William W. Bremer